THE EARLY AND MID-VICTORIAN NOVEL

The work of early and mid-Victorian critics is often held in low esteem, obscuring many of the best earlier insights. This book revives them, showing how challenging many of them remain today. It reflects the great range and diversity of contemporary critical debate, placing the great Victorian novelists within their intellectual framework.

Arranged thematically, the volume covers such topics as literary form, the social responsibility of literature, issues of politics and gender, the influence of criticism, realism, plot and characterisation, imagination and creativity, and the office and social standing of the novelist. Reflecting what the literary world of the time regarded as the most important issues, the collection presents an original and useful body of material for study. Professor Skilton's introductions and notes draw together the large number of voices taking up interrelated themes, and guide the reader through the Victorian literary critical debate.

This accessible and invaluable guide will provide insights and introductions to ideas, critics, and to the classic texts themselves.

David Skilton is Professor of English at the University of Wales, Cardiff.

CRITICAL APPROACH SERIES

General editor: Donald Thomas

THE POST-ROMANTICS *edited by* Donald Thomas
SHAKESPEAREAN TRAGEDY *edited by* D.F. Bratchell
THE EARLY AND MID-VICTORIAN NOVEL
edited by David Skilton

THE EARLY AND MID-VICTORIAN NOVEL

◆

edited by DAVID SKILTON

LONDON AND NEW YORK

First published 1993
by Routledge
11 New Fetter Lane, London EC4P 4EE

Simultaneously published in the USA and Canada
by Routledge
a division of Routledge, Chapman and Hall, Inc.
29 West 35th Street, New York, NY 10001

Typeset in 10/12 Garamond by Witwell Ltd, Southport
Printed in Great Britain by
T.J. Press (Padstow) Ltd, Padstow Cornwall

British Library Cataloguing in Publication Data
A catalogue record for this book is available from the British Library

Library of Congress Cataloging in Publication Data
The Early and Mid-Victorian novel / [edited by] David Skilton.
p.   cm. – (Critical approach series)
Includes bibliographical references and index.
1. English fiction–19th Century–History and criticism.
I. Skilton, David. II. Series.
PR872.E27   1993
823′.809–dc20   92–9415
ISBN 0–415–03256–3
0–415–03257–1 (pbk)

Contents

CONTENTS

Acknowledgements

I am grateful for advice and help received from Andrew Edgar, Stanley Jones, John Percival, Michal Scollen, J.R. Watson, the archivist and proprietors of *The Times*, and the staffs of the Reference Division of the British Library, the London Library, and the University Library, Cardiff.

Introduction

To the Victorians, theirs was the age of the novel, just as the Elizabethan and Jacobean period had been the age of drama: '[T]he novel has displaced the stage. The theatre hardly exists, as an intellectual influence. And this perhaps may be accepted as proof that what was once the strongest current of our literature has been diverted to another channel.'[1] According to one critic of the 1860s:

> within the space of thirty-six days, not long ago, no less than forty-six novels were offered for subscription in Paternoster Row – that is, nine every week for five successive weeks. The number seems to be prodigious, but in truth it gives no adequate idea of the quantity of fiction which is written and printed, published and read, year by year in this country. Not only are there heaps of stories, great and small, produced in single, in double, and in treble volumes, each one by itself, but let it be remembered that there are an infinity of periodicals, weekly and monthly, varying in price from a halfpenny to half-a-crown, which have, with scarcely an exception, each a story on foot, and some of them two.[2]

Thackeray reported an 'appetite for novels extending to the end of the world', and imagined 'far away in the frozen deep, the sailors reading them to one another during the endless night'.[3] For Leigh Hunt the survival of fantastic fiction, like the *Arabian Nights*, into the age of utilitarianism represented a victory for the human imagination:

> Well may the lovers of fiction triumph over the prophecy, that was to see an end put to all poetry and romance by the progress of science;- to care for nothing but what the chemist could analyse, and the manufacturer realize; and take no further delight in nymphs and gnomes, because Sir Humphrey Davy had made a lamp; nor in the story of Iris because, as Peter Parley[4] has it, the public was learning to know 'all about rainbows'.[5]

1

For others the phenomenon spelt cultural decline: 'There has never been anything like it before. To the literary historian it is an unparalleled phænomenon, and brings to mind the remark of Lord Lytton, that the literature of Greece began to exist in poetical literature and expired in prose fiction.'[6] The greatest of the nineteenth-century prophets, Thomas Carlyle, had mocked the fashionable novelist in an influential article of 1832:

> Of no given Book, not even of a Fashionable Novel, can you predicate with certainty that its vacuity is absolute; that there are not other vacuities which shall partially replenish themselves therefrom, and esteem it a *plenum*. How knowest thou, may the distressed Novelwright exclaim, that I, here where I sit, am the Foolishest of existing mortals; that this my Long-ear of a Fictitious Biography shall not find one and the other, into whose still longer ears it may be the means, under Providence, of instilling somewhat? We answer, None knows, none can certainly know: therefore, write on, worthy Brother, even as thou canst, even as it has been given thee.[7]

Although his attack is specifically on fashionable fiction, many later writers, including two successful novelists of modern life, took it as a general remark on the novel. Thackeray draws the novelist in 'Vanity Fair' as a long-eared clown, addressing long-eared listeners, while over forty years after Carlyle's attack, Trollope still takes the trouble to reply to it when he is writing his *Autobiography* (see 2.6). On the other hand Sir Walter Scott was always exempt from this kind of criticism throughout the period, and remained for succeeding generations a stable point of reference when the quality or morality of fiction was under discussion.

Critics clearly saw the importance of prose fiction, and being generally unable to grant to later historical novels the high status they accorded Scott's, they looked for ways to explain the interest they took in the novel of contemporary life. Even the negative aspects of the 'fictitious Biography' Carlyle professed to despise could be turned to advantage:

> Our interest in the private life of our fellow-men has been developed into a system, and there is nothing in the way of study which people seem now to desire so much as to peep into the house of a neighbour, to watch his ways, and to calculate the ups and downs of fortunes. . . . Here is a gossipping propensity in human nature which any man of sense can keep within bounds,

but which none of us can eradicate. To this gossiping sense the novelist appeals. A novel may be described as gossip etherealized, family talk generalized. In the pages of a novel we can pry without shame into the secrets of our neighbour's soul, we can rifle his desk, we can read his love letters, we are present when he first kisses the maiden of his heart, we see that little maiden at her toilet preparing for the interview, we go with her to buy her simple ribands and to choose her bonnet. To transport us into new villages which we have never known, to lodge us in strange houses which we have never dreamt of, to make us at home among new circles of our fellow-creatures, to teach us to sympathize in all their little pursuits, to love their trifling gauds, to partake of their filmy hopes and fears, to be one of them and to join in the petty fluctuations of contracted lives – this may not be a lofty occupation, nor need great genius for its perfect exercise; nevertheless, it is good healthy work, and I know not who in this generation is better employed than he who – even if he cannot boast of genius, yet with tact and clearness – widens through fiction the range of our sympathies, and teaches us not less to care for the narrow aims of small people than for the vast schemes of the great and mighty. We read the village gossip with as much concern as if the fate of the nation depended on it, and we take as much interest in a lawyer's poor daughter as if she were a peeress in her own right. Oh, happy art of fiction which can thus adjust the balance of fortune, raising the humble and weak to an equality in our hearts with the proud and the great![8]

Chapter 1 of this anthology shows early and mid-Victorian critics discussing the significance of the dominant literary form of the day, and at their best and their worst displaying a concern for the well-being of literature as reflecting and perpetuating a healthy or a sick state of society. From a safe distance it is possible to mock their worries, assuming that they are merely another manifestation of the stifling moralism of the Victorian period. But the concern for the education and mental development of the population was real, and the fears of corrupting or weakening influences were no more absurd than those of a later century, when television, not the novel, has been the object of anxiety. (The discussion of 1880 in 3.8 was repeated with variations in 1980.)

Most of the major novelists of the period are referred to in the following chapters, but it is worth remembering that they do not represent the novelistic output of the time: vastly more novels were then published than have since survived changes in taste and fashion. James Payn, himself a novelist, pointed to the existence of a literary 'underclass' of readers:

> It is now nearly a quarter of a century ago since a popular novelist[9] revealed to the world in a well-known periodical the existence of the 'Unknown Public;' and a very curious revelation it was. He showed us that the few thousands of persons who had hitherto imagined themselves to be the public – so far, at least, as their being the arbiters of popularity in respect to writers of fiction was concerned – were in fact nothing of the kind; that the subscription to the circulating libraries, the numbers of book clubs, the purchasers of magazines and railways novels, might indeed have their favourites, but that these last were 'nowhere,' as respected the number of their backers, in comparison with novelists whose names and works appear in penny journals and nowhere else.[10]

Some of these more popular novelists are named in 1.6. Because this collection contains a preponderance of criticism written for that 'few thousand' Payn mentions who 'imagined themselves to be the public', it may underestimate the sociological importance of the mass of cheap, popular fiction which is now known only to bibliographers and scholars. Many Victorians, however, were seriously concerned by the phenomenon, and Matthew Arnold for example discussed it in his essay on Copyright in 1880 (quoted in 3.8), where he doubts whether 'the consumption of the bad and the middling in literature does, of itself, necessarily engender a taste for the good'.

Of course the question of what constituted 'the good' in literature occupied much of Arnold's attention throughout his life, and he rarely seems to have included novels in the category. On the other hand many writers did devote a great deal of trouble to discriminations between different kinds and qualities of fiction, and this collection gives samples of this kind of effort from the work of some of the most significant critics of the period. Most of them are from book reviews, since very little criticism of the novel appeared in the form of books, and the academic study of the novel had scarcely yet begun. (David Masson's book, *British Novelists and Their Styles*, was unique in this respect – see 1.4 and 4.9.) Sensing that a lack of aesthetic respect for prose fiction arose from a lack of 'rules' governing the art form, writers such as Anthony Trollope, George Henry Lewes and Walter Besant concentrated on guiding the tyro novelist, and left it for a later age to produce a systematic terminology in which to express the critical assessment of technical matters. Many later readers have therefore erroneously supposed that no thought was given to questions of fictional technique. Nothing could be further from the truth. A study of the novelistic experiments of Thackeray, Dickens, the Brontës, Collins and Trollope, for example, proves that these matters received sustained attention. Both novelists and critics, however, had other urgent things to write about. It was a great achievement of Henry James and his disciples to make analysis of 'the art of the novel' an intellectually and even academically respectable activity. But much was lost as well as gained.

It must be admitted that not all Victorian criticism reaches the level of intellectual respectability: and in this the period resembles any other. Yet when we look at the huge numbers of reviews that were published, the surprise is not that there was so much mediocrity, but that so much was good. Quite often reviews which appeared within a few days of the book concerned remain useful to this day. The longer, retrospective treatment of a novelist's whole career to date – prompted by a death, a collected edition or a biography or autobiography – is often comparatively ponderous. On the whole, the shorter, hastier reviews contain much of the best work, while the longer, more sober, considered articles are less lively and less provocative; but the overall quality of reviews in the non-specialist press was at least as good as at any time since, and the range of material noticed was equally impressive. There was a considerable body of 'men of letters' (there seems to have been no corresponding term for women writers), producing millions of words in essays, informative articles and criticism. Although the authorship of much of this criticism was known in literary circles, most of it was published anonymously, and anonymity was elevated to an ethical principle. We find Mowbray Morris, the manager of *The Times* rebuking E.S. Dallas for revealing that he had written the review of Tennyson's *Maud*, for example. Then, when Dallas asked to be allowed to use some of his reviews from the paper in a book, Morris replied in terms which reveal that anonymity enjoyed the heightened, irrational prestige of a fetish: 'The only objection that occurs to me against your unacknowledged quotation of what has appeared in the Times is, that if some clever critic should detect & expose the plagiarism, you would have to submit to the charge without explanation.'[11] Certain critics used pseudonyms, or signed their articles with some device like Charles Lamb's pointing hand, while a few periodicals, such as the *Fortnightly Review*, stood out against anonymity in reviewing.

Although it is impossible to make confident attributions in all cases

– five of the pieces printed here are unattributable – it is hoped that the reader of this collection will develop a respect for many of the writers represented here, such as Bagehot, Brimley, Dallas, Forster, Hutton, Lewes, Morley, Roscoe or Simcox, or at very least a healthy awe of the range of the individual achievement of some of them across what later come to be regarded as different and distant disciplines. Hutton, Lewes, Morley and Simcox, for example, were polymaths, as was Marian Evans ('George Eliot'), one of the outstanding intellectuals of the century.[12] The achievement of these people indicates a sincere belief that all areas of intellectual enquiry were interconnected. Not for them a doctrine of 'two cultures', the humane and the scientific, each fortified against the other. Keats's belief that 'Philosophy will clip an angel's wing'[13] is rarely echoed by Victorian writers, few of whom would have understood such a shyness of science.

Although this anthology contains over fifty extracts, there remain many good critics, such as Leslie Stephen, who are not even mentioned, let alone represented. On the other hand a number of the many novelists who wrote on the novel are included: Collins, George Eliot, Gaskell, Bulwer Lytton and Trollope. No particular effort has been made to include specially famous pieces of criticism, and Rigby's attack on *Jane Eyre* and Ruskin's on *Mill on the Floss* are perhaps the only periodical articles extracted here whose existence is known to a large number of readers. The purpose of this volume is rather to bring a sample of early and mid-Victorian writing about the novel back into circulation, and to demonstrate that it is worthy of various kinds of serious attention. The object is not the assessment or evaluation of Victorian critical achievement by the academic standards current in a later age; and certainly it is not the criticism of critics. In 1831 Carlyle warned against such introverted literary activity, which he saw as indicative of a great peril: that book-reviewing might replace literature in the public mind:

[I]s not the diseased self-conscious state of Literature disclosed in this one fact, which lies so near us here, the prevalence of Reviewing! . . . now your Reviewer is a mere *taster*; who tastes, and says, by the evidence of such palate, such tongue, as he has got, It is good, It is bad. Was it thus that the French carried out certain inferior creatures on their Algerine Expedition, to taste the wells for them, and try whether they were poisoned? Far be it from us to disparage our own craft, whereby we have our living! Only we note these things: that Reviewing spreads with strange vigour; that such a man as Byron reckons the Reviewer and the Poet equal;[14] that at the last Leipzig Fair, there was advertised a Review of Reviews. By the by it will be found that all Literature has become one boundless self-devouring Review; and, as in London routs, we have to *do* nothing, but only to *see* others do nothing. Thus does Literature also, like a sick thing, superabundantly 'listen to itself.'[15]

If this seemed to be a danger in 1831, it must have appeared doubly so by the middle of Queen Victoria's reign. Daily and weekly newspapers, magazines and reviews multiplied breathtakingly, and a checklist of Victorian periodicals contains some thousands of titles. Throughout the period as much of the best criticism appeared in *The Times*, the *Spectator* and the *Saturday Review* as in specialist literary papers such as the *Athenaeum*, and there were dozens of other important dailies, weeklies, monthlies and quarterlies carrying notices of fiction besides.

The fact is that literature, including the novel, *mattered* in a direct way to the educated Victorian public to a degree which is now forgotten. Even though ours is an age in which far more people receive a higher education involving the study of literature as a subject, we do not inevitably connect that study to other current subjects of interest. Carlyle's vision of 'one boundless self-devouring Review' is a negative construction placed on a fundamentally healthy state of affairs. All kinds of what we call 'literature', including the novel, had indissoluble social, political, religious and philosophical connections: there was no absolute division between 'literary' and other discourse. Novelists not only wrote novels which through their subject-matter, social settings or fables, dealt explicitly with matters of topical or 'eternal' concern – from the fashions and the politics of the moment, to the prospects of eternal life – but they also felt able to descant in quasi-authorial 'asides' on the whole of human (and supernatural) life as they saw it. Reviewers in their turn responded by tackling all these subjects as they arose in the works under scrutiny. In addition, on a more or less conversational level, a novelist who published frequently, like Trollope, could actually become engaged in a sort of dialogue with some of the reviewers, as can be seen from the example of 7.5, or from the cross-references between the text of *Framley Parsonage* and Thackeray's 'Roundabout Papers' while they were both appearing in the *Cornhill Magazine*, which Thackeray edited. Serial fiction was intertwined with other periodical discourse in yet other ways. As editor of *All the Year Round*, Dickens would sometimes surround a novel with informative articles to help his readers understand unfamiliar things such as current Italian politics, which arose in Wilkie Collins's *Woman in White* (1859–60) for example. The link could also be less direct, as when Trollope's novels referred – by design or by coincidence – to matters that were the subject of articles in the very magazines in which his novels appeared. The literary system was held together by social links too. The male novelists and critics had generally had a common classical education, and habitually used their shared intellectual heritage to maintain the cultural influence of the classically educated élite. (Dickens is, of course, a notable exception to this generalisation.) There was also a high degree of personal interaction between writers of novels and writers about novels in the period. Just as in a later century, the same person often filled both roles, though George Meredith's anonymous and not altogether favourable notice of his own *Farina* in the *Westminster Review* is an extreme case.[16] And just as now, many writers and critics moved in the same limited social circles in London, such as the Garrick Club. They were often friends. To Trollope's disgust, Dickens presented E.S. Dallas with the bound manuscript of *Our Mutual Friend* in recognition of a favourable review.[17] Trollope persuaded his friend G.H. Lewes to take the editorship of the new *Fortnightly Review*, and found his kind of fiction vigorously defended in the pages of that journal, in a series of articles which were later reprinted under the title *The Principles of Success in Literature*. Trollope had in any case deliberately written a book on 'realistic' principles (*The Belton Estate*) as the first novel for the *Fortnightly* on its launch in 1865.[18]

G.H. Lewes provides a good example of the range of interest of these 'men of letters'. He wrote novels, plays, theatre criticism, literary reviews, philosophical works, and books and articles popularising science. A mere list of some of his non-fictional titles is impressive: *A Biographical History of Philosophy* (1845), *Comte's Philosophy of the Sciences* (1853), *The Life and Works of Goethe* (1855), *The Physiology of Common Life* (1859), *Studies in Animal Life* (1862), *Problems of Life and Mind* (1873–9) and *Actors and the Art of Acting* (1875). His book on Goethe received the singular honour of translation into German. Other writers were equally gifted. Richard Holt Hutton, who (like Lewes) was educated in Germany, studied classics, theology and law, prepared for the Unitarian ministry, worked as assistant editor of the *Economist*, joint editor of the *National Review* and literary editor of the *Spectator*, and held the post of Professor of Mathematics at Bedford College, London, from

1856 to 1865. When Hegelian philosophy became fashionable in Britain after about 1869, he was one of very few Englishmen who moved confidently among the new ideas because of an early acquaintance with them at German universities.[19] He was also one of the founders of the Metaphysical Society, which attracted many of the greatest thinkers of the age as members, and which aimed to bridge the gap between religious and scientific thought. Any of his knowledge might at any moment be brought into play in his reviews of *belles-lettres*, with the result that critics of a later age, with new ideas of the 'purity' of literary criticism, accused him of debasing criticism with 'political, or religious, or philosophical, or anthropological, or pantopragmatic adulteration'.[20] This particular polemical attack was published shortly after his death, but from a safer distance we might envy the sheer intellectual variety of the Huttons, Leweses, Evanses, Morleys, Simcoxes and others.

The low esteem in which critics of the 1890s and later held early and mid-Victorian criticism of prose fiction accompanies a turning away from social and political aspects of the novel, such as the social origins of fiction, the expansion of the reading public, and speculation about the determination of fictional form and content by social and economic factors. Such concerns were supplanted for some later critics by technical questions of structure and narrative point of view, and by theories of art as the production of a creator standing apart from society as a gifted individual, and pursuing art purely for the sake of art. The slogan *l'art pour l'art*, which was derived from an earlier anti-utilitarian movement of the 1830s in France, was readily adaptable to a late-century British revolt against the dominant utilitarian ideology of Victorian Britain, and nothing could less resemble the early and mid-Victorian assumption that literature was inevitably involved in debate on all subjects of general public concern. This earlier form of critical interest in fiction can aptly be called 'sociological' (although the word was not current until the mid-1860s), and plenty of examples of it are to be found in this collection, including the *Economist*'s analysis of Dickens's *Christmas Books* in relation to political economy (2.2), and H.L. Mansel's socio-economic explanation of the origin and effect of sensational fiction (3.6). Unfortunately for the later reputation of the critics represented here there was involved in all these strands of thought a strong thread of moral judgement and social and moral control, which has tended ever since to discredit the work of even the best critics of the period. Yet something of real richness was lost when these habits of thought were discarded in the desire to break with the moral imperatives of mid-Victorian cultural life.

Since few critics erected any barrier between 'literary' and 'non-literary' considerations in writing about the novel, it has not seemed appropriate to narrow the selection of extracts in the present collection to coincide with what any particular critics of later periods regarded as appropriate to literary criticism. Extracts are therefore reprinted which cover a considerable diversity of subjects, with the aim of showing what early and mid-Victorian literary people themselves regarded as the important issues of the day in prose fiction. As a result, alongside the discussion of texts, this volume contains examples of the nineteenth-century debate about the office and social standing of the novelist (chapter 7), and even an instance of advice to parents on the attractiveness of writing as a career (7.2). Similarly, the analysis of plot is not left to professional critics, but the founding father of British empirical psychology, Alexander Bain, is also quoted on the workings of 'the literature of plot-interest' (5.3). In this the editor is following the example of his Victorian forebears, who entrusted criticism of *belles-lettres* to soldiers, philosophers and lawyers. (5.1 and 3.6 show examples of the first two, while from its inception the *Saturday Review* employed numbers of young barristers.) The purpose of this choice is not only to demonstrate that there was ample challenging criticism, and at least as much competent reviewing as in the following century, but to argue for the study of Victorian fiction in an appropriate critical setting, in the belief that we do considerable violence to the great Victorian novelists if we ignore the intellectual framework in which their work was originally set, and take the persuasive but misleading word of Henry James's disciples for what should be regarded as the proper subjects for critical examination.

The theoretical motivation behind this selection is not new, of course. A great deal of the most stimulating work on Victorian fiction in the later twentieth century has concerned interconnections: between the fiction and socio-economic aspects of the systems of publication and distribution; between the narratives of fiction and the narratives of science; between the theory and practice of realism; and – most expansively – between women authors and their world, and novels by women and readings by men. This collection will have served its purpose if it reminds students or general readers of the importance of such specialist studies, and enables them to read these in a larger context of intellectual and aesthetic history. The point is that 'background' studies, however well done – and there are some very fine books available on Victorian 'background' – stand somewhat apart from the literature of the period, and cannot on their own foster the useful habit of reading not only the novels, but the historical, ideological and aesthetic significance of the literary choices they embody.

The better understanding of writing by and about Victorian women is of such importance that a book of limited length can only provide a small sample of the relevant available material. Rather than collecting together all the extracts bearing on the subject, I have dispersed them throughout the work, to indicate my contention that, while the subject should also be pursued in separate books and separate academic courses, it is deeply implicated in all aspects of literary study. In the present instance I felt that there was a positive advantage in including materials of feminist significance among rather than detached from the utterances of unselfcritical patriarchy. Arguably there is too much of the latter and too little of the former, but that is how the literary institutions of the age present themselves. Aware readers will know how to exploit the material in this volume to their own ends, particularly since I have made no attempt to sanitise it, and have left my favourite critics with all their ideological imperfections full-blown upon them. As will be clear, I admire Eneas Sweetland Dallas from some points of view, but have also represented him at his ideological worst in his attack on Gaskell's *Life of Charlotte Brontë* (7.1).

This kind of tolerance is necessary in approaching the whole subject of early and mid-Victorian criticism. For instance, those today who most appreciate R.H. Hutton's almost semiological approach to characterisation and interpersonal perceptions in the 'drawing-room' novel (5.6 and 6.4), are least likely to be comfortable with his assumptions about female characterisation, or his insistence that literature should be written in the 'awe-struck awareness' of heaven above and hell beneath (introduction to chapter 5 and 3.3). The truth is that any age takes from its predecessors what it wants of positive and negative, and this volume, even if it attempts some kind of 'fairness', must be guilty of the same fault in working out the terms of that 'fairness'. For example, there is next-to-nothing in this collection on the historical novel as a genre, and very little on science fiction. To use one of Carlyle's famous images, there is a boundless sea of knowledge surrounding us, of which any book can only include an infinitesimal part. Then again, Victorian book reviews were nearly always substantial and frequently very long – 30,000 words was not unknown. Hence each extract which has been chosen is but a short portion of a long whole, omitting far more than it prints, and concealing far more than it shows. Victorian literary criticism is like a large and complex city: a guided tour will show one aspect of selected buildings, but round the corner may be quite other features; squalor may be hidden behind respectability; and by turning round we might have seen townscapes made up of altogether different combinations of social and architectural styles.

Not all the extracts reprinted here deal with the sort of fiction still widely known and respected over a hundred years later. At the time of publication, the future standing of a new novel cannot be known, and some of the most revealing criticism was then, as later, a response to less enduring works. This volume certainly does not attempt to do what the Critical Heritage series so admirably does, and provide coherent representation of opinion on any given novelist, though a great deal of information on the reception of different writing can obviously be gleaned from any broadly based selection. Of course readers are always curious to know whether a particular novel or novelist found favour with contemporary reviewers, and like to know that in the 1830s it was commonly said that Dickens was too popular, and that having risen like a rocket, he would come down like a stick; that both Charlotte and Emily Brontë were attacked by the Tory press; that the best-educated critics generally wrote of Thackeray with admiration and affection; that Trollope was 'the Apollo of the circulating library', and George Eliot everywhere spoken of in terms of intellectual respect. Such facts as these are relevant to literary biography, contribute to an understanding of the context in which the novelists' works appeared, and tell us a great deal of how the literary system worked.

It is arguable that on some occasions critical opinions on a book had a direct influence on a writer's subsequent work, but in general it is safe to agree with E.S. Dallas that it is not within the power of criticism to instruct perfect poets, any more than physics or chemistry textbooks make practitioners in those fields; and Dallas goes so far as to quote G.H. Lewes to the effect that 'The good effected by criticism is small, the evil incalculable.'[21] William Caldwell Roscoe, too, maintained that criticism does not in general improve literature:

A writer or labourer of any sort rarely profits by criticism on his productions; here and there a very candid man may gather a hint; but for the most part criticism is only used by an author as a test of the good taste of his judge. It is a fiction, in fact, long religiously maintained in the forms of our reviews, that we write for the benefit of the reviewee. In most cases, and at any rate in that of a mature and established author, this didactic figment would be as well put aside. A new work, a body of writings, by a man who has attained a wide audience and produced a considerable impression on his times, constitutes a subject for investigation; we examine it as we do other matters of interest, we analyse, we dissect, we compare notes about it; we estimate its influences; and as man is the most interesting of all studies, we examine what light it throws on the producing mind, and endeavour to penetrate through the work to some insight into the special genius of the writer; – and all this for our own pleasure and profit, not because we think our remarks will prove beneficial to him who is the subject of them.[22]

It is a salutary idea that all human activity should be subject to intellectual inquiry, and our admiration of this characteristically Victorian stance should not be deflected by the realisation that the study of 'the producing mind' has passed through various phases of unfashionableness in the twentieth century. To the later reader there may also seem to be an inordinate stress on morality, truth-to-life and 'correctness' of language in the advice typically given by Victorian reviewers, but it may be that these matters strike us more forcibly as readers of another period. As I pointed out above, many important subjects came under review, and the overt moralism of the age should not be allowed to obscure other things of interest, and the variety of critical postures involved. 'Truth-to-life' – judged by how 'recognisable' the characters in the novel were – was regarded by most critics as an indispensable quality in fiction, and only Dallas and Lytton among those reprinted here were openly contemptuous of this naïve mimetic standard. Certain reviews, notably some in the *Spectator* while R.H. Hutton was literary editor, turn their attention to interpersonal perceptions and the 'language of manners', thus anticipating concerns of a century later, and opening up for perhaps the first time in British intellectual history the possibility of a semiotics of social behaviour. (See the introduction to chapter 5.)

On the whole reviewers did as well then as they have ever done since. Edith Simcox put their problems in clear terms:

Contemporary criticism of great works is apt to prove unsatisfactory, for even when their greatness is recognised at once, the critic labours under a double disadvantage: an unwonted sense of responsibility restrains the free expression of unmotivated admiration, and the easy volubility of praise, which is enough for slighter merits, makes way for a guarded tone of respect that looks like coldness on the surface. Nor is this all; for the vocabulary of positive eulogium is soon exhausted; criticism to be significant must be comparative, and there is an obvious difficulty in estimating by old-fashioned standards of excellence a new work that may contain within itself a fresh standard for the guidance and imitation of futurity. (1.8)

Despite moments of insight which might contribute to a theory of fiction, most of our critics were unsystematically empirical in their approach. Simcox goes on to make an attractively comfortable case for this approach:

For the theory of art is after all only a patchwork of inference from the practice of artists, and, to quit generalities, in one clearly defined and admirable branch of imaginative art – the English novel – our ideal is simply one or other of the masterpieces of one or other of the great novelists between Fielding and George Eliot. *Tom Jones, Clarissa Harlowe, Waverley, Pride and Prejudice, Vanity Fair, Adam Bede* – to which some might wish to add *Eugene Aram, Pickwick*, and *Jane Eyre* – are the sources from whence all theories of the novel, as a prose narrative representation of manners, character and passion, ultimately derive.

She proceeds to add *Middlemarch* to her list, and in this has been followed by many critics since. Unfortunately there is no adequate study of the works used by Victorian reviewers for the purposes of comparison, and hence we can merely guess at the shape of their literary and intellectual universe. The following extracts from criticism of the novel, 1837 to 1880, may provide evidence which helps that guesswork to be more reliable.

The volume is organised in thematic chapters, which move in towards a consideration of textual matters, and out again. The 'subjects' of individual chapters are inevitably somewhat arbitrary, and some passages in almost any extract could find homes equally well in other chapters, while in most cases, if the bounds of the extract had been differently drawn, the dominant theme would have been changed, and the item would have rightly belonged to another part of the book. To avoid forcing an artificially coherent shape on the criticism of the period, the items in each chapter are printed chronologically. The first chapter, 'The age of the novel', proves the importance of the novel in the period, and represents some of the conflicting emotions the dominant form aroused, while the second exemplifies one of the characteristics of this fiction: its willingness to take on any social, religious or philosophical question of the day. Chapter 3, 'Social, moral and religious judgements', concentrates on kinds of criticism which are less frequent in a later century, and which erected serious obstacles to the writing of certain types of fiction on certain sorts of subject. Chapters 4 and 5 introduce the major Victorian topics of realism, idealism, sensationalism, humour, character, plot and 'truth-to-life', which are so intimately woven together that up to half-a-dozen of them are often implicated in a single, short utterance. Chapter 6 deals with creativity and the imagination, while the final chapter moves further from the text to investigate the author and authorship. With so many voices taking up related points, it is hoped that a feeling of debate will be created, and that this debate will be seen to have been of enormous importance not only to the authors and critics of the early and mid-Victorian period, but to a large section of the literate public as well. An age in which literary criticism is too often partitioned off from other intelligent concerns might well envy the vigour and commitment of a previous century.

Notes

1 'The Novel and the Drama', *Saturday Review* 17 (12 March 1864), 312–14.
2 E.S. Dallas, *The Gay Science*, 2 vols, 1866, vol. 2, p. 284.
3 'On a Lazy Idle Boy', *Roundabout Papers* no. 1, *Cornhill Magazine* 1 (January 1860), 124–8.
4 Pseudonym for William Martin (1801–67), author (with George Mogridge, 1787–1854) of *Peter Parley's Annual* for young people, 1840–67.
5 Leigh Hunt, 'New Translations of the *Arabian Nights*', *Westminster Review* 33 (January 1840), 101–37.
6 Dallas, *Gay Science*, vol. 2, p. 285.
7 'Biography', *Fraser's Magazine* (April–May 1832), 253–60, 379–413 (review of Boswell's *Life of Johnson*).
8 Dallas, *Gay Science*, vol. 2, pp. 285–6. Dallas based part of this passage on his earlier review of Trollope's *Rachel Ray* in *The Times*, 25 December 1863, 4.
9 Wilkie Collins.
10 James Payn, 'Penny Fiction', in *Some Private Views: Being Essays from 'The Nineteenth Century' Review with Some Occasional Articles from 'The Times'*, 1881, p. 116.
11 MS letter-books of *The Times*, vol. 5, 516 (5 September 1855), and vol. 13, 618 (1 November 1865). I am grateful to the archivist and proprietors of Times Newspapers for access to these letters.
12 For an account of many of these writers and their importance, see John Gross, *The Rise and Fall of the English Man of Letters*, London,

Weidenfeld and Nicolson, 1969.
13 *Lamia*, II, 234.
14 A reference to Byron's poem, 'English Bards and Scotch Reviewers', 1809.
15 'Characteristics', *Edinburgh Review* 54 (December 1831), 369–70.
16 See G. S. Haight, 'George Meredith and the *Westminster Review*', *Modern Language Review* 53 (January 1958), 1–16.
17 Anthony Trollope, *An Autobiography*, London, Oxford University Press, 1980, pp. 264 and 387.
18 See David Skilton, Introduction to Anthony Trollope, *The Belton Estate*, The Trollope Society Edition of the novels of Anthony Trollope, 1991.
19 4.10, for example, contains a small and witty but precise reference to Hegel, which suggests that Hutton had developed at least the germ of a Hegelian theory of humour.
20 George Saintsbury, *A History of English Criticism*, Edinburgh, William Blackwood & Sons Ltd, 1962, p. 496 (first published 1900–4).
21 Dallas, *Gay Science*, vol. 1, pp. 63–5 and 13.
22 William Caldwell Roscoe (anon.), 'W. M. Thackeray, Artist and Moralist', 264–308; review of *The Newcomes* and *Miscellanies, Prose and Verse*, *National Review* 2 (January 1856), 177–213.

1

The age of the novel

Since the late eighteenth century the novel had been greeted with antagonism by evangelicals and Utilitarians alike, as a danger to the reader's moral and mental well-being, and with grudging acceptance by the more open-minded, as a form far inferior to poetry and drama, and fit only for ephemeral amusement. In 1848, in what is usually regarded as a most remarkably fertile period for the English novel, De Quincey put the matter unequivocally: 'All novels whatever, the best equally with the worst, have faded almost with the generation that produced them. This is a curse written as a superscription above the whole class.'[1] In general, however, as the extraordinary amount of good new fiction forced itself on the attention of all thinking people in the early and mid-Victorian period, it became apparent that the novel was the literary form most characteristic of the day, and the question arose as to whether the dominance of prose fiction represented wholescale cultural degradation. It might be true that '[a] chain of novels like Mr. Anthony Trollope's Barsetshire set is essentially a birth of our own time', as the Oresteia was of fifth-century Athens[2] but how did that fact reflect on the new age? By the 1860s, however, the aesthetic importance of the form was becoming accepted by many. In 1863 a culturally élitist weekly like the *Saturday Review* could write:

> Novels have become so large a part of our literature . . . that they cannot be dismissed as so much 'light literature', nor their character be considered a matter of indifference. In the hands of some writers, they have almost risen to the dignity of the drama and the epic, and have become models of thought and style to all who come after them.[3]

To a critic in the *North British Review* in 1864 this was the age of the novel, as the Elizabethan and Jacobean period had been the age of drama, while for the *Westminster Review* in 1867, '[t]o say that the novel is the modern substitute for the drama is only to repeat one of the commonplaces of criticism'.[4] In 1881, at the end of the period covered by this book, there was no incongruity in Leslie Stephen's comparison of George Eliot's death with that of Shakespeare in its potential significance for the history of English literature.[5] The high status of prose fiction had finally been confirmed in relation to *Middlemarch*, a novel which gives an account of the political, social and economic foundation of mid-nineteenth-century prosperity, and hereby arguably did for the Victorians what Virgil's *Aeneid* did for Imperial Rome.

The dominant literary form had its admirers and detractors, but everybody agreed in attributing the success and peculiarities of each kind of novel to social and economic factors. De Quincey (1.2) puts the growth in the fiction industry down to an increase in basic literacy, and ascribes the shortcomings of the mass of novels to the fact that authors become corrupted by pandering to the debased tastes of the inadequately educated lower classes. For Bagehot (1.3) the tastes of young readers are allowed too much influence in the choice of subject-matter, while the *Saturday Review* (1.5) looks down on fiction which it feels to have arrived at success through the vagaries of fashion. E.S. Dallas (1.6) for his part recognises serialisation as an effective way of reaching a large readership, and finds it in turn a determining factor in the development of plot-interest in novels in the period.

The age of the novel had brought with it new methods of distributing and consuming fiction. Extracts 1.5, 1.6 and 1.7 highlight the importance of part-issue and serialisation, which were crucial in creating a wider readership at a time when a three-volume novel cost £1 11s 6d. The particular sort of continuing interest wound up by serialisation leads Jeaffreson (1.7) to ask on behalf of his readers for the further adventures of Trollope's Barsetshire characters. The other system of distribution most characteristic of the age was the large circulating library, notably the one founded in 1842 by Charles Mudie, whose fortune, the *Saturday Review* jokes (1.5), Trollope was born to make, and who quickly, as De Quincey notes (1.2), made use of improved communications in the age of steam to transport books to his readers all over the country, and indeed over the entire globe. (A box of books from Mudie's even accompanied Sir John Franklin on his fatal arctic expedition of 1845–7.)[6]

We know less about the individual experience of reading than we do of the workings of the literary market-place. It is unsafe to assume that original readers took in the major works of Victorian fiction in the way that we are likely to read current fiction. According to Dallas

(5.4), 'a novel-reader will go on reading novels to all eternity, and sometimes even will have several in hand at once – a serial of Mr. Trollope's here, a serial of Mr. Dickens's there, and the last three-volume tale into the bargain'. Illustration was an integral part of much serial fiction from *Pickwick* onwards, including a majority of the works of Dickens, Thackeray and Trollope, and George Eliot's *Romola*, and the very fact of the inclusion of illustrations in each instalment could change the way in which the fiction was approached. The actor William Macready's records in his diary for 22 January 1841 his reaction to the issue of *Master Humphrey's Clock* containing the death of Little Nell in *The Old Curiosity Shop*: 'I saw one print in it of the dear dead child that gave a dead chill through my blood. I dread to read it, but I must get it over.' Macready's reading was a kind of ritual, aided by the illustration.[7]

There was a widespread belief in this period that the novel could do anything, from bringing about social reform, to setting forth the entire life of the nineteenth century. According to Bagehot (1.2) it was capable of 'describing the whole of human life in all its spheres, in all its aspects, with all its varied interests, aims and objects. It searches through the whole life of man; his practical pursuits, his speculative attempts, his romantic youth, and his domestic age', while for Bulwer (1.1) it drew its force from the fact that '[T]he passions of men are the most useful field for the metaphysics of the imagination, and yet the grandest and the most inexhaustible'.

Notes

1 See extract 1.2 below.
2 Review of *The Last Chronicle of Barset*, *Examiner* (20 July 1867), 452–3, reprinted in D. Smalley, *Trollope: the Critical Heritage*, London, Routledge & Kegan Paul, 1969, p. 297.
3 *Saturday Review* 15 (28 February 1863), 280, quoted in Richard Stang, *The Theory of the Novel in England 1850–1870*, London, Routledge & Kegan Paul, 1959, p. 47, which includes a useful discussion of the status of prose fiction in the period.
4 A.S. Kinnear (anon.) in *North British Review* 40 (May 1864), 369, and J.R. Wise (anon.) in *Westminster Review* 88 (October 1867), 593.
5 *Cornhill Magazine* 43 (February 1881), 152–68.
6 For the production and circulation of Victorian fiction see John A. Sutherland, *Victorian Novelists and Publishers*, London, Athlone Press, 1978 and N.N. Feltes, *Modes of Production of Victorian Novels*, Chicago, University of Chicago Press, 1986; and for circulating libraries see Guinevere L. Griest, *Mudie's Circulating Library and the Victorian Novel*, Newton Abbot, David & Charles, 1970.
7 *Macready's Reminiscences, and Selections from his Diaries and Letters*, ed

Sir Frederick Pollock, Bart., 2 vols, London, 1871, vol. 2, p. 69. For a discussion of illustration and the reading process in Victorian fiction see David Skilton, 'The Relation between Illustration and Narrative in the Victorian Novel', in P.M. Daly, K.J. Höltgen and W. Lottes (eds), *The Word and the Visual Imagination. A Symposium of Studies Relating to English Literature*, Erlangen, Erlangen Forschungen, 1987.

1.1 Edward Bulwer, *England and the English*, 2 vols, 1833, vol. 2, pp. 109–12

This passage is taken from a survey of English life, politics and culture published four years before Victoria came to the throne. It is included here because it expresses an influential view which had currency at the opening of the period covered by the present volume. The author is the novelist Edward Bulwer (1803–73; subsequently Edward Bulwer Lytton, and still later Lord Lytton). His bestseller Pelham *(1828) was a hugely popular social study of fashionable life in London, and he was equally successful with* Paul Clifford *(1830), which founded the 'Newgate novel', a genre of fiction dealing with criminals recorded in the* Newgate Calendar. *Throughout his life Bulwer wrote general statements about the novel and the nature of fiction, often in the form of prefaces to the various editions of his own novels. One of these (the preface to the 1845 edition of* Night and Morning) *is partly reproduced in extract 1.2, below. In an age which is uncomfortable with grand abstractions, personifications and the liberal use of capital letters, Bulwer is not now widely admired, but the intellectual respect in which he was once held can be judged from David Masson's remark in* British Novelists and Their Styles *that of all novelists he had 'worked most consciously on a theory of the Novel as a form of literature'.[1] The passage reproduced follows a discussion of the popularity of novels of fashionable life, and makes a case for fiction as a major vehicle for social thought and reform – a role which many novelists were happy to adopt for the next half century or more.*

Few writers ever produced so great an effect on the political spirit of their generation as some of these novelists, who, without any other merit, unconsciously exposed the falsehood, the hypocrisy, the arrogant and vulgar insolence of patrician life. Read by all classes, in every town, in every village, these works, as I have before stated, could not but engender a mingled indignation and disgust at the parade of frivolity, the ridiculous disdain of truth, nature, and mankind, the self-consequence and absurdity, which, falsely or truly, these novels exhibited as a picture of aristocratic society. The Utilitarians railed against them, and they were effecting with unspeakable rapidity the very purposes the Utilitarians desired.

While these light works were converting the multitude, graver writers were soberly confirming their effect, society itself knew not the change in feeling which had crept over it; till a sudden flash, as it were, revealed the change electrically to itself. Just at the time when with George the Fourth an *old* era expired, the excitement of a popular election at home concurred with the three days of July in France,[2] to give a decisive tone to the *new*. The question of Reform came on, and, to the astonishment of the nation itself, it was hailed at once by the national heart. From that moment, the intellectual spirit hitherto partially directed to, became *wholly* absorbed in, politics; and whatever lighter works have since obtained a warm and general hearing, have either developed the errors of the social system, or the vices of the legislative. Of the first, I refrain from giving an example; of the last, I instance as a sign of the times, the searching fictions of Miss Martineau, and the wide reputation they have acquired.[3]

A description of the mere frivolities of fashion is no longer coveted; for the public mind, once settled towards an examination of the aristocracy, has pierced from the surface to the depth; it has *probed* the wound, and it now desires to *cure*.

It is in this state that the Intellectual Spirit of the age rests, demanding the Useful, but prepared to receive it through familiar shapes: a state at present favourable to ordinary knowledge, to narrow views, or to mediocre genius; but adapted to prepare the way and to found the success for the coming triumphs of a bold philosophy, or a profound and subtle imagination. Some cause, indeed, there is of fear, lest the desire for immediate and palpable utility should stint the capacities of genius to the trite and familiar truths. But as Criticism takes a more wide and liberal view of the true and unbounded sphere of the Beneficial, we may trust that this cause of fear will be removed. The passions of men are the most useful field for the metaphysics of the imagination, and yet the grandest and the most inexhaustible. Let us take care that we do not, as in the old Greek fable, cut the wings of our bees and set flowers before them, as the most sensible mode of filling the Hives of Truth!

But the great prevailing characteristic of the present intellectual spirit is one most encouraging to human hopes; it is Benevolence. There has grown up among us a sympathy with the great mass of mankind. For this we are indebted in no small measure to the philosophers (with whom Benevolence is, in all times, the foundation of philosophy); and that more decided and emphatic expression of the sentiment which was common, despite their errors, to the French moralists of the last century, has been kept alive and applied to immediate legislation by the English moralists of the present. We owe also the popularity of the growing principle to the writings of Miss Edgeworth and of Scott,[4] who sought their characters among the people, and who interested us by a picture of (and not a declamation upon) their life and its humble vicissitudes, their errors and their virtues.

Notes

1 David Masson, *British Novelists and Their Styles: Being a Critical Sketch of the History of British Prose Fiction*, Cambridge, 1859, pp. 228–9.
2 The 'popular election' was dominated by the issue of parliamentary reform, and followed the succession of William IV on George IV's death on 26 June 1830. The 'days of July', or 'les journées de juillet', in the same year saw the exiling of Charles X and the installation in France of the so-called 'July monarchy' of Louis-Philippe.
3 As an example of the first category he is presumably thinking of his own *Paul Clifford* (1830), which was a highly successful novel attacking the law's excessive reliance on capital punishment. It is not clear to which of the writings of Harriet Martineau (1802–76) he is alluding. She was best known at the time for her *Illustrations of Political Economy* (1832) in the form of didactic short tales.
4 Throughout the 1800s Maria Edgeworth (1767–1849) and Sir Walter Scott (1771–1832) were regarded as the founders of the type of novel which concerned itself with the lives of individuals in society. Jane Austen was widely undervalued until much later in the century.

1.2 Thomas De Quincey, review of John Forster, *The Life and Adventures of Oliver Goldsmith*, *North British Review* 9 (May 1848), 187–212, pp. 193–5

The novelist, essayist and poet Oliver Goldsmith (1728–74) was a figure held in great historical affection by Victorian literary people. He combined physical unattractiveness with amiability, generosity and a notable inability to deal with the affairs of the world, and as an intimate acquaintance of many of the great cultural figures of his day, such as Samuel Johnson and Sir Joshua Reynolds, he seemed to provide the ordinary person's entrée into the world of the immortals.

De Quincey's opinion that prose narrative was generally ephemeral and of comparatively little worth typifies the negative side to the recognition of the period as the 'age of the novel'. To make matters worse, he says, urbanisation and popular education were lowering cultural standards, and the new age was rightly but disgracefully characterised by its mass of mediocre fiction. To Forster's claim that Goldsmith was at a disadvantage in writing after the great period of aristocratic patronage and before the establishment of the large Victorian literary market, De Quincey retorts that a reliance on the latter is necessarily degrading. His disdain for plotting and suspense in particular is characteristic of many of the opponents of sensational fiction a dozen years later. For examples of various positions on this question see extracts 3.6, 5.3, 5.4 and 5.9.

We are not . . . of Mr. Forster's opinion, that Goldsmith fell upon an age less favourable to the expansion of literary powers, or to the attainment of literary distinction, than any other. The patron might be a tradition – but the public was not therefore a prophecy. My lord's trumpets had ceased to sound, but the *vox populi*[1] was not therefore muffled. The means indeed of diffusive advertisement and of rapid circulation, the combinations of readers into reading societies, and of roads into iron net-works, were as yet imperfectly developed. These gave a potent stimulus to periodic literature. And a still more operative difference between ourselves and them is – that a new class of people has since then entered our reading public, viz. – the class of artisans and of all below the gentry, which (taken generally) was in Goldsmith's day a cipher as regarded any real encouragement to literature. In our days, if *The Vicar of Wakefield* had been published as a Christmas tale, it would have produced a fortune to the writer.[2] In Goldsmith's time, few below the gentry were readers on any large scale. So far there really *was* a disadvantage. But it was a disadvantage which applied chiefly to novels. The new influx of readers in our times, the collateral affluents into the main stream from the mechanic and provincial sections of our population, which have centupled the volume of the original current, cannot be held as telling favourably upon literature, or telling at all, except in the departments of popularized science, of religion, of fictitious tales, and of journalism. To be a reader, is no longer as once it was, to be of a meditative turn. To be a *very* popular author is no longer that honorary distinction which once it might have been amongst a more elevated because more select body of readers. We do not say this invidiously, or with any special reference. But it is evident that writers and readers must often act and react for reciprocal degradation. A writer of this day, either in France or England, to be *very* popular, must be a story-teller; which is a function of literature neither very noble in itself, nor, secondly, tending to permanence. All novels whatever, the best equally with the worst, have faded almost with the generation that produced them. This is a curse written as a superscription above the whole class. The modes of combining characters, the particular objects selected for sympathy, the diction, and often the manners,[3] hold up an imperfect mirror to any generation that is not their own. And the reader of novels belonging to an obsolete era, whilst acknowledging the skill of the groupings, or the beauty of the situations, misses the echo to that particular revelation of human nature which has met him in the social aspects of his own day; or too often he is perplexed by an expression which, having dropped into a lower use, disturbs the unity of the impression, or is revolted by a coarse sentiment, which increasing refinement has made unsuitable to the sex or to the rank of the character. How bestial and degrading at this day seem many of the scenes in Smollett! How coarse are the ideals of Fielding! – his odious Squire Western, his odious Tom Jones! What a gallery of histrionic masqueraders is thrown open in the novels of Richardson, powerful as they were once found by the two leading nations of the earth.[4] A popular writer, therefore, who, *in order* to be popular, must speak through novels, speaks to what is least permanent in human sensibilities. That is already to be self-degraded. *Secondly*, because the novel-reading class is by far the most comprehensive one, and being such, must count as a large majority amongst its members those who are poor in capacities of thinking, and are passively resigned to the instinct of immediate pleasure – to these the writer must chiefly humble himself: he must study *their* sympathies, must assume them, must give them back. In our days he must give them back even their own street slang; so servile is the modern novelist's dependence on his *canaille* of an audience.[5] In France, amongst the Sues, &c., it has been found necessary to give back even the closest portraits of obscene atrocities that shun the light, and burrow only in the charnel-houses of vast manufacturing towns. Finally, the very principle of command-ing attention only by the interest of a tale, which means the interest of a momentary curiosity that is to vanish for ever in a sense of satiation, and of a momentary suspense that, having once collapsed, can never be rekindled, is in itself a confession of reliance upon the meaner offices of the mind. The result from all which is that to be popular in the most extensive walk of popularity, that is, as a novelist, a writer must generally be in a very considerable degree self-degraded by sycophancy to the lowest order of minds, and cannot (except for mercenary purposes) think himself advantageously placed.

Notes

1   *vox populi* (Latin): 'voice of the people'; from Alcuin's dictum *vox populi vox dei*: 'the voice of the people is the voice of God'.

2   According to Forster, Samuel Johnson sold *The Vicar of Wakefield* on Goldsmith's behalf for 60, when the latter had been arrested for debt in 1764. The novel was not immediately successful but became one of the best loved novels in the Victorian period. In contrast, Dickens made very large sums from his *Christmas Books*.

3   De Quincey's footnote: Often, but not so uniformly (the reader will think) as the diction, because the manners are sometimes not those of the writer's own age, being ingenious adaptations to meet the modern writer's conjectural ideas of ancient manners. These, however, (even in Sir Walter Scott), are precisely the most mouldering parts in the entire architecture, being always (as, for instance, in *Ivanhoe*) fantastic, caricatured, and betraying the true modern ground gleaming through the artifical tarnish of antiquity. All novels, in every language, are hurrying to decay; and hurrying by *internal* changes – were those all; but in the meantime, the everlasting life and fertility of the human mind is for ever accelerating this hurry by *superseding* them, *i.e.*, by an external change. Old forms, fading from the interest, or even from the apprehension, have no chance at all as against new forms embodying the same passions. It is only in the grander passions of poetry, allying themselves with forms more abstract and permanent, that such a conflict of the old with the new is possible.

4   Richardson was as much admired and imitated in France as in Britain, with readers such as Rousseau and Diderot from among the greatest thinkers of the day.

5   Middle- and upper-class critics in Britain regarded the works of Eugène Sue (1804–57) (*The Mysteries of Paris, The Wandering Jew* and *The Seven Deadly Sins*) as highly improper and distasteful, but they were widely imitated by writers of cheap serial fiction.

1.3 Walter Bagehot, 'The Waverley Novels', *National Review* 6 (April 1858), 444–72, p. 445

In an article on Sir Walter Scott, Walter Bagehot (1826–77), businessman, economist, political scientist, critic and later editor of the Economist, *regrets the dominance of love interest in so many novels of his age, and accords a higher place to fiction characterised by ideas and knowledge of the world. In particular he feels that the 'romantic plot' in a Dickens novel is generally a sop to young readers. About the time that this article appeared a greater integration of questions of love, marriage and personal development with social or philosophical analysis was being developed in the realistic novels of Trollope and George Eliot. (See 1.8 below.)*

There are two kinds of fiction which, though in common literature they may run very much into one another, are yet in reality distinguishable and separate. One of these, which we may call the *ubiquitous*, aims at describing the whole of human life in all its spheres, in all its aspects, with all its varied interests, aims and objects. It searches through the whole life of man; his practical pursuits, his speculative attempts, his romantic youth, and his domestic age. It gives an entire picture of all these; or if there are any lineaments which it forbears to depict, they are only such as the inevitable repression of a regulated society excludes from the admitted province of literary art. Of this kind are the novels of Cervantes and Le Sage,[1] and, to a certain extent, of Smollett or Fielding. In our own time, Mr. Dickens is an author whom nature intended to write to a certain extent with this aim. He should have given us *not* disjointed novels, with a vague attempt at a romantic plot, but sketches of diversified scenes, and the obvious life of varied mankind. The literary fates, however, if such beings there are, allotted otherwise. By a very terrible example of the way in which in this world great interests are postponed to little ones, the genius of authors is habitually sacrificed to the tastes of readers. In this age, the great readers of fiction are young people. The 'addiction' of these is to romance; and accordingly a kind of novel has become so familiar to us as almost to engross the name, which deals solely with the passion of love; and if it uses other parts of human life for the occasions of its art, it does so only cursorily and occasionally, and with a view of throwing into a stronger or more delicate light those sentimental parts of earthly affairs which are the special objects of delineation. All prolonged delineation of other parts of human life is considered 'dry,' stupid, and distracts the mind of the youthful generation from the 'fantasies' which peculiarly charm it.

Note

1 Since the mid-eighteenth century Cervantes (1547–1616) and Lesage (1668–1747) have been credited with a formative influence on the English novel.

1.4 David Masson, *British Novelists and Their Styles: being a critical sketch of the history of British prose fiction*, Cambridge, 1859, pp. 233–40

David Masson (1822–1907) was born and brought up in Aberdeen, and was appointed Professor of English Literature in University College, London, in 1852. British Novelists and Their Styles *is probably the first book on the subject aimed at a university audience, and shows many rhetorical signs of the lectures in which it originated. The extract reproduced here follows a laborious classification of the novel into 'thirteen distinct varieties' by subject matter. The enterprise is typical of a widespread Victorian desire to apply Baconian scientific method to all subjects of investigation. In describing the domination of the world of fiction by Dickens and Thackeray, Masson is expressing a common feeling of the day. In a further extract from Masson's long comparison of Dickens and Thackeray (4.9), he contrasts them as novelists of the 'Real' and 'Ideal' schools.*

Prose fiction in Britain – nay, in the rest of Europe and in America too – has received a fresh impulse and has taken on a new set of characteristics, since Dickens and Thackeray became, for us, its chief representatives. . . . Dickens, as you are aware, was the first in the field. His *Sketches by Boz* appeared in 1837 followed, within the next ten years, by his *Pickwick*, his *Nicholas Nickleby*, his *Oliver Twist* (previously published in magazine parts), his *Humphrey's Clock* (including *The Old Curiosity Shop* and *Barnaby Rudge*), his *Martin Chuzzlewit*, and several of his Christmas Stories. It was not till after these ten years of Dickens's established popularity, or till about the year 1847, that Mr. Thackeray – whose extraordinary powers had already, however, been long recognized within a limited circle of intellectual men, in virtue of his numerous scattered publications and papers – stepped forth into equally extensive celebrity. His *Vanity Fair* was the first efficient proclamation to the public at large of the existence of this signal British talent, increasingly known since by the republication of those *Miscellanies* which had been buried in magazines and other periodicals, and by the successive triumphs of the *Snob Papers*, *Pendennis*, *Esmond*, the *Newcomes*, and various Christmas Books. Parallel with these had been running later fictions from Mr. Dickens's pen – *Dombey and Son*, *David Copperfield*, and *Bleak House*. Mr. Dickens also had the last word in his *Little Dorrit*, until the other day, when Mr. Thackeray recommenced in his *Virginians*. For, with the two writers, according to the serial system, it seems to be, whether by arrangement or by necessity, as with Castor and Pollux; both cannot be above the horizon of the publishing world at once, and, when the one is there, the other takes his turn in Tartarus. But whether simultaneously visible or alternate, the two are now so closely associated in the public mind that whenever the one is mentioned the other is thought of. It is now Dickens and Thackeray,

Thackeray and Dickens, all the world over. Nay, not content with associating them, people have got into the habit of contrasting them and naming them in opposition to each other. There is a Dickens faction, and there is a Thackeray faction; and there is no debate more common, wherever literary talk goes on, than the debate as to the respective merits of Dickens and Thackeray. . . .

Both novelists belong, in the main, though by no means exclusively, to the order of Humorists, or writers of Comic Fiction. Moreover, under this distinction, both stand very much in the same relation to their predecessors in respect of the kind or kinds of fiction, previously in use, to which they have attached themselves, and in respect of the extension of range which that kind or those kinds of fiction have received at their hands. The connexions of both at first were chiefly with that which we have distinguished as the Novel of English Life and Manners; and both, in working this kind of Novel, have added immensely to its achievements and capabilities in one particular field – that of the Metropolis. The Novels of Dickens and Thackeray are, most of them, novels of London; it is in the multifarious circumstances of London life and its peculiar humours that they move most frequently and have their most characteristic being. A fact not unimportant in the appreciation of both! As the greatest aggregate of human beings on the face of the earth, a population of several millions crushed together in one dense mass on a space of a few square miles – this mass consisting, for the most part of Englishmen, but containing also as many Scotchmen as there are in Edinburgh, as many Irishmen as there are in Dublin, and a perfect Polyglot of other nations in addition – London is as good an epitome of the world as anywhere exists, presenting all those phenomena of interest, whether serious or humorous, which result from great numbers, heterogeneousness of composition, and close social packing; besides which, as metropolis of the British Empire, it is the centre whither all the sensations of the Empire tend, and whence the motive currents issue that thrill to the extremities. If any city could generate and sustain a species of Novel entirely out of its own resources, it might surely be London; nor would ten thousand novels exhaust it. After all the mining efforts of previous novelists in so rich a field, Dickens and Thackeray have certainly sunk new shafts in it, and have come upon valuable veins not previously disturbed. So much is this the case that, without injustice to Fielding and others, Dickens and Thackeray might well be considered as the founders of a peculiar sub-variety of the Novel of English Life and Manners, to be called 'The British Metropolitan Novel.' As Londoners, however, do not always stay in

London, or, while in London, are not always engrossed by what is passing there, so our two novelists both range and equally, beyond the bounds of the kind of fiction thus designated. They do give us English life and manners out of London; nay, they have both, as we have seen, given us specimens also of their ability in at least two varieties of the Novel distinct from that of English life and manners – the Traveller's Novel, and the Historical Novel. If, in the respect of external range, either has the advantage, it is perhaps Dickens – who, in his Christmas stories, and in stories interspersed through his larger fictions, has given us specimens of his skill in a kind of prose phantasy which Thackeray has not attempted.

1.5 Review of Trollope's *Framley Parsonage*, *Saturday Review* 11 (4 May 1861), 451–2

The anonymous reviewer gives a lively account of how important a social phenomenon a successful novel could be. Framley Parsonage *was the first of Trollope's novels to be serialised, and the fourth in his* Chronicles of Barsetshire. *It was illustrated by no less an artist than John Everett Millais, and ran from the first number of the new* Cornhill Magazine *which was dated January 1860, but published early, presumably to catch the Christmas market. Under its editor, Thackeray, the* Cornhill *attracted the very best contributors, and, with sales exceeding 100,000, a very large number of middle- and upper-class readers. Among its serial fiction in the first few years were novels by George Eliot, Thackeray and Trollope, alongside poems by Tennyson and articles by Matthew Arnold and Ruskin. The* Saturday Review *and the* Cornhill *early on established themselves as sparring partners, and sometimes generated real acrimony. The reviewer adopts the* Saturday's *characteristic tone of intellectual superiority in making clear the important role of Mudie's, and by implication the other circulating libraries such as W.H. Smith's, in the consumption of fiction. The last remark in this extract alerts the modern reader to the fact that much mid-Victorian reviewing concentrated on the 'truth-to-life' of fictional characters.*

Mr. Anthony Trollope has agreeably entertained for the last eighteen months that portion of society whose intellectual food is taken monthly in the shape of magazines. In looking back on the result of his labours we must confess that he writes as good a book as is often written by a clever and pleasant man in the intervals of business.[1]

With his love of fun and caricature he combines much kindliness and good feeling; he is always readable and pleasant, even if he does not assume to be severe; and few readers can complain of having ever risen from a chapter of *Framley Parsonage* in either too serious or too cynical a mood. If Mr. Mudie is 'a man,' and not merely the system that Madame de Staël pronounced the first Bonaparte to be, he has much reason to be grateful to Mr. Trollope.[2] The author of *Framley Parsonage* is a writer who is born to make the fortune of circulating libraries. At the beginning of every month the new number of his book has ranked almost as one of the delicacies of the season; and no London belle dared to pretend to consider herself literary, who did not know the very latest intelligence about the state of Lucy Robarts' heart, and of Griselda Grantley's flounces. It is a difficult thing to estimate the exact position and merit of a book with which we are all so familiar, and which has diverted us so long. It seems a kind of breach of hospitality to criticise *Framley Parsonage* at all. It has been an intimate of the drawing-room – it has travelled with us in the train – it has lain on the breakfast table. We feel as if we had met Lady Lufton at a country house, admired Lord Dumbello at a ball, and seen Mrs. Proudie at an episcopal evening party. How is it possible, after so much friendly intercourse, to turn round upon the book and its leading characters, and to dissect and analyse them as a critic should?

Notes

1 Trollope was a full-time Civil Servant in the Post Office from 1834 until 1867.
2 Charles Edward Mudie (1818–90) founded his circulating library in 1842, and it rapidly became the largest such business in the country, acquiring volumes at the rate of 180,000 a year around 1861, and delivering books to subscribers throughout the world. The writer Madame de Staël (1766–1817) was exiled by Napoleon I for her liberal opinions.

1.6 E.S. Dallas (anon.), review of Dickens's *Great Expectations*, *The Times*, 17 October 1861, 6

Eneas Sweetland Dallas (1828–79) was one of the most interesting critics of the mid-Victorian period, whose principal work on literary theory, The Gay Science *(2 vols, 1866), is still worth reading, and was perhaps the first work in English to attribute a key role to the unconscious in artistic creativity. (For a brief introduction to his aesthetic position see extract 6.5 and its headnote.) Dallas was born in*

Jamaica and studied at Edinburgh University, where he became a disciple of the philosopher Sir William Hamilton, rejecting the Utilitarians, whose influence was so widespread in the period. In this extract he discusses the effect of serial and part publication of novels on the kind of fiction produced. Publication in instalments made novels available to many people who could not afford the cost of them as books, a three-volume work normally costing £1 1s 6d. Dallas makes it clear, however, that although Dickens catered in part for a lower class of reader than most of the novelists who continued to be read over a century later, there existed cheaper, more popular kinds of fiction, whose circulation far surpassed that of even Dickens's most popular work.

The method of publishing an important work of fiction in monthly instalments was considered a hazardous experiment, which could not fail to set its mark upon the novel as a whole. Mr. Dickens led the way in making the experiment,[1] and his enterprise was crowned with such success that most of the good novels now find their way to the public in the form of a monthly dole. We cannot say that we have ever met with a man who would confess to having read a tale regularly month by month, and who, if asked how he liked Dickens's or Thackeray's last number, did not instantly insist upon the impossibility of his getting through a story piecemeal. Nevertheless, the monthly publication succeeds, and thousands of a novel are sold in minute doses, where only hundreds would have been disposed of in the lump. . . . On the whole, perhaps, the periodical publication of the novel has been of use to it, and has forced English writers to develop a plot and work up the incidents. Lingering over the delineation of character and of manners, our novelists began to lose sight of the story and to avoid action. Periodical publication compelled them to a different course. They could not afford, like Scheherazade, to let the devourers of their tales go to sleep at the end of a chapter. As modern stories are intended not to set people to sleep, but to keep them awake, instead of the narrative breaking down into a soporific dulness, it was necessary that it should rise at the close into startling incident. Hence a disposition to wind up every month with a melodramatic surprise that awakens curiosity in the succeeding number. Even the least melodramatic novelist of the day, Mr. Thackeray, who, so far from feasting us with surprises, goes to the other extreme, and is at particular pains to assure us that the conduct and the character of his personages are not in the least surprising, falls into the way of

31

finishing off his monthly work with a flourish of some sort to sustain the interest.

But what are we to say to the new experiment which is now being tried of publishing good novels week by week? Hitherto the weekly issue of fiction has been connected with publications of the lowest class – small penny and halfpenny serials that found in the multitude some compensation for the degradation of their readers. The sale of these journals extended to hundreds of thousands, and so largely did this circulation depend on the weekly tale, that on the conclusion of a good story it has been known to suffer a fall of 40,000 or 50,000. The favourite authors were Mr. J.F. Smith, Mr. Pierce Egan, and Mr. G.W.M. Reynolds,[2] and the favourite subjects were stories from high life, in which the vices of an aristocracy were portrayed, now with withering sarcasm, and now with fascinating allurements. Lust was the alpha and murder the omega of these tales. When the attempt was made to introduce the readers of the penny journals to better authors and to a more wholesome species of fiction, it was an ignominious failure. . . . Mr. Dickens has tried another experiment. The periodical which he conducts is addressed to a much higher class of readers than any which the penny journals would reach, and he has spread before them novel after novel specially adapted to their tastes.[3] The first of these fictions which achieved a decided success was that of Mr. Wilkie Collins – *The Woman in White*. . . . After Mr. Wilkie Collins's tale, the next great hit was this story of Mr. Dickens's to which we invite the attention of our readers. It is quite equal to *The Woman in White* in the management of the plot, but, perhaps, this is not saying much when we have to add that the story, though not impossible like Mr. Wilkie Collins's, is very improbable. If Mr. Dickens, however, chose to keep the common herd of readers together by the marvels of an improbable story, he attracted the better class of readers by his fancy, his fun, and his sentiment. Altogether, his success was so great as to warrant the conclusion, which four goodly editions already justify, that the weekly form of publication is not incompatible with a very high order of fiction.

Notes

1 *Pickwick Papers* was published in nineteen illustrated monthly parts from April 1836 to November 1837 (with one month omitted), at a shilling per part, the last month's being a 'double number'.

2 J.F. Smith (1803–90) was a voluminous writer of cheap romance in serial form, and was well known as a writer who could vastly increase the circulation of a periodical by the clever use of suspense. Pierce Egan the

younger (1814–80), another writer of cheap serial fiction, specialised in historical romances, and is regarded as the founder of the popular Robin Hood industry. G.W.M. Reynolds (1814–79), was a plagiarist of Dickens with his successful *Pickwick Abroad* (1839), editor of the highly successful *Reynold's Miscellany* from 1846, and in the 1840s and 1850s the author of *The Mysteries of London*, the most celebrated imitation of the French novelist Eugène Sue.

3   In April 1859 Dickens launched the second weekly venture of his career, a paper selling at 2d and called *All the Year Round*. *A Tale of Two Cities* (30 April to 26 November 1859) was the first serial, followed by Wilkie Collins's phenomenal success *The Woman in White* (26 November 1859 to 25 August 1860). *Great Expectations* appeared in *All the Year Round* in weekly instalments from 1 December 1860 to 3 August 1861. At the peak of its success sales of *All the Year Round* exceeded 300,000.

1.7 J.C. Jeaffreson (anon.), review of Trollope's *The Small House at Allington*, *Athenaeum* 1900 (26 March 1864), 437–8, p. 437

The author of this extract, a regular contributor to the Athenaeum, *describes emphatically the tension created by serialised fiction, even when it was as 'unsensational' as Trollope's* The Small House at Allington, *which ran in the* Cornhill Magazine *from September 1862 to April 1864. The illustrations by John Everett Millais were clearly a factor in the novel's success. Trollope concluded the story of Lily Dale, Johnny Eames and Adolphus Crosbie in* The Last Chronicle of Barset *(1866–7).*

'The Small House at Allington' has already been as thronged with interested visitors as Strawberry Hill the ten days before the sale![1] Nearly everybody has heard of it, most people have read it, and now that it has come before the public complete in two beautiful volumes, with Mr. Millais's illustrations retained, those who have possessed their soul in patience until it should be completed, will be able to reap their reward; whilst those who have taken it in monthly fractions will go over the ground again with something of regret, recognizing the old landmarks where the story broke off, leaving them hungry and impatient at the month's pause that must intervene before the next instalment. Certainly if the dietary rule 'to rise from table with an appetite' holds good for the reading of novels, 'The Small House at Allington' has strenuously enforced it, and many readers at the moment would have rashly offered to forfeit three weeks in the month, if they might thus have learnt the progress of the story a little further ahead. It is characteristic of this story, that the characters are all living, human beings; and there has been as much speculation whether Lily Dale would marry Johnny Eames, as about any 'marriage on the *tapis*' (as the *Morning Post* phrases it) in any town or village in Great Britain. Readers have made it a personal question, and there have been vehement discussions as to the probability of her forgiving Adolphus Crosbie, and being happy with him at last, after he had been punished sufficiently for the sake of the moral, and had profited by his sufferings so as to come to his right mind. Many hoped that he would break loose from his slavery to Lady Alexandrina and her family before the wedding-day, and go back to his lawful queen. . . . The story cannot be considered as concluded. In the interest of a wide circle of readers, we demand, with emphasis, of Mr. Trollope that he tell us the further fortunes of the characters in 'The Small House at Allington' . . .

Note

1 Strawberry Hill, the fantastic 'gothic' villa of the writer Horace Walpole (1717–97) aroused enormous public curiosity when it and its contents were sold in 1842.

1.8 Review of George Eliot's *Middlemarch, Academy* 4 (1 January 1873), 1–4, p. 1; signed 'H. Lawrenny', pseudonym of Edith Simcox

This is an extract from one of the most intelligently sympathetic reviews of George Eliot's novel, and brought the critic and novelist into contact. Edith Simcox (1844–1901), a brilliant writer on a wide variety of subjects, including fine art, literature, philosophy, folklore and economics, became the most extravagant of George Eliot's younger female admirers, considering herself the older woman's 'spiritual daughter', and treating her with an almost religious reverence.

Finding the principles of novel criticism to be derived from the practice of the best novelists of the past and present, Simcox suggests that Middlemarch *will in future demonstrate a new set of standards which can be applied in criticism. The favourable reception of this novel, of which this review is an example, in fact marks a moment in the history of English criticism of the novel after which adherents to the Victorian standards of realism were able for over a century to use*

Middlemarch *as a point of reference marking the highest achievement of their favoured genre. Simcox is notably up-to-date in the high seriousness with which she treats prose fiction, without a hint that it is a form which is read in the absence of great modern epic poetry or tragic drama. Despite her statement that nineteenth-century England is less 'heroic' than late fifteenth-century Florence, there is no cultural disgrace to living in the age of the novel. With her high moral seriousness, philosophical analysis and density of cultural awareness, George Eliot did as much as any author to establish in the ideology of the English literary system the idea of the lasting value of the novel as a literary form and social phenomenon. The references in this extract to Goethe and Balzac demonstrate an aesthetic confidence in the possibilities of English fiction and show for the first time that assertions of English moral superiority no longer need to be trumpeted forth to conceal the English inferiority complex in relation to continental artistic standards.*

Contemporary criticism of great works is apt to prove unsatisfactory, for even when their greatness is recognised at once, the critic labours under a double disadvantage: an unwonted sense of responsibility restrains the free expression of unmotivated admiration, and the easy volubility of praise, which is enough for slighter merits, makes way for a guarded tone of respect that looks like coldness on the surface. Nor is this all; for the vocabulary of positive eulogium is soon exhausted; criticism to be significant must be comparative, and there is an obvious difficulty in estimating by old-established standards of excellence a new work that may contain within itself a fresh standard for the guidance and imitation of futurity. For the theory of art is after all only a patchwork of inference from the practice of artists, and, to quit generalities, in one clearly defined and admirable branch of imaginative art – the English novel – our ideal is simply one or other of the masterpieces of one or other of the great novelists between Fielding and George Eliot. *Tom Jones, Clarissa Harlowe, Waverley, Pride and Prejudice, Vanity Fair, Adam Bede* – to which some might wish to add *Eugene Aram, Pickwick,* and *Jane Eyre* – are the sources from whence all theories of the novel, as a prose narrative representation of manners, character and passion, ultimately derive. In truth, variety and intensity, the best of these works left something to be supplied by excellence of a different type: there are stronger as well as more complex passions than Fielding has drawn; Richardson's subtlety works in a narrow field; Miss Austen's knowledge of the world was scanty, and Thackeray's theory of human nature one-sided, while on the other hand it might be argued that an over-systematic plot or too thrilling situations give a *primâ facie* look of unreality to scenes of modern life. No one of course makes it a ground of complaint against these authors that they failed to combine incompatible perfections, but a reference to the natural limitations of the styles in which they severally succeeded may help to show what space was left for a fresh combination of the old ingredients.

Middlemarch marks an epoch in the history of fiction in so far as its incidents are taken from the inner life, as the action is developed by the direct influence of mind on mind and character on character, as the material circumstances of the outer world are made subordinate and accessory to the artistic presentation of a definite passage of mental experience, but chiefly as giving a background of perfect realistic truth to a profoundly imaginative psychological study. The effect is as new as if we could suppose a *Wilhelm Meister* written by Balzac.[1] In *Silas Marner*, *Romola*, and the author's other works there is the same power, but it does not so completely and exclusively determine the form in which the conception is placed before us. In *Silas Marner* there is a natural and obvious unity in the life of the weaver, but in *Romola* – where alone the interest is at once as varied and as profound as in *Middlemarch* – though the historic glories of Florence, the passions belonging to what, as compared with the nineteenth century, is an heroic age, are in perfect harmony with the grand manner of treating spiritual problems, yet the realism, the positive background of fact, which we can scarcely better bear to miss, has necessarily some of the character of an hypothesis, and does not inspire us with the same confidence as truths we can verify for ourselves. For that reason alone, on the mere point of artistic harmony of construction, we should rate the last work as the greatest; and to say that *Middlemarch* is George Eliot's greatest work is to say that it has scarcely a superior and very few equals in the whole wide range of English fiction.

Note

1 Goethe's *Wilhelm Meister* was commonly referred to in the mid-Victorian period as the supreme example in fiction of the psychological study of individual development, while Balzac was admired as the analyst of vast tracts of society and social history.

2

Fiction with a purpose

The Victorian novel offered all manner of religious and moral teaching, and undertook to inculcate almost anything from particular varieties of religious belief to social manners. Prose fiction had always been regarded as a less elevated genre than drama and poetry, and some defence of it was required that should be stronger than the claim that it could be made morally harmless. Fanny Burney (1752–1840) had made the form eminently respectable, by dealing adequately with the individual moral dilemmas of young women embarking on the world – 'the difficulties of the female heart', as one of her characters put it. For his part Sir Walter Scott (1771–1832) dealt with the great movements of history and the foundation of the modern Scottish nation, and immensely raised popular perceptions of what the novel could achieve. In the early Victorian period there was a widespread confidence that prose fiction could use this inherited seriousness to take on any social or religious topic of the day; and of course the 'seriousness' did not necessarily imply solemnity, as Dickens's novels show.

So successful were the novelists of the period that it could be boasted that they had exerted a recognisable influence on the course of social and institutional reform. It was not felt to be strange for novels to deal with the social, political or religious issues of the day. Dickens did it in his very first novel, and never lost the habit. In *Pickwick Papers* (1836–7) he had written about the state of the prisons, and he was still increasing the scale of his attacks in *Little Dorrit* (1855–7), with the whole of the Civil Service now the object of his satire. As one reviewer put it in 1845: '[h]e aspires to be a social reformer, to make each year happier than the last, by making all classes better' (2.2). The reading public came to expect to be informed and moved by fictional as well as factual accounts of the 'Condition of England' – the apparently inexplicable state of things whereby the Industrial Revolution had simultaneously produced the greatest wealth and the most abject misery the country had ever seen. The 'Condition of England' novel, by authors like Elizabeth Tonna, Frances Trollope, Elizabeth Gaskell, Charlotte Brontë, Charles Reade and Charles Dickens, aimed to awaken the social conscience and the mind. At the same time there was an immense outpouring of fiction intended to stir religious feelings, or to proselytise for a particular Christian sect, one example of which is the novel *Perversion* which is under review in extract 3.3. It would be impossible to represent this mass of work at all fairly, and probably uninteresting for the later reader to go into any amount of detail about it. The fact is that it amounted to an industry on its own, and one that is underrepresented in this present collection.

On the other hand, the fiction of middle- and upper-class life, which called forth some of the best criticism in the period, is well represented here. For the novelist aspiring to 'truth-to-life', moral instruction was still an imperative. Trollope and George Eliot (7.6) agreed on the assumption that (in Trollope's words) 'the novelist, if he have a conscience, must preach his sermons with the same purpose as the clergyman, and must have his own system of ethics' (2.6). This 'teaching' was to constitute a general ethical education, and unlike 'Condition of England' fiction was not directed at specific social evils. George Eliot maintained that her function was 'that of the aesthetic, not the doctrinal teacher – the rousing of the nobler emotions which make mankind desire the social right, not the prescribing of special measures, concerning which the artistic mind, however strongly moved by social sympathy, is often not the best judge' (2.7). The debate was not about whether the novel could and should teach, but whether the moral or aesthetic impulse was uppermost. For Bulwer Lytton (2.3) the aesthetic impulse was primary, but moral lessons came with it, the artist 'taking care that they be not too sharply defined, and too obviously meant to contract the Poet into the Lecturer – the Fiction into the Homily'. For him the moral lesson of 'idealist' art came from 'elevation' of the subject-matter. George Eliot was to make a parallel claim for realistic art: 'I think aesthetic teaching is the highest of all teaching because it deals with life in its highest complexity. But if it ceases to be purely aesthetic – if it lapses anywhere from the picture to the diagram – it becomes the most offensive of all teaching.'[1] Dallas mocks this claim to the general inculcation of virtue, by reference to absurdly outmoded ideas of literary utility, and boldly proposes instead that the purpose of art is pleasure, and that other effects are incidental (2.4). The *Saturday Review*, which was generally dismissive of the moral and aesthetic claims of English prose fiction, and very much opposed to preaching anywhere but in the pulpit, doubted the ostensible ethical purpose of most novels:

> Our English conception of a novel, as a sort of moral anodyne, more or less harmless according to circumstances, implies that novelists should confine themselves to a low range of thought, and should abstain from any *bona fide* attempt to investigate the great problems of life. . . . It would be hard to mention a single modern English novelist of eminence who has written either as an artist or as a philosopher. They mostly write in the spirit either of pamphleteers, or of tradesmen whose chief object is to sell their goods, but who have no objection to put in their shop-windows placards about charity sermons.[2]

The only thing not in dispute was that practically all novelists laid claim to moral utility for their art as, if not the best, then at least the most important selling-point with their publics.

Notes

1 Letter to Frederic Harrison, 15 August 1866, *The George Eliot Letters*, ed G. Haight, New Haven, Yale University Press, 1954–78, vol. 4, p. 300.
2 Notice of Balzac's *Balthazar* (a translation of *La Recherche de l'absolu*), *Saturday Review* 3 (3 January 1857), 8–9.

2.1 T.H. Lister (anon.), review of *Sketches by Boz*, *The Pickwick Papers*, *Nicholas Nickleby* and *Oliver Twist*, *Edinburgh Review* 68 (October 1838), 75–97, pp. 76–8

Thomas Henry Lister (1800–42), novelist and dramatist, was also the first Registrar-General of England and Wales and a commissioner of inquiry into the state of education in Ireland. The Edinburgh Review, *the first of the great, heavyweight quarterlies, was founded in Edinburgh in 1802, and maintained a decidedly Whig line in the early decades of the century. Its greatest editor, Francis Jeffrey, who presided over it from 1803 to 1829, later became an intimate friend of Dickens.*

Lister identifies Dickens's aim as directing human sympathy into practical philanthropy, and finds the novelist's roots in the humorists of the eighteenth century, including the painter Hogarth, whose narrative art is commonly used as a point of reference for novelists and their illustrators in the early and mid-Victorian period. In view of the fetish of female 'purity' in the period, the difficulties facing the

Victorian satirist are well exemplified in the expectation that fiction should cause no offence 'if read aloud in female society'. The praise of 'unmixed' characters, which are not combinations of good and evil, had been an eighteenth-century commonplace, and found its most influential form in Samuel Johnson's essay on prose fiction in the Rambler *no. 4. Lister's remarks on this subject, though still quite simplistic, signal a move towards more complex notions of realism.*

We think him a very original writer – well entitled to his popularity – and not likely to lose it – and the truest and most spirited delineator of English life, amongst the middle and lower classes, since the days of Smollett and Fielding. He has remarkable powers of observation, and great skill in communicating what he has observed – a keen sense of the ludicrous – exuberant humour – and that mastery in the pathetic which, though it seems opposed to the gift of humour, is often found in conjunction with it. Add to these qualities, an unaffected style, fluent, easy, spirited, and terse – a good deal of dramatic power – and great truthfulness and ability in description. We know no other English writer to whom he bears a marked resemblance. He sometimes imitates other writers, such as Fielding in his introductions, and Washington Irving in his detached tales, and thus exhibits his skill as a parodist. But his own manner is very distinct – and comparison with any other would not serve to illustrate and describe it. We would compare him rather with the painter Hogarth. What Hogarth was in painting, such very nearly is Mr Dickens in prose fiction. The same turn of mind – the same species of power displays itself strongly in each. Like Hogarth he takes a keen and practical view of life – is an able satirist – very successful in depicting the ludicrous side of human nature, and rendering its follies more apparent by humorous exaggeration – peculiarly skilful in his management of details, throwing in circumstances which serve not only to complete the picture before us, but to suggest indirectly antecedent events which cannot be brought before our eyes. Hogarth's cobweb over the poor-box, and the plan for paying off the national debt, hanging from the pocket of the prisoner in the Fleet, are strokes of satire very similar to some in the writings of Mr Dickens. It is fair, in making this comparison, to add, that it does not hold good throughout; and that Mr Dickens is exempt from two of Hogarth's least agreeable qualities – his cynicism and his coarseness. There is no misanthropy in his satire, and no coarseness in his descriptions – a merit enhanced by the nature of his subjects. His works are chiefly pictures of humble life – frequently of the humblest. The reader is led through scenes of poverty and crime, and all the characters are made to discourse in the appropriate language of their respective classes – and yet we recollect no passage which ought to cause pain to the most sensitive delicacy, if read aloud in female society.

We have said that his satire was not misanthropic. This is eminently true. One of the qualities we most admire in him is his comprehensive spirit of humanity. The tendency of his writings is to make us practically benevolent – to excite our sympathy in behalf of the aggrieved and suffering in all classes; and especially in those who are most removed from observation. He especially directs our attention to the helpless victims of untoward circumstances, or a vicious system – to the imprisoned debtor – the orphan pauper – the parish apprentice – the juvenile criminal – and to the tyranny, which, under the combination of parental neglect, with the mercenary brutality of a pedagogue, may be exercised with impunity in schools. His humanity is plain, practical, and manly. It is quite untainted with sentimentality. There is no mawkish wailing for ideal distresses – no morbid exaggeration of the evils incident to our lot – no disposition to excite unavailing discontent, or to turn our attention from remediable grievances to those which do not admit a remedy. Though he appeals much to our feelings, we can detect no instance in which he has employed the verbiage of spurious philanthropy.

He is equally exempt from the meretricious cant of spurious philosophy. He never endeavours to mislead our sympathies – to pervert plain notions of right and wrong – to make vice interesting in our eyes – and shake our confidence in those whose conduct is irreproachable, by dwelling on the hollowness of seeming virtue. His vicious characters are just what experience shows the average to be; and what natural operation of those circumstances to which they have been exposed would lead us to expect. We are made to feel both what they are, and *why* they are what we find them. We find no monsters of unmitigated and unredeemable villainy; no creatures blending with their crimes the most incongruous and romantic virtues; but very natural and unattractive combinations of human qualities, in which the bad is found to predominate in such a proportion as the position of the party would render probable. In short, he has eschewed that vulgar and theatrical device for producing effect – the representation of human beings as they are likely *not* to be.

Good feeling and sound sense are shown in his application of ridicule. It is never levelled at poverty or misfortune; or at circumstances which can be rendered ludicrous only by their deviation from artificial forms; or by regarding them through the medium of a conventional standard. Residence in the regions of Bloomsbury, ill-dressed dinners, and ill-made liveries, are crimes which he suffers to go unlashed; but follies or abuses, such as would be admitted alike in every sphere of society to be fit objects for his satire, are hit with remarkable vigour and precision. Nor does he confine himself to such as are obvious; but elicits and illustrates absurdities which, though at once acknowledged when displayed, are plausible and comparatively unobserved.

2.2 Anonymous review of Dickens's *The Chimes*, *Economist*, 18 January 1845, 53–4

The Chimes was written in Genoa in the autumn of 1844, and was the second of Dickens's Christmas Books. *It exemplifies the cruelty which results from mechanically applying the 'rules' of political economy to the poor, and traces the reliance on these 'rules' to the economic interests of privileged social groups. The dominance of what Carlyle called 'the Dismal Science' can be seen from Dickens's remark in a letter to Forster that the* Westminster Review *'considered Scrooge's presentation of the turkey to Bob Cratchit [in* Christmas Carol] *as grossly inconsistent with political economy'. When writing it he declared, 'I am in a regular, ferocious excitement with* The Chimes . . . *I am fierce to finish off in a spirit bearing some affinity to those of truth and mercy, and to shame the cruel and the canting.' When Dickens returned to London he read it privately to two groups of friends, whose highly emotional reactions were soon widely reported throughout literary and radical London.*[1]

The Economist *was founded in 1843 to propagate the radical reforming politics of Cobden and Bright, and it responds strongly to the topicality of* The Chimes. *The anonymous reviewer's explanation of the way in which Dickens embodies social facts and ideologies in his fiction may seem to prefigure later sociological criticism in its reference to the representativeness of 'the different characters in the book, each of which is the type of a class', but the word 'class' is used in its philosophical rather than its sociological sense. And what additionally distinguishes this criticism from its twentieth-century successors is its sentimental belief in the innate goodness of all humankind, and in the mechanism of tearful sympathy which it assumes to have the power actually to effect political and economic change.*

Mr Dickens, in his 'Christmas Carol', published a twelvemonth ago, impressed on all his readers the loveliness of the kind affections; in his Chimes he has a solemn purpose – he sets forth the terrible consequences of social and political injustice. At the conclusion of the work he thus speaks:

> If it be a dream, oh! Listener, dear to him in all his visions, *try to bear in mind the stern realities from which these shadows come*, and in your sphere, none is too wide and none is too limited for such an end, *endeavour to correct, improve, and soften them.* So may the new year be a happy one to you, happy to many more whose happiness depends on you: so may each year be happier than the last, and *not the meanest of our brethren or sisterhood be debarred their rightful share in what our great Creator formed them to enjoy.*

The Chimes is a picture of the condition of England, and an earnest exhortation to all classes to amend it, by giving to the meanest of our brethren their rightful share in the advantages of society. The author has been heretofore merely a novelist – in the Chimes he is a political philosopher and a social reformer. His book is a political and social essay of intense interest. This is its true character; and the mere story, which some critics have carped at, is of the least importance. It is but the filmy down which, on the wings of the wind, carries from the ripened plant the seeds of wisdom over the earth.

Nevertheless the Chimes has a story; it is a tale, or rather it contains, within the compass of 175 pages, a great many thrilling histories. Each person describes, by deeds or words, an interesting life, and, in the large drama, embracing all ranks. There are no walking gentlemen, or mere confidants introduced, as in a French tragedy, merely to listen to the hero's exploits.

It has been said by way of censure, that the tales are police reports, which is the highest praise. What are they? Accurate representations of everyday events, embracing the lives of all classes; and what but genius can impart to them, trite and vulgar, such interest, while all their truthfulness is preserved, and the story made to read with the extreme interest of a romance? The book is remarkable for impressing on the public, by the commonest events, after the manner of all great moralists, the most valuable lessons. It exactly corresponds to the common definition of History – it is Philosophy teaching by example. . . .

We would fain advert, at some length, to the different characters in the book, each of which is the type of a class, and the voice and practical exponent of some social error, but our space forbids; and we must limit ourselves to briefly illustrating the principle with which Mr Dickens seems himself to be imbued through and through, and which, as it were, oozes out of him in every page. One of the remarkable circumstances of the day is the passion – we call it so designedly – which prevails to improve the condition of the working classes. In fact, that is felt by every thinking and feeling man to be an imperative social necessity. Under the influence of this passion, all the so-called *light* writers, who catch their inspiration from the prevailing events, have turned political philosophers, perhaps without knowing it; and, after having lived for years by the practice of ridiculing all serious thought as a bore, have nearly one and all begun to write long articles, in prose and verse, on the most abstruse questions of social economy. Mr Dickens shares this national feeling; and, sharing it, a cruel injustice is done him by those who believe that he has employed the elaborate imagery of the Chimes, and described some heart-rending effects of the most natural affections, for the mere purpose of exciting fictitious emotion. If at the moment when the heart of England is filled to overflowing with intense woe, in spite of 'facts and figures' announcing a flourishing revenue, proving that the interest of men in office is terribly at variance with the interest of the industrious people, Dickens could have touched the national misery and its sources with no other object than to tickle his readers into a forgetfulness of their duty, and to put a few pieces of paltry coin into his own pocket, as has been more unworthily and ignorantly imputed to him – he would have been in our estimation one of the meanest spirits, and one of the most degraded writers, of the day. But he aspires to be a social reformer, to make each year happier than the last, by making all classes better. This is the clue to his book. Read merely as a tale, it may perhaps be regarded as a piece of pathetic and impressive writing – read as a reproof of a wide-spread and debasing error, it is not merely a pathetic tale – it is one of the most philosophical works which has for a long period issued from the public press. Under this aspect the *Economist* meets Mr Dickens as a brother, and hails his work as a real light in our now darkened paths. In briefly stating the principle which Dickens has in view, the *Economist* has only to regret that he cannot do justice to the estimable author; and bring shame on some of his ignorant and carping critics.

What, then, is the principle which Dickens enforces. Here is it described in so many words. 'I have learnt it, cried the old man, Oh, have mercy on me in this hour, if, in my love for her so young and good, I *slandered Nature*, in the breasts of mothers rendered desperate. Pity my *presumption, wickedness*, and *ignorance* (in slandering nature), and save her.' 'I know there is a sea of time to rise one day, before which all who wrong us or oppress us will be swept away like leaves. I see it on the flow. I know that we must *trust and hope*, and *neither doubt ourselves, nor doubt* the GOOD *in one another*.' The opposite error – the mistrust of one another, the mistrust of ourselves, or of human nature and human affections – the assertion that all men are 'born bad,' and require some anti-natural coercion to keep them from destroying themselves and others – the overstrained and debasing humbleness of the many, which is the source of arrogance in the few – of their confidence in one another, and their looking only to goals and governments for protection and safety; this error is reproved by Dickens from the beginning to the end of the Chimes.

Note

1   Edgar Johnson, *Charles Dickens: His Tragedy and Triumph*, 2 vols, New York, Simon and Schuster, 1952, vol. 1, pp. 520 and 530–2.

2.3 Preface to the 1845 edition of Edward Bulwer Lytton, *Night and Morning*; from *Lord Lytton's Novels*, the Knebworth Edition, vol. 2, pp. vii–xi

This novel, which was first published in 1841, concerns an unhappy marriage. Despite Lytton's claim that he wrote without a view to popularity, he had been extremely successful for over a decade, with a line of best-sellers to his credit. He is distinguished in the period by the fact that he championed prose fiction as a serious form, but that he did so on the basis of the high efforts of imagination supposedly required to produce his kind of works, and of a wild overstatement of the influence for good a novelist exerts, makes him a little ridiculous to later readers. Equally difficult for today's reader is his almost religious respect for his own version of German idealism, which provided a rationale for his habit of using many Abstractions and Personifications (each with its own capital letter) and which proved attractive in some circles because it was so obviously at variance with the dominant utilitarian ideology of the day. William Caldwell Roscoe went so far as to claim that 'in his prefaces you hear him screaming, "I will be a philosopher: I am a great poet;" and his only difficulty as to those who disagree with him is as to whether they are most knave or fool.' [1] *See also the headnote to extract 1.1.*

Much has been written by critics, especially by those in Germany, (the native land of criticism,)[2] upon the important question, whether to please or to instruct should be the end of Fiction – whether a moral purpose is or is not in harmony with the undidactic spirit perceptible in the higher works of the imagination: And the general result of the discussion has been in favour of those who have contended that Moral Design, rigidly so called, should be excluded from the aims of the Poet; that his Art should regard only the Beautiful, and be contented with the indirect moral *tendencies*, which can never fail the creation of the Beautiful. Certainly, in fiction, to interest, to please, and sportively to elevate – to take man from the low passions, and to beguile weary and selfish pain, to excite a generous sorrow at vicissitudes not his own, to raise the passions into sympathy with heroic struggles – and to admit the soul into that serener atmosphere from which it rarely returns to ordinary existence, without some memory or association which ought to enlarge the domain of thought and exalt the motives of action; – Such, without the other moral result or object, may satisfy the Poet,[3] and constitute the highest and most universal morality he can effect. But subordinate to this, which is not the duty, but the *necessity*, of all Fiction that outlasts the hour, the writer of imagination may well permit to himself other purposes and objects, taking care that they be not too sharply defined, and too obviously meant to contract the Poet into the Lecturer – the Fiction into the Homily. The delight in 'Shylock' is not less vivid for the Humanity it latently but profoundly inculcates; the healthful merriment of the 'Tartuffe' is not less enjoyed for the exposure of the Hypocrisy it denounces. We need not demand from Shakespeare or from Molière other morality than that which Genius unconsciously throws around it – the natural light which it reflects; but if some great principle which guides us practically in the daily intercourse with men becomes in the general lustre more clear and more pronounced – we gain doubly, by the general tendency and the particular result.

Long since, in searching for new regions in the Art to which I am a servant, it seemed to me that they might be found lying far, and rarely trodden, beyond that range of conventional morality in which Novelist after Novelist had entrenched himself – amongst those subtle recesses in the ethics of human life in which Truth and Falsehood dwell undisturbed and unseparated. The vast and dark

Poetry around us – the Poetry of Modern Civilisation and Daily Existence, is shut out from us in much, by the shadowy giants of Prejudice and Fear. He who would arrive at the Fairy Land, must face the Phantoms. Betimes, I set myself to the task of investigating the motley world to which our progress in humanity has attained, caring little what misrepresentation I incurred, what hostility I provoked, in searching through a devious labyrinth for the foot-tracks of Truth.

In pursuit of this object, I am, not vainly, conscious that I have had my influence on my time – that I have contributed, though humbly and indirectly, to the benefits which Public Opinion has extorted from Governments and Laws. While (to content myself with a single example) the ignorant or malicious were decrying the moral of 'Paul Clifford,'[4] I consoled myself with perceiving that its truths had stricken deep – that many, whom formal essays might not reach, were enlisted by the picture and the popular force of Fiction into the service of that large and Catholic Humanity which frankly examines into the causes of crime, which ameliorates the ills of society by seeking to amend the circumstances by which they are occasioned; and commences the great work of justice to mankind, by proportioning the punishment to the offence. That work, I know, had its share in the wise and great relaxation of our Criminal Code – it has had its share in results yet more valuable, because leading to more comprehensive reforms – viz., in the courageous facing of the ills which the mock decorum of timidity would shun to contemplate, but which, till fairly fronted, in the spirit of practical Christianity, sap daily, more and more, the walls in which blind Indolence would protect itself from restless Misery and rampant Hunger. For it is not till Art has told the unthinking that nothing (*rightly treated*) is too low for its breath to vivify, and its wings to raise, that the Herd awaken from their chronic lethargy of contempt, and the Lawgiver is compelled to redress what the Poet has lifted into esteem. In thus enlarging the boundaries of the Novelist, from trite and conventional to untrodden ends, I have seen, not with the jealousy of an Author, but with the pride of an Originator, that I have served as a guide to later and abler writers, both in England and abroad. If at times, while imitating, they have mistaken me, I am not answerable for their errors; or if, more often, they have improved where they borrowed, I am not envious of their laurels. They owe me at least this, that I prepared the way for their reception, and that they would have been less popular and more misrepresented, if the outcry which bursts upon the first researches into new directions, had not exhausted its noisy vehemence upon me.

In the Novel of 'Night and Morning' I have had various ends in view – subordinate, I grant, to the higher and more durable morality which belongs to the Ideal, and instructs us playfully while it interests, in the passions, and through the heart. First – to deal fearlessly with that universal unsoundness in social justice which makes distinctions so marked and iniquitous between Vice and Crime – viz., between the corrupting habits and the violent act – which scarce touches the former with the lightest twig of the fasces – which lifts against the latter the edge of the Lictor's axe.[5] Let a child steal an apple in sport, let a starveling steal a roll in despair, and Law conducts them to the Prison, for evil commune to mellow them for the gibbet. But let a man spend one apprenticeship from youth to old age in vice – let him devote a fortune, perhaps colossal, to the wholesale demoralisation of his kind – and he may be surrounded with the adulation of the so-called virtuous, and be served upon its knee, by that Lackey – the Modern World! I say not that Law can or that Law should, reach the Vice as it does Crime; but I say, that Opinion may be more than the servile shadow of Law. I impress not here, as in 'Paul Clifford,' a material moral to work its effect on the Journals, at the Hustings, through constituents, and on Legislation; – I direct myself to a channel less active, more tardy, but as sure – to Conscience that reigns, elder and superior to all Law, in men's hearts and souls; I utter boldly and loudly a truth, if not all untold, murmured feebly and falteringly before, – sooner or later it will find its way into the judgement and the conduct, and shape out a tribunal which requires no robe or ermine.

Secondly – In this work I have sought to lift the mask from the timid selfishness which too often with us bears the name of *Respectability*. Purposely avoiding all attraction that may savour of extravagance, patiently subduing every tone and every hue to the aspect of those whom we meet daily in our thoroughfares, I have shown in Robert Beaufort the man of decorous phrase – in whom the world forgive [sic] the lack of all that is generous, warm, and noble, in order to respect the passive acquiescence in methodical conventions and hollow forms. And how common such men are with us in this century, and how inviting and how necessary their delineation, may be seen in this, – that the popular and pre-eminent Observer of the age in which we live, has since placed their prototype in vigorous colours upon imperishable canvas.[6]

There is yet another object with which I have identified my tale. I trust that I am not insensible to such advantages as arise from the diffusion of education really sound, and knowledge really available; – for these, as the right of my countrymen, I have contended always. But of late years there has been danger that what ought to be an important truth may be perverted into a pestilent fallacy. Whether for rich or for poor, disappointment must ever await the endeavour to give knowledge without labour, and experience without trial. Cheap literature and popular treatises do not in themselves suffice to fit the nerves of man for the strife below, and lift his aspirations, in healthful confidence above. He who seeks to divorce toil from knowledge deprives knowledge of its most valuable property, – the strengthening of the mind by exercise. We learn what really braces and elevates us only in proportion to the *effort* it costs us. Nor is it in Books alone, not in Books chiefly, that we are made conscious of our strength as Men; Life is the great Schoolmaster, Experience the mighty Volume. He who has made one stern sacrifice of self, has acquired more than he will ever glean from the odds-and-ends of popular philosophy: And the man, the least scholastic, may be more robust in the power that *is* knowledge, and approach nearer to the Arch-Seraphim, than Bacon himself,[7] if he cling fast to two simple maxims – 'Be honest in temptation, and in Adversity believe in God.' Such moral, attempted before in 'Eugene Aram,' I have enforced more directly here; and out of such convictions I have created hero and heroine, placing them in their primitive and natural characters, with aid more from life than books – from courage the one, from affection the other – amidst the feeble Hermaphrodites of our sickly civilisation; – examples of resolute Manhood and tender Womanhood.

The opinions I have here put forth are not in fashion at the day. But I have never consulted the popular any more than the sectarian, Prejudice. Alone and unaided, I have hewn out my way, from first to last, by the force of my own convictions. The corn springs up in the field centuries after the first sower is forgotten. Works may perish with the workman; but, if truthful, their results are in the works of others, imitating, borrowing, enlarging, and improving, in the everlasting Cycle of Industry and Thought.

Notes

1 W.C. Roscoe, 'Sir E.B. Lytton, Novelist, Philosopher, and Poet', *Poems and Essays*, ed R.H. Hutton, 1860, vol. 2, p. 359.
2 Germany was 'the native land of criticism' in philosophical and religious contexts, rather than simply in terms of what is later called 'literary criticism'. The term was used in particular to refer to Kant's criticism of speculative and practical reason and to the so-called 'Higher Criticism' of biblical texts.
3 Lytton's footnote: I use the word Poet in its proper sense, as applicable to any writer whether in verse or prose, who invents or creates.

4 See headnote to extract 1.1.

5 Lictors were officers who preceded Roman magistrates and carried the fasces, or bundle of rods with an axe at the centre, which were symbols of the authority of law and of punishment.

6 Lytton's footnote: Need I say that I allude to the 'Pecksniff' of Mr. Dickens?

7 Francis Bacon's *Novum Organum* (1620) was the work which established the inductive method which the Victorians regarded as the basis of all modern scientific advance.

2.4 E.S. Dallas, *The Gay Science*, 2 vols, London, 1866, vol. 2, pp. 158–63

For information about E.S. Dallas, see the headnote to extract 1.6, and for a brief introduction to his aesthetic position see extract 6.5 and its headnote. The argument in this extract springs from Dallas's contention in The Gay Science *that the characteristic quality of art is its ability to give pleasure, and the theory of literature should therefore be based upon the premise that 'the immediate end of art is to give pleasure'. In an age as unrelaxed about pleasure as the high Victorian period, this doctrine was not likely to meet with universal approval, and Dallas implies that the emphasis on mimesis in literary theory results from a distrust of pleasure. As he recognises, '[w]ord and thing, pleasure is in very bad odour' (vol. 1, p. 89). As part of his argument he satirically attacks the case for the moral usefulness of art by reference to some extraordinary examples of writers who believed in the medical efficacy of literature.*

It is no doubt a great fact that many prophets and sages have ascended each his peculiar hill, to fling down curses on art; but it is a fact which must be resolved into a still more general phenomenon. The condemnation of poetry is but a part of the condemnation pronounced upon all pleasure. We are all more intolerant of pleasure than even of opinion. If we desire to crush the opinions of our neighbours, we at least hug our own; but the tyranny of taste is still more oppressive, for we not only frown on the pleasure of a neighbour – we are often dissatisfied with our own; it is our nature to pant after the bliss which is in store, and to find rottenness in that which we possess. We do not see the jokes of our ancestors. An Englishman imagines that it requires a surgical operation to make a Scotchman understand wit.[1] A Frenchman long ago declared that the English take their pleasure sadly.[2] A ban goes forth now against the delights of knowledge; now against marriage; now wine is accursed; now poetry, the wine of devils, shares that curse. . . . The frequent condemnation of art is, I say, but a part of this general law by which, at some time or other, we malign our own joys, and almost always despise the joys of our neighbours. . . . If Plato turned the poets out of his republic, he made the philosophers kings of it. This is the egotism of pleasure; as in Bacon's objection to poetry that it is the pleasure of a lie,[3] we see chiefly the discontent of it. The prevalence of such facts leads us straight to the conclusion, that the mere statement of dislike to art, and the mere assertion of its moral wrong, must – aloof from intelligible reasoning – go for nought. It is but part of a widespread asceticism, which clings like a parasite to the sense of enjoyment, always irritates it, and sometimes sucks it dry. We may reject assertion, therefore, and insist on dealing only with facts and arguments.

Now, in pushing any inquiry into the moral influence of art, I suppose it is almost needless to begin by explaining that here there is no question as to the direct lesson which art *professes* to teach, if it make any profession at all. Its worth is not to be measured by the lower – that is, the more palpable order of utilities. Bartholin declared that ailments, chiefly the falling sickness, were curable by rhymes; Dr. Serenus Sammonicus offered to cure a quartan ague by laying the fourth book of the Iliad under the patient's head;[4] Virgil was once believed to be an excellent fortune-teller. The moral usefulness which we expect from art bears no sort of resemblance to these physical utilities. Any one who will look for conscious moral aim in art, will find it nearly purposeless. The troubadour gave to his calling the name of El Gai Saber, the gay science. To conclude, however, that nobleness of tendency may not flourish under gaiety of mien, is to imitate the poor satyr, puzzled to understand how a man could blow hot and cold with one and the same mouth. The avowed object of the poet is pleasure, and he seems to have his eye set only on present enjoyment, but it is like a rower, that looks one way and pulls another.[5] Shenstone paints the village schoolmistress as disguised in looks profound.[6] On the contrary, it was a reproach to the greatest of all teachers that he was a wine-bibber and a friend of sinners.[7] The artist has still less the air of a teacher, and if he puts on the air of one, it sometimes happens that his influence is directly the reverse of his precepts.

Take the novelist, Richardson, for example, as he appears in his earliest work, which Fielding could not refrain from satirising.[8] No book has even been written in which there is such a parade of morality as in *Pamela*: nevertheless, it is a mischievous work that makes one sympathise with the disgust which it excited in Fielding. There is no end to the morals which it professes to instil – morals for husbands, morals for wives, morals for parents, morals for children, morals for masters, morals for servants. Ostensibly we are taught to admire the strength of virtue, and to note the reward of victory; but to understand the virtue, we are introduced to all the arts of the deceiver. There is a continual handling of pitch, in order to see how well it can be washed off: there is a continual drinking of poison, in order to show the potency of the antidote. The girl resists the seducer; but the pleasure of the story consists in entering into all the details of the struggle, and seeing how the squire takes liberties with the maid. When our senses have been duly tickled by these glowing descriptions, our consciences are soothed by a thick varnish of moral reflections and warnings that are entirely out of place. Notwithstanding its great show of virtue, such an exhibition seems to have a much more immoral tendency than the frank sinfulness of Fielding's works. 'Here is my hero,' says Fielding, 'full of wickedness and good heart: come and read of his doings.' 'Here is my heroine, full of virtue,' says Richardson: 'come and read of her goodness.' But the descriptions of both are equally indelicate. It may be safely taken for granted that the force of Richardson's preachings goes for very little in comparison with the force of his pictures.

In justice, however, to so great a writer as Richardson, I should take particular care to state that these strictures apply only to his earliest work. In all his novels there is a parade of moral laws, but that parade is not offensive and hollow in the later ones. Notwithstanding the tediousness of its commencement, it is not risking much to say that *Clarissa Harlowe* is the finest novel in the English language. No one thinks of Richardson, with all his weak vanity, as a great genius; yet we have to recognise the existence of this curious phenomenon that, as a grig like Boswell produced our best piece of biography, so a squat, homely burgess, who fed his mind on 'says he' and 'says she,' produced what is still our best novel. It is not Richardson, however, that we have now to do with. The point I wish to bring out is this, that it is not moral sermons which constitute the moral force of a novel: it is example.

Notes

1   A remark of Sydney Smith's, recorded in Lady Holland's *Memoir*: 'It

requires a surgical operation to get a joke well into a Scotch understanding.'

2 *Memoirs* of Maximilian, Duc de Sully, 1539–1641.

3 Bacon's essay 'Of Truth': 'A mixture of a lie doth ever add pleasure.'

4 Thomas Bartholin (1619–80), Danish literary scholar and professor of medicine at Copenhagen University, was an admirer of the second- or third-century empiric physician, Quintus Serenus Sammonicus, author of the poem *De medicina*.

5 See James Mabbe, *The Rogue or the Life of Guzman de Alfarache* (1623) 'To the Discreet Reader': 'Some perhaps will say, That having (like unto Watermen) turned my backe and eyes contrarie way, (who looke one way, and rowe another) I direct this little Barke of mine, where I have most desire to land. But upon mine honest word, hee is deceived, that so thinketh.'

6 William Shenstone, 'The Schoolmistress' (1742), l.44.

7 In Matthew 11.19 and Luke 7.34 Jesus reports this as said of himself and adds 'But wisdom is justified of her children.'

8 Soon after the appearance of Samuel Richardson's *Pamela* in 1740, Fielding issued a vigorous parody entitled *Shamela*, while his novel *Joseph Andrews* (1742) is in some degree also parodic of the Richardson work.

2.5 Edward Dowden, 'George Eliot', *Contemporary Review* 20 (August 1872), 403–22, pp. 418–21

Edward Dowden (1843–1913), the Irish critic and Shakespearian scholar, was appointed Professor of English at Trinity College, Dublin at the age of twenty-four, and continued in the post until he died. In this extract he is responding to the amalgam in George Eliot's work of the social science of Herbert Spencer and Auguste Comte with the moral imperatives of religious humanism.

The scientific observation of man, and in particular the study of the mutual relations of the individual and society, come to reinforce the self-renouncing dictates of the heart. To understand any individual apart from the whole life of the race is impossible. We are the heirs intellectual and moral of the past; there is no such thing as naked manhood; the heart of each of us wears livery which it cannot throw off. Our very bodies differ from those of primeval savages – differ, it maybe, from those of extinct apes only by the gradual gains of successive generations of ancestors. Our instincts, physical and mental, our habits of thought and feeling, the main tendency of our activity, these are assigned to us by the common life which has preceded and which surrounds our own. 'There is no private life,' writes George Eliot in 'Felix Holt', 'which has not been determined by a wider public life, from the time when the primeval milkmaid had to wander with the wanderings of her clan, because the cow she milked was one of a herd which had made the pastures bare.'

If this be so, any attempt to render our individual life independent of the general life of past and present, any attempt to erect a system of thought and conduct out of merely personal convictions and personal desires must be a piece of slight, idealistic fatuity. . . .

It will be readily seen how this way of thinking abolishes rights, and substitutes duties in their place. Of rights of man, rights of woman, we never hear speech from George Eliot. But we hear much of the duties of each. The claim asserted by the individual on behalf of this or that disappears, because the individual surrenders his independence to collective humanity, of which he is a part. And it is another consequence of this way of thinking that the leadings of duty are most often looked for, not within, in the promptings of the heart, but without, in the relations of external life, which connect us with our fellow-men. Our great English novelist does not preach as her favourite doctrine the indefeasible right of love to gratify itself at the expense of law; with the correlative right, equally indefeasible, to cast away the marriage bond as soon as it has become a painful encumbrance. She regards the formal contract, even when its spirit has long since died, as sacred and of binding force. Why? Because it is a formal contract. 'The light abandonment of ties, whether inherited or voluntary, because they had ceased to be pleasant, would be the uprooting of social and personal virtue.' Law is sacred. Rebellion, it is true, may be sacred also. There are moments of life 'when the soul must dare to act upon its warrant, not only without external law to appeal to, but in the face of a law which is not unarmed with Divine lightnings – lightnings that may yet fall if the warrant has been false.' These moments, however, are of rare occurrence, and arise only in extreme necessity. . . . Maggie returns to St. Oggs: Fedalma and Don Silva part: Romola goes back to her husband's house.[1] We can imagine how unintelligible such moral situations, and such moral solutions, would appear to a great female novelist of France.[2] 'If the past is not to bind us, where can duty lie?' As the life of the race lying behind our individual life points out the direction in which alone it can move with dignity and strength, so our own past months and years lying behind the present hour and minute deliver over to these a heritage and a tradition which it is their wisdom joyfully to accept when that is possible. . . . All that helps to hold our past and present together is therefore precious and sacred. It is well that our affections should twine tenderly about all material tokens and memorials of bygone days. Why should Tito keep his father's ring?[3] Why indulge a foolish sentiment, a piece of mere superstition, about an inanimate object? And so Tito sells the ring, and with it closes the bargain by which he sells his soul. There is, indeed, a noble pressing forward to things that are before, and forgetting of things that are behind. George Eliot is not attracted to represent a character in which such an ardour is predominant, and the base forgetting of things behind alarms and shocks her.

Notes

1 In *The Mill on the Floss* (1860) and *Romola* (1862–3).
2 Presumably George Sand (1804–76), whose influence on the Victorian novel in terms of romantic passion, social and political ideas, and feminism was immeasurable.
3 In *Romola*.

2.6 Anthony Trollope on moral teaching, *An Autobiography*, written 1875–6, 3 vols, 1883, vol. 2, pp. 31–5

The great novelist, Anthony Trollope (1815–82), was well aware how narrow was the path between dulness and immorality. At the same time he was convinced that prose fiction had a direct effect on the moral conduct of the young, and that novelists therefore found themselves, whether they liked it or not, being taken as exemplifying virtue and vice in action, and hence acting as teachers. In this (like many of his contemporaries) he was a follower of Samuel Johnson, who maintained in his Rambler *essay on prose fiction that novels were 'written chiefly to the young, the ignorant, and the idle, to whom they serve as lectures on conduct, and introductions to life'. Trollope was a true Victorian believer in progress, and for him the line between the permissible and the impermissible in conduct and knowledge had almost certainly moved since Johnson's day, but he would still have agreed with Johnson that '[t]he purpose of these writings is ... to initiate youth by mock encounters in the art of necessary defence, and to encrease prudence without impairing virtue'.[1] In this extract Trollope is surveying some of the changes that have taken place in his lifetime, including the spread of novel-reading into almost all literate social groups.*

Trollope wrote more on the subject of the writing and reading of prose fiction than any of his great novelist contemporaries. His Autobiography *in part takes a form which was not to disappear for some decades: that of advice to the aspiring novelist. The theory of the novel was not yet recognised in Britain as an activity in its own right, and in consequence it was often practised under the guise of moral analysis or professional advice. (In France, by contrast, Henry James found that prose fiction was* discutable.) *The result was that English novelists were far better at experimenting than at articulating the principles underlying their practice.*

Novels are read right and left, above stairs and below, in town houses and in country parsonages, by young countesses and by farmers' daughters, by old lawyers and by young students. It has not only come to pass that a special provision of them has to be made for the godly, but that the provision so made must now include books which a few years since the godly would have thought to be profane. It was this necessity which, a few years since, induced the editor of *Good Words* to apply to me for a novel, – which, indeed, when supplied was rejected,[2] but which now, probably, owing to further change in the same direction, would have been accepted.

If such be the case – if the extension of novel-reading be so wide as I have described it – then very much good or harm must be done by novels. The amusement of the time can hardly be the only result of any book that is read, and certainly not so with a novel, which appeals especially to the imagination, and solicits the sympathy of the young. A vast proportion of the teaching of the day, – greater probably than many of us have acknowledged to ourselves,[3] – comes from these books, which are in the hands of all readers. It is from them that girls learn what is expected from them, and what they are to expect when lovers come; and also from them that young men unconsciously learn what are, or should be, or may be, the charms of love, – though I fancy that few young men will think so little of their natural instincts and powers as to believe that I am right in saying so. Many other lessons are also taught. In these times, when the desire to be honest is pressed so hard, is so violently assaulted, by the ambition to be great; in which riches are the easiest road to greatness; when the temptations to which men are subjected dull their eyes to the perfected iniquities of others; when it is so hard for a man to decide vigorously that the pitch, which so many are handling, will defile him if it be touched; men's conduct will be actuated much by that which is from day to day depicted to them as leading to glorious or inglorious results. The woman who is described as having obtained all the world holds to be precious, by lavishing her charms and her caresses unworthily and heartlessly, will induce other women to do the same with theirs, – as will she who is made interesting by exhibitions of bold passion teach others to be spuriously passionate. The young man who in a novel becomes a hero, perhaps a Member of Parliament, and almost a Prime Minister, by trickery, falsehood, and flash cleverness, will have many followers, whose attempts to rise in the world ought to lie heavily on the conscience of the novelists who create fictitious Cagliostros[4] There are Jack Sheppards other than those who break into houses and out of prisons, – Macheaths, who deserve the gallows more than Gay's hero.[5]

Thinking of all this, as a novelist surely must do, – as I certainly have done through my whole career, – it becomes to him a matter of deep conscience how he shall handle those characters by whose words and doings he hopes to interest his readers. It will very frequently be the case that he will be tempted to sacrifice something for effect, to say a word or two here, or to draw a picture there, for which he feels that he has the power, and which when spoken or drawn would be alluring. The regions of absolute vice are foul and odious. The savour of them, till custom has hardened the palate and the nose, is disgusting. In these he will hardly tread. But there are outskirts on these regions, on which sweet-smelling flowers seem to grow, and grass to be green. It is in these border-lands that the danger lies. The novelist may not be dull. If he commit that fault he can do neither harm nor good. He must please, and the flowers and the grass in these neutral territories sometimes seem to give him so easy an opportunity of pleasing!

The writer of stories must please, or he will be nothing. And he must teach whether he wish to teach or no. How shall he teach lessons of virtue and at the same time make himself a delight to his readers? That sermons are not in themselves often thought to be agreeable we all know. Nor are disquisitions on moral philosophy supposed to be pleasant reading for our idle hours. But the novelist, if he have a conscience, must preach his sermons with the same purpose as the clergyman, and must have his own system of ethics. If he can do this efficiently, if he can make virtue alluring and vice ugly, while he charms his reader instead of wearying him, then I think Mr. Carlyle need not call him distressed, nor talk of that long ear of fiction, nor question whether he be or not the most foolish of existing mortals.[6]

Notes

1 Samuel Johnson, *Rambler* no. 4, 31 March 1750.
2 *Rachel Ray* had been commissioned in 1863 by the editor of *Good Words*,

Norman Macleod, who refused to print it on the grounds that it was unsuitable for a periodical 'in the field of cheap Christian literature'. Trollope disingenuously reports that the trouble lay in 'some dancing in one of the early chapters, described, no doubt, with that approval of the amusement which I have always entertained', but the real problem lay in the unsympathetic portrayal of an Evangelical clergyman, Mr Prong, a character ill-calculated to suit a periodical whose editor was a Scottish Presbyterian divine, and one of the founders of the Evangelical Alliance. See A. Trollope, *An Autobiography*, London, Oxford University Press, 1950, p. 188; Donald Macleod, *Memoir of Norman Macleod, D.D.*, London, 1882, p. 330, and *The Letters of Anthony Trollope*, ed N. John Hall, 2 vols, Stanford, CA, Stanford University Press, 1983, pp. 177–80 and 220–5.

3 The manuscript reads 'greater probably than many of us have as yet acknowledged to ourselves'. See *An Autobiography*, p. 379.

4 Guiseppe Balsamo, Count of Cagliostro (1743–95) was a mountebank doctor, who offered everlasting youth to his customers.

5 Jack Sheppard, the eighteenth-century highwayman, was glamourised in a novel named after him by Harrison Ainsworth in 1839, and Macheath was the attractive highwayman in Gay's *Beggar's Opera* (1728).

6 In a passage cancelled from the manuscript of his *Autobiography* Trollope quotes the relevant passage from Thomas Carlyle's essay, 'Biography', of 1832. See above (p. 2).

2.7 John Morley, 'The Life of George Eliot', review of J.W. Cross, *George Eliot's Life*, 3 vols, Edinburgh, 1885, *Macmillan's Magazine* 51 (February 1885), 253

John Morley (1838–1923), distinguished man of letters, polymath and liberal statesman, was a notable contributor to the Saturday Review *and succeeded G.H. Lewes as editor of the* Fortnightly Review *from 1867 to 1882. It was reputedly an article on her novels in* Macmillan's Magazine *in 1866 which gained him the friendship of George Eliot. In the present article he is reviewing the life of George Eliot by her widower, and giving a brief but effective account of the literary and intellectual context in which the fiction of this period was appearing.*

Like many Victorian men of letters Morley has an equal interest in things political and things literary, and seeks to convey the effect of George Eliot's work in educating the public mind in the new thought and new attitudes appropriate to the age of science and religious scepticism. He cites evidence of George Eliot's intention to be a teacher in what she wrote, and goes on to show that on the other hand she was not an inspiration to political activity, because what she imparted was 'not a very strenuous, aggressive, and operative desire'. She gave very little of a political welcome to the events of 1848, 'the year of revolutions', and felt that the American Civil War would be most useful as, in her own words, 'a check to the arid narrow antagonism which in some quarters is held to be the only form of liberal thought'.

The period of George Eliot's productions was from 1856, the date of her first stories, down to 1876, when she wrote, not under her brightest star, her last novel of *Daniel Deronda*. During this time the great literary influences of the epoch immediately preceding had not indeed fallen silent, but the most fruitful seeds had been sown. Carlyle's *Sartor* (1833–4), and his *Miscellaneous Essays* (collected, 1839), were in all hands; but he had fallen into the terrible slough of his Prussian history (1858–65), and the last word of his evangel had gone forth to all whom it concerned. *In Memoriam*, whose noble music and deep-browed thought awoke such new and wide response in men's hearts, was published in 1850. The second volume of *Modern Painters*, of which I have heard George Eliot say, as of *In Memoriam* too, that she owed much and very much to it, belongs to an earlier date still (1846), and when it appeared, though George Eliot was born in the same year as its author, she was still translating Strauss at Coventry.[1] Mr. Browning, for whose genius she had such admiration, and who was always so good a friend, did indeed produce during this period some work which the adepts find as full of power and beauty as any that ever came from his pen. But Mr. Browning's genius has moved rather apart from the general currents of his time, creating character and working out motives from within, undisturbed by transient shadows from the passing questions and answers of the day.

The romantic movement was then upon its fall. The great Oxford movement, which besides its purely ecclesiastical effects, had linked English religion once more to human history, and which was itself one of the unexpected outcomes of the romantic movement, had spent its original force, and no longer interested the stronger minds among the rising generation. The hour had sounded for the scientific movement. In 1859 was published the *Origin of Species*, undoubtedly the most far-reaching agency of the time, supported as it was by a volume of new knowledge which came pouring in from many sides. The same period saw the important speculations of Mr. Spencer, whose influence on George Eliot had from their first acquaintance been of a very decisive kind. Two years after the *Origin of Species* came Maine's *Ancient Law*, and that was followed by the accumulations of Mr. Tylor and others, exhibiting order and fixed correlation among great sets of facts which had hitherto lain in that cheerful chaos of general knowledge which has been called general ignorance. The excitement was immense. Evolution, development, heredity, adaptation, variety, survival, natural selection, were so many patent pass-keys that were to open every chamber.

George Eliot's novels, as they were the imaginative application of this great influx of new ideas, so they fitted in with the moods which those ideas had called up. 'My function,' she said (iii.330), 'is that of the aesthetic, not the doctrinal teacher – the rousing of the nobler emotions which make mankind desire the social right, not the prescribing of special measures, concerning which the artistic mind, however strongly moved by social sympathy, is often not the best judge.' Her influence in this direction over serious and impressionable minds was great indeed. The spirit of her art exactly harmonised with the new thoughts that were shaking the world of her contemporaries. Other artists had drawn their pictures with a strong ethical background, but she gave a finer colour and a more spacious air to her ethics, by showing the individual passions and emotions of her characters, their adventures and their fortunes, as evolving themselves from long series of antecedent causes, and bound up with many widely operating forces and distant events. Here, too, we find ourselves in the full stream of evolution, heredity, survival, and fixed inexorable law.

Note

1 Marian Evans spent the years 1844–6 translating David Strauss's *The Life of Jesus* from the German – a book which examined the gospels as myth and history rather than as revelation. The works alluded to in this paragraph are Carlyle's *Sartor Resartus* and *Frederick the Great*, Tennyson's *In Memoriam* and Ruskin's *Modern Painters*.

3

Social, moral and religious judgements

One of the problems facing us as interpreters of Victorian literature is assessing how far the prevailing standards of religious and social morality and conformity had a formative influence on the texts transmitted to us. It is not difficult to find examples of novels from which sexually 'warm' language, indelicacy or profanity were edited out, and anecdotes abound to show the risible lengths to which editors, publishers and publishers' readers went to avoid offending the susceptibilities of what Thackeray, when editor of the *Cornhill Magazine*, used to call his 'squeamish public'. Longman's reader had 'fat stomach' changed to 'deep chest' in Trollope's *Barchester Towers* (1857), and 'foul breathing' totally deleted.[1] More seriously certain subjects were proscribed, while others, most notably sexuality in women, could only be presented in terms of conventions where ideology and supposedly 'literary' standards were tightly plaited together. Hence we lose most of our 'fallen women' by premature death, like Martha's in *David Copperfield* (1849–50), or emigration, like Emily's in the same novel. Merely staying out over night transforms Susan in Margaret Oliphant's *Salem Chapel* (1862–3, chs 23 and 29) into a 'grand form' of 'marble', so that although she is 'spotless', death seems the logical next step to her family, who could then categorise her as a tragic figure and a guilty memory.

From a myriad of such examples it is not difficult to build up a picture of the generation of texts, in which authors had carefully to adapt themselves to standards which were a matter of the social respectability and sensitivities of certain sections of the literate middle classes, and not grounded in any acute ethical or literary awareness. It is clear that the standards exercised by the unofficial censors of literature not only shaped individual novels by excluding 'unsafe' subjects, words and attitudes, but themselves became the subject-matter of fiction. Given sufficient space, this proposition could be demonstrated with respect to a wide range of moral, religious and social issues. For economy, I shall take a few examples from the same highly charged area mentioned above – women's sexuality in relation to the construction of gender stereotypes – and shall content myself with the assertion that a similar introduction of socio-literary conventions into the *subject* of fiction occurs in most areas of Victorian moral, religious and social sensibility. In *Mill on the Floss* (1860, VII.2), George Eliot uses the social disgrace of Maggie Tulliver after her episode on the river with Stephen Guest, to introduce a discussion of the difference between judgement on the basis of 'maxims' and sympathetic moral understanding, and this discussion remains central to her fictional material and teaching. The literary as much as the social rehabilitation of a prostitute becomes Trollope's subject in *The Vicar of Bullhampton* (1869–70). Gaskell's *Ruth* (1853) centres on the idea that an unmarried mother can be socially and morally unexceptionable if her unmarried status is not recognised. In all of these cases characters seem at first sight to be representations of attempts to navigate some very difficult waters in their fictional societies, and this is often taken to be the subject-matter of these novels. It is not, however, apparent that such subject-matter could be presented without itself falling foul of the prevailing unofficial censorship, and the irresistible conclusion is that it is the novelists' skill in negotiating the obstacles presented by social and trading restrictions to such subject-matter that is in its turn the subject of the fiction.

The struggle for moral control in the Victorian period was untiring, and everyone took part, the extracts printed below showing some of the modes of participation. Rigby's celebrated attack on *Jane Eyre* (3.1) shows the intertwining of moral, religious and political factors in the protection of the propertied classes, in whose interest it was to maintain that the world was as God had ordained it, a place in which – in Richard Chenevix Trench's words –

> Thou cam'st not to thy place by accident:
> It is the very place He meant for thee.

In a related spirit Mansel (3.6) castigates literature which is widely read and commercially distributed, and which does not require the education of a lady or a gentleman to understand it. The review of Trollope's *Eustace Diamonds* (3.7) makes the author's specifically *literary* choices in the presentation of individual immorality the subject of the review, and registers them as central in the production of meaning during the reading process. The present volume does not attempt to trace these or any other specific examples in detail, since to do so would require an amount of space not available here. Instead insights are offered into the kind of judgements which contributed to the socio-literary debate as it became part of the subject-matter of fiction.

During the second half of the twentieth century, literary critics and historians have increasingly come to regard literary conventions as socially constructed – not, it must be emphasised, socially and economically determined in a one-way process, but reacting in complex ways with non-literary factors, jointly to develop social and literary ways of perceiving and understanding the world. Literature – in the narrow sense of texts which are read with a certain respect and solemnity, or which feature on reading lists for literature degrees – must be supplemented in this account by many other written forms, including, crucially, the commentary, semi-literary, semi-social, which surrounds texts and produces some of their meanings, and produces these meanings both at the stage of production (or writing) and consumption (or reading). All this is to say, more briefly, that literature plays important roles both as contributor to and register of the social construction of reality, and that the following extracts help to give an insight into how these roles were played.

Naturally, Victorian attempts to draw up standards by which to judge the morality of works of literature are fascinating in their own right, as part of the history of ideas and as examples of the resourcefulness of the human mind in proposing again and again to erect a whole intellectual and aesthetic system on frankly unpromising foundations. Bagehot (3.5) reveals the centrality of this problem about moral standards to the Victorian understanding of literature, while confirming that the problem itself became part of the subject-matter, as well as an unavoidable factor in the reading experience:

No one can read Mr. Thackeray's writings without feeling that he is perpetually treading as close as he dare to the border-line that separates the world which may be described in books from the world which it is prohibited so to describe. No one knows better than this accomplished artist where that line is, and how curious are its windings and turns.

An extract from R.H. Hutton's long article, 'The Hard Church Novel', is included by way of apology for not adequately exploring religious judgement in this anthology. Hutton's piece should serve to indicate the highly specialised sympathies and understandings required in a reader of a later age fully to engage with this vast subject, while allowing one to see, by extrapolation as it were, the endless extent of the religious debate in and on prose fiction.

In his two pieces printed here, E.S. Dallas attempts to bring some sanity into the discussion, in accordance with his sceptical view of the moral efficacy of literature, as expressed in 2.4. Finally, an extract from *Cope's Tobacco Plant* stands in a long and continuing line of debate about whether social delinquency can be attributed to books – or, in another age, to films and television programmes. It is refreshing to look a little further back in history at a remark characteristically Scottish in its challenge to received 'wisdom' on this subject, when Dugald Stewart (1753–1828) reports one of Adam Smith's comments on morality and the effect of literature. He is discussing

> the effect of those writers who unite with any transcendent excellencies, some affected peculiarities of manner and style, in misleading and corrupting the taste of their contemporaries. 'How many great qualities,' says Mr Smith, 'must that writer possess, who can thus render his very faults agreeable! After the praise of refining the taste of a nation, the highest eulogy, perhaps, which can be bestowed on any author, is to say that he corrupted it.'[2]

Notes

1 *The Letters of Anthony Trollope*, ed N. John Hall, Stanford, CA, Stanford University Press, 1983, pp. 51–4.
2 Dugald Stewart, *Philosophical Essays*, vol. 3, 'On the Faculty of Taste', *Collected Works*, ed Sir William Hamilton, 10 vols, 1854–8, vol. 5, p. 365.

3.1 Elizabeth Rigby (anon.), review of *Vanity Fair, Jane Eyre* and *Governesses' Benevolent Institution Report for 1847*, *Quarterly Review* 84 (December 1848), 162–75

In her biography of Charlotte Brontë, Elizabeth Gaskell cites this article as an example of the 'cowardly insolence' of anonymous criticism. 'I am not aware that Miss Brontë took any greater notice of the article than to place a few sentences out of it in the mouth of a hard and vulgar woman in "Shirley," where they are so much in character, that few have recognised them as a quotation.' The 'hard and vulgar woman' is Mrs Pryor, and the quotations occur in chapter 21 of Shirley. Brontë originally wanted to preface the novel with a reply to Rigby's review, but her publishers would not agree.[1]

Brontë accurately diagnoses the social basis of Rigby's attack, which is most clearly exposed in the suggestion that the reader should 'wince' when Rochester – however immoral he may be – is exposed to the indignity of intimate contact with a social inferior. Although this article is generally and deservedly pilloried by later critics, Rigby was right to identify the attitudes in the Brontës' works as progressive and disruptive, and from her standpoint they must indeed have looked as though they tended to undermine the social order. The Quarterly Review *is certainly fulfilling the purpose for which it was founded, which was to uphold Church, State and the social order.*

Jane Eyre is merely another Pamela,[2] who, by the force of her character and the strength of her principles, is carried victoriously through great trials and temptations from the man she loves. Nor is she even a Pamela adapted and refined to modern notions; for though the story is conducted without those derelictions of decorum which we are to believe had their excuse in the manners of Richardson's time, yet it is stamped with a coarseness of language and laxity of tone which have certainly no excuse in ours. It is a very remarkable book: we have no remembrance of another combining such genuine power with such horrid taste. Both together have equally assisted to gain the great popularity it has enjoyed; for in these days of extravagant adoration of all that bears the stamp of novelty and originality, sheer rudeness and vulgarity have come in for a most mistaken worship. . . .

Mr. Rochester is a man who deliberately and secretly seeks to violate the laws both of God and man, and yet we will be bound half our lady readers are enchanted with him for a model of generosity and honour. We would have thought that such a hero had had no chance, in the purer taste of the present day; but the popularity of Jane Eyre is a proof how deeply the love for illegitimate romance is implanted in our nature. Not that the author is strictly responsible for this. Mr. Rochester's character is tolerably consistent. He is made as coarse and as brutal as can in all conscience be required to keep our sympathies at a distance. In point of literary consistency the hero is at all events impugnable, though we cannot say as much for the heroine.

As to Jane's character – there is none of that harmonious unity about it which made little Becky so grateful a subject of analysis[3] – nor are the discrepancies of that kind which have their excuse and their response in our nature. The inconsistencies of Jane's character lie mainly not in her own imperfections, though of course she has her share, but in the author's. There is that confusion in the relations between cause and effect, which is not so much untrue to human nature as to human art. The error in Jane Eyre is, not that her character is this or that, but that she is made one thing in the eyes of her imaginary companions, and another in that of the actual reader. There is a perpetual disparity between the account she herself gives of the effect she produces, and the means shown us by which she brings that effect about. We hear nothing but self-eulogiums on the perfect tact and wondrous penetration with which she is gifted, and yet almost every word she utters offends us, not only with the absence of these qualities, but with the positive contrasts of them, in either her pedantry, stupidity, or gross vulgarity. . . .

Jane Eyre is throughout the personification of an unregenerate and undisciplined spirit, the more dangerous to exhibit from that prestige of principle and self-control which is liable to dazzle the eye too much for it to observe the inefficient and unsound foundation on which it rests. It is true Jane does right, and exerts great moral strength, but it is the strength of a mere heathen mind which is a law unto itself. No Christian grace is perceptible upon her. She has inherited in fullest measure the worst sin of our fallen nature – the sin of pride. Jane Eyre is proud, and therefore she is ungrateful too. It pleased God to make her an orphan, friendless, and penniless – yet she thanks nobody, and least of all Him, for the food and raimant, the friends, companions, and instructors of her helpless youth – for the care and education vouchsafed to her till she was capable in mind as fitted in years to provide for herself. On the contrary, she looks upon all that has been done for her not only as her undoubted right, but as falling far short of it. The doctrine of humility is not more foreign to her mind than it is repudiated by her heart. It is by her own talents, virtues, and courage that she is made to attain the summit of human happiness, and, as far as Jane Eyre's own statement is concerned, no one would think she owed anything either to God above or to man below. . . .

Altogether the auto-biography of Jane Eyre is pre-eminently an anti-Christian composition. There is throughout it a murmuring against the comforts of the rich and against the privations of the poor, which, as far as each individual is concerned, is a murmuring against God's appointment – there is a proud and perpetual assertion of the rights of man, for which we find no authority in God's word or in God's providence – there is that pervading tone of ungodly discontent which is at once the most prominent and the most subtle evil which the law and the pulpit, which all civilized society in fact has at the present day to contend with. We do not hesitate to say that the tone of mind and thought which has overthrown authority and violated every code human and divine abroad, and fostered Chartism and rebellion at home, is the same which has also written Jane Eyre.[4]

Still we say again this is a very remarkable book. We are painfully alive to the moral, religious, and literary deficiencies of the picture, and such passages of beauty and power as we have quoted cannot redeem it, but it is impossible not to be spell-bound with the very freedom of the touch. It would be mere hackneyed courtesy to call it 'fine writing.' It bears no impress of being written at all, but is poured out rather in the heat and hurry of an instinct, which flows ungovernably on to its object, indifferent by what means it reaches it, and unconscious too. As regards the author's chief object, however, it is a failure – that, namely of making a plain, odd woman, destitute of all the conventional features of feminine attraction, interesting in our sight. We deny that he[5] has succeeded in this. Jane Eyre, in spite of some grand things about her, is a being totally uncongenial to our feelings from beginning to end. We acknowledge her firmness – we respect her determination – we feel for her struggles; but, for all that, and setting aside higher considerations, the impression she leaves on our mind is that of a decidedly vulgar-minded woman – one whom we should not care for as an acquaintance, whom we should not seek as a friend, whom we should not desire for a relation, and whom we should scrupulously avoid for a governess.

Notes

1   E.C. Gaskell, *The Life of Charlotte Brontë*, 2nd edn, 1857, vol. 2, p. 87.
2   In Samuel Richardson's *Pamela* the heroine's virtue in resisting her employer's advances while fuelling his sexual desire, is rewarded by marriage to him. See extract 2.4 for E.S. Dallas's comments on *Pamela*, which he regards as 'a mischievous work' of 'immoral tendency'.
3   Thackeray's *Vanity Fair* appeared as a serial from January 1847 to July 1848.
4   Rigby is referring to the French Revolution and to the political turmoil in continental Europe in the year in which she is writing (1848, 'the Year of Revolutions'), as well as to Chartist agitation in Britain.
5   Rigby claims to believe that the author must be a man, because of certain domestic and sartorial inaccuracies, but is almost certainly being deliberately offensive in suggesting that the 'indelicacy' of the novel is 'unwomanly'. *The Dictionary of National Biography* records that '[e]lsewhere she expressed her conviction that Currer, Acton, and Ellis Bell were three Lancashire brothers of the weaving order'.

3.2 E.S. Dallas (anon.), review of Geraldine Jewsbury, *Constance Herbert, The Times*, 1 June 1855, 10

This and extract 3.4 are brief examples of the work of the critic Eneas Sweetland Dallas, whose views on moral didacticism in prose fiction are developed at greater length in his book, The Gay Science, *from which a few pages are reprinted as extract 2.4. In this review he clearly outlines one of the perpetual problems facing moral criticism of the novel. Though unsurprising, it acts as a useful antidote to some of the simpler-minded criticism and fiction of the period. For E.S. Dallas see the headnotes to extracts 1.6 and 2.4 and extract 6.5 and its headnote.*

Geraldine Jewsbury (1812–80), daughter of a Manchester cotton merchant, was simultaneously a prominent disciple of George Sand as regards fiction on 'the woman question', and of Thomas Carlyle in many other social matters. Rather unfairly she is now best remembered for her exchange of letters with Jane Carlyle, but she was equally prominent in her day as a novelist and essayist. Constance Herbert *(1855) is the story of a woman who refuses to marry for fear of passing on an hereditary insanity from her mother.*

The tendency of a book is by no means to be inferred from its ostensible moral, – indeed, most authors, whatever be their tone or their principle, generally come to pretty nearly the same result on the last page. For instance, though among writers who are hostile to the ordinary prejudices of society there is no more favourite subject than that of a pair of ardent lovers oppressed by social restraint, scarcely any of them dream of making an illicit or even an imprudent amour the basis of perfect happiness. The famous novel *Indiana*[1] is an exception to the general rule.

It is from the preponderance of interest that is given to either of the opposite sides in the discussion of a grand moral question that the ethical purport of a work is to be judged. There is no good in hanging an erring hero at the end of a third volume, if he has already fascinated his readers by his gallantry and heroism, as exhibited during two volumes and a-half. When passion and duty are brought into collision, we can guess very well that the latter will come off nominally victorious, but as to the amount of sympathy that will be claimed for the fallen combatant we are by no means so certain about the matter. If the reader mourns over the hard fate of unruly passion, while duty coldly writes its uninspiring epitaph, the moral operation of the story is at best questionable.

Note

1   George Sand, *Indiana* (1832). Dallas's 'famous' is ironic, since while the
    novel had a scandalous reputation, it was not available in Britain, where
    no translation was ever published, although it appeared in translation in
    the USA in various editions from 1843.

3.3 Richard Holt Hutton (anon.), 'The Hard Church Novel', review of *Perversion*, 3 vols, 1856, *National Review* 3 (July 1856), 127–46

*R.H. Hutton (1826-97) was one of the most influential critics of the
second half of the nineteenth century. He was educated at University
College, London and at the universities of Berlin and Heidelberg,
where he imbibed the latest German philosophical, theological and
critical thought, and was consequently better able than many of his
contemporaries to sustain the shock of new ideas such as the limited
authority of the Bible and the scientific theory of evolution, which
caused major traumas in the period. Society's loss of an older,
unquestioning religious faith remained a source of sorrow to him, but
he was more thoroughly prepared by his education to accept the new
than were the graduates of the intellectually moribund ancient
universities of Oxford and Cambridge in England. He mastered an
impressive range of subjects, studying law and later working as
assistant editor of the* Economist, *and holding the post of Professor of
Mathematics at Bedford College, London, from 1856 to 1865. Having
been brought up a Unitarian (he prepared for the Unitarian ministry
in 1847), he was also able to be intelligently detached from English
Establishment ideology, though he later converted to the Church of
England. He was joint editor of the* National Review *with Walter
Bagehot (see 1.3 and 3.5) from 1855 to 1865, and literary editor and
part-proprietor of the* Spectator *from 1861 until his death in 1897. By
the 1880s and 1890s his criticism had lost favour with many younger
thinkers, and George Saintsbury for one attacked him for allaying and
sweetening his articles 'by sentimental, or political, or religious, or
philosophical, or anthropological, or pantopragmatic adulteration'.[1] It
is one of the attractions of the best mid-Victorian criticism that it did
take all human learning as its sphere, and of course in its turn
Saintsbury's 'pure criticism' has since been assailed because it claimed
to steer clear of 'non-literary' systems of thought.*

Perversion; or the Causes and Consequences of Infidelity *was
published anonymously by William John Conybeare (1815-57), vicar
of Axminster, Devon. It critically surveys the varieties of belief and*

unbelief current at the time by following a man's career through successive allegiances to High and Low Church, and experiments with free thought. In his long review Hutton distinguishes between the fiction of 'the Church of Commonsense' and that of 'the Hard Church', which he sees as 'a degradation of the solid, sagacious form of Christianity . . . [and] a hard arrogant infliction, uniting the tone of a schoolmaster to a spirit of intellectual scorn'. An extract from his review is printed here as an example of the intelligent application of theological principles to intellectual history and literary criticism. Religious analysis of prose fiction took so many forms and occupied so many acres in so many periodicals, that it cannot be fairly represented in the present volume. The reader is assured that for almost any conceivable Christian position there existed a body of polemic attacking some or all current fiction on more-or-less religious grounds.

There has recently been a considerable influx into the world of theological speculation, as well from Nonconformist as from Conformist sources, which may fairly be classed together as manifestoes of the *Hard Church*. It is a degradation of the solid, sagacious form of Christianity. . . . In its worst type it is a hard arrogant infliction, uniting the tone of a schoolmaster to a spirit of intellectual scorn, essentially a *Hard* Church . . .

[E]xceedingly as we dislike that hybrid species of composition of which religious novels almost always consist, we yet believe there is no better sign for the theology of the present day than its disposition to try itself by literary tests. Theology and Literature – the study of God and the study of Man – need to go hand in hand, and are only just beginning to know it. It was not so always. Although it was the return of literature that heralded the free theology of the Reformation, yet in the first era of that theology there was too intense a straining of the newly-recovered sight for the divine love and mercy, to permit any quiet and perfect union between human duties and religious trust. . . . Luther and the Puritans found the only literature they needed in the Bible, and their great yearning was to concede as little hold over themselves to the anxious cares of this life as a Hebrew prophet or a Christian apostle. They desired to drown the memory of human labours in the springs of a divine life. . . . It was not with the affectionate minuteness of joy that human cares and duties were discharged; and human literature was therefore little valued. As the objects of God's love and care, all men were equally precious; as mere human studies, all were equally insignificant. In the one vast thought of free mercy and personal love, all thought of the special windings of that love through the varying lives of various men was for a time merged and forgotten. And when the first tide of fresh religious life had rolled away, the new theology, thus separated from special human interests, necessarily tended to become inorganic, – a series of fixed truths as to what God had done, not a revelation of what He was doing.

Literature, on the other hand, set free from the control of the Church, ran riot in its liberty, and man's image was reproduced in every modification of distortion, until literary genius was almost habituated to regard new specimens of character with as little relation to any standard of character as if each specimen were an independent species of Nature's own making, which it would be idle to compare with any central type. As it is the tendency of theology without literature to recede into a set of distant, discontinuous, inorganic truths, so it is the tendency of literature without theology to lose all trace of unity, and break up into numberless accidental forms of discoloured humanity. The object of literature is not the mere delineation of actual men; it is the delineation of men drawn with a full insight into *man*. Wherever individual characters are merely copied without reference to any such vision of man, – wherever, for instance, human evil is pictured without the consciousness that it is also human *degradation*, – wherever meanness is painted without any glimpse of its sadness, – there literature becomes grovelling, decrepit, dead; it chokes and nauseates the mind: it is *human* literature no longer. And this insight into what man *is*, and men *might* be, is but too apt to die out of the imagination, if the diversity of living images be not seen in relation to the one life in which they were made. Indeed, it is the natural tendency of mere literary pursuits to weaken the belief in any unchangeable moral standard of character; and, except in cases of the highest conceivable imaginative inspiration, such as Shakespeare's (in whom there was such fulness of humanity, that no familiarity, however close, with the varieties of human weakness and evil could have disturbed his calm insight into the inexhaustible varieties of possible greatness), it is almost inevitable that the habit of taking up all moral and immoral attitudes in turn must dizzy the brain and confound the steadiness of personal convictions, unless there be a real inward hold on that spiritual image, which is the same yesterday, to-day, and for ever. No theology, of course, however living and true, will lend the artistic power to paint human character vividly, but it will secure the imagination against the dangers of its own flexibility, – it will tinge with a divine pathos the picture of misery and guilt, – it will suggest an inward perspective for grouping the creations of the poet, – and it will involuntarily open new vistas in the tragedy of human story by giving a spiritual transparence to the brooding cloud of calamity, or mixing a watery gleam of unreality with the triumphant sunshine of selfish prosperity. Literature has a right to ask Theology to show that it can assimilate closely with all the various forms of human life, and solve in detail the individual problems of individual lives; Theology has a right to ask literature to show that it aims at some unity of spirit amid its diversity of gifts, that it . . . will not shrink therefore from connecting the flying tints of human nature by regarding them with conscious reference to the One presence in whom it is *fulness* of life that prevents the possibility of change.

Note

1   George Saintsbury, *A History of English Criticism*, 1962, p. 496 (first published 1900–4).

3.4 E.S. Dallas (anon.), review of Charles Kingsley, *Two Years Ago*, *The Times*, 29 December 1857, 5

This three-volume novel by Charles Kingsley, clergyman, 'muscular Christian', Christian socialist and novelist, is set in a Cornish village during the cholera epidemic of 1855, and advances the author's case for better sanitation. For Dallas, see the headnote to 3.2.

A novelist may '*teach lessons.*' We cordially allow that a novelist may write all the better for having a purpose; but the purpose of the novelist is to act upon the reader, and not to convert the characters of his creation. He is most likely to effect his purpose by representations of life which the reader will find probable, in which the characters for the most part act as we might expect them to act, in which they are tolerably consistent with their imaginary antecedents, or inconsistent only to the limits of our experience, and not of our dreams, our aspirations, or our theories. Under such conditions of representation virtue and vice will be fairly sequential; the one may be made to bear the palm and the other the penalty to encourage or deter the interested observer, who is unconscious of the purpose till the work is completed. The purpose should never be patent or obtrusive; still less should it involve the pantomimic expedient of a change of nature in the *dramatis personae* in the face of the audience and in the course of the piece. . . . Keep the moral out of the fable, or you will spoil the fable and moral together; and don't distort facts to inculcate doctrines . . .

Mr. Thackeray rarely writes without a purpose, yet all is natural, persistent, and accordant; his characters are true to themselves . . . and it is only on seeking the purport of their exhibition that we find out, when the curtain has dropped and the actors are dismissed, that we have been listening to a grand homily against some meanness or affectation. The purpose is more impressive as a moral lesson if the artist is not sacrificed to the impatience of the teacher, and if the moral is simply suggested while the act remains unimpeachable.

3.5 Walter Bagehot (anon.), 'Charles Dickens', review of Chapman and Hall's cheap edition of Dickens's novels, 1857–8, *National Review* 7 (October 1858), 476–98

The following passage clearly indicates the moral 'double-bind' of mid-Victorian criticism. Both Dickens and Thackeray are found wanting in their own ways, and the modern reader is left wondering whether there really is room for another more 'moral' path in the minute space that this critic has identified between Thackeray's knowing avoidance of open offence and Dickens's innocence. This article was published more than two years before the start of the serialisation of Great Expectations, *a novel which for many critics answers Bagehot's criticism of Dickens's ineptitude in presenting sexual desire. For Bagehot, see the headnote to extract 1.3.*

It perhaps follows from what has been said of the characteristics of Mr. Dickens's genius, that he would be little skilled in planning plots for his novels. He certainly is not so skilled. . . . The defect of plot is heightened by Mr. Dickens's great, we might say complete, inability to make a love-story. A pair of lovers is by custom a necessity of narrative fiction, and writers who possess a great general range of mundane knowledge, and but little knowledge of the special sentimental subject, are often in amusing difficulties. The watchful reader observes the transition from the hearty description of well-known scenes, of prosaic streets, or journeys by wood and river, to the pale colours of ill-attempted poetry, to such sights as the novelist wishes he need not try to see. But few writers exhibit the difficulty in so aggravated a form as Mr. Dickens. Most men by taking thought can make a lay figure to look not so very unlike a young gentleman, and can compose a telling schedule of ladylike charms. Mr. Dickens has no power of doing either. . . .

This deficiency is probably nearly connected with one of Mr. Dickens's most remarkable excellencies. No one can read Mr. Thackeray's writings without feeling that he is perpetually treading as close as he dare to the border-line that separates the world which may be described in books from the world which it is prohibited so to describe. No one knows better than this accomplished artist where that line is, and how curious are its windings and turns. The charge against him is that he knows it but too well; that with an anxious care and a wistful eye he is ever approximating to its edge, and hinting with subtle art how thoroughly he is familiar with, and how interesting he could make the interdicted region on the other side. He never violates a single conventional rule; but at the same time the shadow of the immorality that is not seen is scarcely ever wanting to his delineation of the society that is seen. Every one may perceive what is passing in his fancy. Mr. Dickens is chargeable with no such defect: he does not seem to feel the temptation. By what we may fairly call an instinctive purity of genius, he not only observes the conventional rules, but makes excursions into topics which no other novelist could safely handle, and, by a felicitous instinct, deprives them of all impropriety. No other writer could have managed the humour of Mrs. Gamp without becoming unendurable.[1] At the same time it is difficult not to believe that this singular insensibility to the temptations to which many of the greatest novelists have succumbed is in some measure connected with his utter inaptitude for delineating the portion of life to which their art is specially inclined. He delineates neither the love-affairs which ought to be nor those which ought not to be.

Note

1   Mrs Gamp, the nurse in *Martin Chuzzlewit* (1843–4), is interestingly discussed by R.H. Hutton in 4.10.

3.6 Henry Longueville Mansel (anon.), 'Sensation Novels', *Quarterly Review* 113 (April 1862), 481–9

H.L. Mansel (1820–71), an Oxford philosopher and later Professor of Ecclesiastical History, was a High Church High Tory. His article exemplifies the classically educated man's scorn for popular fiction, and sensational novels in particular, and expresses alarm at the development of cultural forms appropriate for ways of life and social groups which seem to him to be undermining the traditional social and religious order. He singles out for special attack the three principal ways in which the circulation of literature was increased in the days when publishers maintained a very high retail price on novels, which put them beyond the reach of most of the population - that is £1 11s 6d for a standard three-volume work. These means of circulation were the serialisation of fiction, the lending library and the cheap reprint.[1] This extract is a good example of a kind of socio-economic analysis often applied in the Victorian period to more popular types of fiction.

'I don't like preaching to the nerves instead of the judgement,' was the remark of a shrewd observer of human nature, in relation to a certain class of popular sermons. A class of literature has grown up around us, usurping in many respects, intentionally or unintentionally, a portion of the preacher's office, playing no inconsiderable part in moulding the minds and forming the habits and tastes of its generation; and doing so principally, we had almost said exclusively, by 'preaching to the nerves.' It would almost seem as if the paradox of Cabanis, *les nerfs, voilà tout l'homme*,[2] had been banished from the realm of philosophy only to claim a wider empire in the domain of fiction – at least if we may judge by the very large class of writers who seem to acknowledge no other element in human nature to which they can appeal. Excitement, and excitement alone, seems to be the great end at which they aim – an end which must be accomplished at any cost by some means or other, 'si possis, recte; si non, quocumque modo.'[3] And as excitement, even when harmless in kind, cannot be continually produced without becoming morbid in degree, works of this class manifest themselves as belonging, some more, some less, but all to some extent, to the morbid phenomena of literature – indications of a wide-spread corruption, of which they are in part both the effect and the cause; called into existence to supply the cravings of a diseased appetite, and contributing themselves to foster the disease, and to stimulate the want which they supply. . . .

Various causes have been at work to produce this phenomenon of our literature. Three principal ones may be named as having had a large share in it – periodicals, circulating libraries, and railway bookstalls. A periodical, from its very nature, must contain many articles of an ephemeral interest, and of the character of goods made to order. The material part of it is a fixed quantity, determined by rigid boundaries of space and time; and on this Procrustean bed the spiritual part must needs be stretched to fit. A given number of sheets of print, containing so many lines per sheet, must be produced weekly or monthly, and the diviner element must accommodate itself to these conditions. A periodical, moreover, belongs to the class of works which most men borrow, and do not buy, and in which, therefore, they take only a transitory interest. Few men will burden their shelves with a series of volumes which have no coherence in their parts, and no limit in their number, whose articles of personal interest may be as one halfpennyworth of bread to an intolerable quantity of sack,[4] and which have no other termination to their issue than the point at which they cease to be profitable. Under these circumstances, no small stimulus is given to the production of tales of the marketable stamp, which, after appearing piecemeal in weekly or monthly instalments, generally enter upon a second stage of their insect-life in the form of a handsome reprint under the auspices of the circulating library.

This last-named institution is the oldest of the three . . . From the days of the 'Minerva Press' (that synonym for the dullest specimens of the light reading of our grandmothers)[5] to those of the thousand and one tales of the current season, the circulating library has been the chief hot-bed for forcing a crop of writers without talent and readers without discrimination. It is to literature what a *magasin de modes* is to dress, giving us the latest fashion, and little more. . . . Subscription, as compared with purchase, produces no doubt a great increase in the quantity of books procurable, but with a corresponding deterioration in the quality. The buyer of books is generally careful to select what for his own purposes is worth buying; the subscriber is often content to take the good the gods provide him,[6] glancing lazily down the library catalogue, and picking out some title which promises amusement or excitement. . . .

The railway stall, like the circulating library, consists partly of books written expressly for its use, partly of reprints in a new phase of their existence – a phase internally that of the grub, with small print and cheap paper, externally that of the butterfly, with a tawdry cover, ornamented with a highly-coloured picture, hung out like a signboard, to give promise of the entertainment to be had within. The picture, like the book, is generally of the sensation kind, announcing some exciting scene to follow. A pale young lady in a white dress, with a dagger in her hand, evidently prepared for some desperate struggle, or a Red Indian in his war-paint; or, if the plot turns on smooth instead of violent villany, a priest persuading a dying man to sign a paper; or a disappointed heir burning a will; or a treacherous lover telling his flattering tale to some deluded maid or wife. The exigencies of railway travelling do not allow much time for examining the merits of a book before purchasing it; and keepers of bookstalls, as well as of refreshment-rooms, find an advantage in offering their customers something hot and strong, something that may catch the eye of the hurried passenger, and promise temporary excitement to relieve the dulness of a journey.

These circumstances of production naturally have their effect on the quality of the articles produced. Written to meet an ephemeral demand, aspiring only to an ephemeral existence, it is natural that they should have recourse to rapid and ephemeral methods of awakening the interest of their readers, striving to act as the dram or the dose, rather than as the solid food, because the effect is more immediately perceptible. And as the perpetual cravings of the dram-drinker or the valetudinarian for the spirits or physic are hardly intelligible to the man of sound health and regular appetites, so, to one called from more wholesome studies to survey the wide field of sensational literature, it is difficult to realise the idea which its multifarious contents necessarily suggest, that these books must form the staple mental food of a very large class of readers. . . .

The sensation novel, be it mere trash or something worse, is usually a tale of our own times. Proximity is, indeed, one great element of sensation. It is necessary to be near a mine to be blown up by its explosion; and a tale which aims at electrifying the nerves of the reader is never thoroughly effective unless the scene be laid in our own days and among the people we are in the habit of meeting. We read with little emotion, though it comes in the form of history, Livy's narrative of the secret poisonings carried on by nearly two hundred Roman ladies; we feel but a feeble interest in an authentic record of the crimes of a Borgia or a Brinvilliers; but we are thrilled with horror, even in fiction, by the thought that such things may be going on around us and among us. The man who shook our hand with a hearty English grasp half an hour ago – the woman whose beauty and grace were the charm of last night, and whose gentle words sent us home better pleased with the world and with ourselves – how exciting to think that under these pleasing outsides may be concealed some demon in human shape, a Count Fosco or a Lady Audley! He may have assumed all that heartiness to conceal some dark plot against our life or honour, or against the life and honour of one yet dearer: she may have left that gay scene to muffle herself in a thick veil and steal to a midnight meeting with some villanous accomplice. He may have a mysterious female, immured in a solitary tower or a private lunatic asylum, destined to come forth hereafter to menace the name and position of the excellent lady whom the world acknowledges as his wife: she may have a husband lying dead at the bottom of a well, and a fatherless child nobody knows where. All this is no doubt very exciting; but even excitement may be purchased too dearly; and we may be permitted to doubt whether the pleasure of a nervous shock is worth the cost of so much morbid anatomy if the picture be true, or so much slanderous misrepresentation if it be false.

Notes

1 See John A. Sutherland, *Victorian Novelists and Publishers*, London, Athlone Press, 1976, and Guinevere L. Griest, *Mudie's Circulating Library and the Victorian Novel*, Newton Abbot, David & Charles, 1970.

2 'les nerfs, voilà tout l'homme' (French): 'the nerves – there is the whole Man.' George Cabanis (1757–1808) was a French man of medicine, and one of the 'Idéologues', who adhered to the sensualism of the eighteenth-century philosopher, Condillac.

3 *si possis, recte; si non, quocumque modo* (Latin): '[make money] by right means if you can, but, if not, by any means [make money]' – Horace, *Epistles* I.i.66. Mansel's abbreviated version of this tag omits mention of money, but the mercenary implications of the quotation would have been clear to the classically educated Victorian reader.

4 'but one halfpennyworth of bread to this intolerable deal of sack!' *Henry IV, Part One*, II.iv.524–6.

5 The Minerva Press, in Leadenhall Street in London, was famous at the turn of the previous century for publishing ultra-sentimental novels with complex plots and happy outcomes.

6 See Dryden, 'Alexander's Feast', ll.106–7:
> Lovely Thais sits beside thee,
> Take the good the gods provide thee.

The idea of cheap literature as prostitution is introduced by this allusion, since Thais was an Athenian courtesan who accompanied Alexander the Great on his Asian campaign.

3.7 Anonymous review of Anthony Trollope's *The Eustace Diamonds*, *Spectator* 45 (26 October 1872), 1365–6

Judging from its style and concerns this review is unlikely to be by R.H. Hutton, the literary editor of the Spectator, *whose criticism is represented by extracts 3.3, 4.10 and 6.4. Its moral stance more resembles the review of Trollope's* The Way We Live Now *by Hutton's co-editor, Meredith Townsend, in the* Spectator *of 26 June*

1875 (48: 825-6). The Eustace Diamonds centres on Lady Eustace's felonious attempts to retain a valuable set of diamonds which should pass down her late husband's family as an heirloom, and it has distinctly sensational elements of surprise, although as usual in Trollope the principal interest is in the psychology and morality of the characters' actions. This review is characteristic of the period in its demand for a system of moral contrasts. It also accepts evil on a grand scale but distrusts sordid, as-it-were 'everyday' evil. While tragedy or 'elevated', Byronic evil would redeem the work by elevating it above the ordinary run of daily life, realism in the sense of adherence to observable reality is seen as degrading. Another key idea is the need for a conscience in the wicked characters and the consequent possibility of moral reformation. The critic puts forward the notion that Becky Sharp is a more acceptable character than Lizzie Eustace because she knows that she is doing wrong, whereas Lizzie is a self-deceiver. At the centre of Becky, as it were, the critic perceives an essence of 'character', whereas Lizzie represents a Victorian nightmare of emptiness – a person defined by the mere accident of circumstances, and not possessing a due proportion of that 'human nature' which the Victorian humanist assumed was common to all people at all times and in all places.

The *Eustace Diamonds*, though as full of good painting as most of Mr. Trollope's tales, has hardly fulfilled the promise of its commencement. We had supposed that in Lady Eustace we were to have Mr. Trollope's equivalent for Thackeray's 'Becky Sharp,' but we hardly think we have got it; or if we have, Mr. Trollope's equivalent for Thackeray's 'Becky Sharp' is but a poor one. It is quite true that Lady Eustace, though she is never guilty of murder, as Becky Sharp certainly is, is a much meaner and more contemptible creature than Becky. She is far less enterprising, far more cowardly, equally selfish, less capable of a disinterested regard such as Becky certainly feels at the end of *Vanity Fair* for Amelia, and more wholly false, more utterly incapable of discriminating between truth and falsehood in herself. Becky is the most daring and cruel of adventuresses. . . . It is hardly possible not to feel it on the cards even to the last that her character might under certain circumstances assert its power, and break through that labyrinth of intrigues in the construction of which it has delighted. Becky in her deepest depths of evil is still herself, and the evil is subsidiary to her ambition and love of ease. Lizzie Eustace is too utterly false to understand where her falsehood begins, – when she is using it deliberately as a means, and when she is toying with it out of mere inability to be true. She is [a] liar by nature, not by policy. Even her cleverness is not like Becky's cleverness, a power in itself, something in the exercise of which the owner so delights that she can always be good-humoured in her villainy, whether she wins or loses. . . . There is something, in its way, grand about Becky's evil. She is wicked and cruel by free choice. Lizzie Eustace is wicked by the law of a mean, and cunning, and greedy nature, with no power in it to be otherwise. Indeed, throughout the long story of her craft and meanness, we do not remember a single occasion on which Mr. Trollope suggests that there was even a glimpse on her part of a better and a worse, or the faintest possible struggle to choose the former. Yet with a will so lost in temptations as hers, one wants, at least for the purposes of Art, the consciousness of evil and the struggle against it, however faint, to relieve the oppressive sordidness of the story. . . .

Lizzie Eustace is a mere greedy and cunning reptile, who seems to give a bad flavour to the story without giving to it the dignity of voluntary wickedness. If you can create a man or woman *above* conscience, deliberately substituting their own interest for conscience, the picture has, at least, a grandeur of its own. But with creatures like Lizzie Eustace, you want to have some glimpse of conscience to give you the sense that she is worthy of moral portraiture at all. There is something a little too suffocating for Art in this picture. . . . Nor is there much tending to relieve the dead-level sordidness of the story in the better class of characters. . . .

[W]e cannot doubt that the defect of the novel is its want of anything like moral contrasts, its horrors in the way of sordidness and coarseness without any adequate foils, the feeling it gives one that the meannesses, basenesses, and moral vulgarities of life, overshadow the heavens and shut out the sun. It is a depressing story, in which all that is coarse and base is painted with lavish power, but where evil itself is not on a grand scale, and where the few good characters are so insignificant that you almost resent the author's expectation that you shall sorrow in their sorrows and rejoice in their joys.

3.8 'Literature and Morality', *Cope's Tobacco Plant* 2 (September 1880), 525–6

Cope's Tobacco Plant *was the house journal of a Liverpool tobacco importer, and has its place in literary history because its chief literary*

critic was the poet James Thomson ('B.V.') (1834–82), author of The
City of Dreadful Night. *However, this article cannot be safely
identified as his. It is tempting to see in this piece the emergence of
the late-century view made familiar by Oscar Wilde in the preface to*
The Portrait of Dorian Gray *(1891): 'There is no such thing as a
moral book or an immoral book. Books are well written, or badly
written. That is all.' But in the end the consideration in this article is
not aesthetic but moral, and for this critic the quality of the work of
art ultimately depends upon the moral qualities of its author.*

The influence of low-class literature on the morals of young readers is
a subject of painful interest to certain worthy persons. Magistrates
from the bench, and parents from the arm-chair, must have their say
about it. From time to time the columns of the newspaper are made a
vehicle for their sentiments. When Tom Jones, ten years old, son of
most respectable parents, takes to amateur housebreaking, and, being
found trying to pick a stable lock with a broken penknife, is whipped
and sent to prison for a week, these magistrates are at no loss to
account for it all. They are confident the sad business is directly
traceable to the fact that Tom has been reading the weekly numbers of
that delectable serial 'The Bad Burgling Brothers of Britain,' whose
publishers guarantee not less than five crimes to the page. When the
boy was captured a copy of it was found in his pockets, together with a
toy pistol that would not fire. These wiseacres do not see that,
supposing the adventure to have been anything more than a harmless
boyish freak, there must have been, beforehand, something in the
character and disposition of Tom himself to incline him to read this
thing. Good Sammy Wilkins, who loves his Sunday school and the
pious little stories he gets there, would not even have looked at it.
They do not comprehend that the something which thus inclined
Tom is precisely the force which moved him to play at housebreaking.
If there had been no dreadful boy, the dreadful book could have done
no harm; a well-disposed boy would have enjoyed it innocently
enough, or would not have enjoyed it at all. But, given the dreadful
boy, and the absence of dreadful books will not keep him out of
mischief.

Dash a little more grossness into the amiable and worthy Anti-Vice
Associations, Societies for the Promotion of Superfine Morals, and the
like. Henceforth, all kinds of literature which in your simplicity you
fancied innocent, prove to be hot-beds of nastiness. The 'maiden's
blush' is now called into play. Even the respectable daily broadsheet is

reckoned 'unfit for the family circle,' if it does not suppress one-half the facts of life and carefully trim the rest. The male members of the family now come to evince the greatest anxiety for the morals of the female members, and the married to exhibit the utmost concern on behalf of the unmarried. If they have anything of doubtful character to say – one of those loose witticisms which married people love – they whisper it. With all the looking after which young people get, one wonders how any of them have even enough knowledge to go wrong, or, for that matter, to go right either, whatever be their individual dispositions. Or one would wonder this, if the story of a young couple who were protected with utmost care from the fruit of a poisonous tree, of which nevertheless they ate, did not recur to us.

Well, then, are some books really *in themselves* immoral, and others essentially moral? Are we to conclude that 'Don Juan,' Ouida's novels,[1] Whitman, Swinburne, and Rossetti's poems are very naughty and exceedingly dangerous? If so, how shall we explain the fact that some good, intelligent people see much beauty and no badness in them, discovering, even in passages which have been pronounced 'improper,' splendid spiritual significance? Wordsworth, as we know, abused 'Wilhelm Meister'[2] heartily: 'It was full of all manner of fornication. It was like the crossing of flies in the air. He had never gone further than the first part; so disgusted was he, that he threw the book across the room.'[3]

When I read that book, many years ago, I confess I would not have been disinclined to endorse Wordsworth's verdict, although I did not throw the volume away. But remembering as I do, the time when I looked upon 'Sartor Resartus'[4] as unreadable for dulness, while now I do not praise it because to praise so grand a work would seem an insult, I feel bound to suspend my judgement about 'Wilhelm Meister,' lest haply the time should come when I shall appreciate it also. I must withhold my decision until I have read it again once or twice. Does not the author of 'Sartor Resartus' himself love this book of Goethe's and rank it very high? and Carlyle, at least, is not addicted to careless or inferior judgements. 'It is with "Meister," ' he tells us, 'as with every work of real and abiding excellence, the first glance is the least favourable. A picture of Raphael, a Greek statue, a play of Sophocles or Shakespeare, appears insignificant to the unpractised eye; and not till after long and patient and intense examination do we begin to descry the earnest features of that beauty which has its foundations in the deepest nature of man, and will continue to be pleasing through all ages.'[5] When Miss Alcott – the well-known author of 'Little Women' – was a girl, she one day went to Mr.

Emerson for a 'real, good, interesting book' to read, and he at once chose for her this very 'Wilhelm Meister.'[6] Of course, the British Parent of the type referred to would take this opinion of Carlyle's to be unimportant, and this behaviour of Emerson's as nothing short of disgraceful. He can see for himself that the book is 'immoral,' and though he may perhaps read it in the privacy of his own room, he will by no means permit it to fall into the hands of his sons and daughters – or at least into the hands of his daughters.

Perhaps the truth of the matter simply is, that books are very much what we take them to be. 'Sartor Resartus' was, years ago, unreadable – to me. *It* has not changed since: the square, brown cover, white paper, black print, are all – saving that a little more dust has fallen on them – just the same now as they were when I first laid the book aside. Now, as I take it up again, it is readable; yes, a book inspired of God, bearing a Divine Message to me! Surely the message was offered all along; but *then* I was dull of hearing, and *now* I can partly understand it. So, perhaps, the forbidden and naughty books also, about which there is such complaint, are not so much naughty as are some of the people who read them, who, having an affinity for nastiness, find its traces everywhere; or who, wearing coloured spectacles, see nothing in the world purely. Thackeray tells us, in his 'Roundabout Papers,' that he never knew there were any indecencies in Shakespeare and 'Arabian Nights' until he read household editions.[7]

Touching this question of the influence and tendency of books, a few thoughtful remarks of George Sand are quoted by Mr. Matthew Arnold in his recent essay on 'Copyright.' They are as follows:- 'It was thought when railways came that we had seen the last of conveyance by horses and carriages, and that the providers of it must all be ruined; but it turns out that railways have created business for horses and carriages greater than there ever was before. In the same way the abundant consumption of middling literature has stimulated the appetite for knowing and judging books. Second-rate, common-place literature is what the ignorant require for catching the first gleam; the day will dawn for them as it does for the child who, by degrees, as he learns to read, learns to understand also; and in fifty years from this time the bad and the middling in literature will be unable to find a publisher because they will be unable to find a market.'[8]

Mr. Arnold himself, however, does not altogether agree with this:- 'I do not think it safe to say that the consumption of the bad and middling in literature does, of itself, necessarily engender a taste for the good, and that out of the multiplication of second-rate books for the million, the multiplication of first-rate books does, as a natural consequence, spring.'

Shall we adopt another standard by which we will judge books, from that employed by our over-anxious friends, the magistrate and the parent? We will not say that a book is to be reckoned good or bad by what is called its 'effect' on those who read it, for this influence we find to arise from a quality in the reader rather than in the book itself. But we will call that book good whose author is competent and conscientious. A writer who has heart and brain will produce a good book if he put the best powers of his heart and brain into his work. But if his aim is nothing more than to turn out so many sheets of 'copy' with the least labour to himself, then, depend upon it, whatever be his talents and his reputation, the product will be bad. That is what we find so much of in the present-day – careless and worthless work; and only once and again a conscientious, true BOOK. If our friends who are so sadly perplexed about pernicious literature would turn their attention to this aspect of the question, and devise means of preventing the publication of literary work which was not the author's best, then the taste for good, sound books would be strengthened, and 'the bad and the middling in literature' would tend to die out. For the rest, we may trust the young people that their morals – when they have any – will not be corrupted by the reading of any books whose authors in the writing of them have been *honest*.

Notes

1 Byron's *Don Juan* is presumably intended. 'Ouida' was the pen-name of Marie Louise de la Ramée (1839–1908), who from the 1860s to the 1890s wrote a large number of novels, most typically high-flown romances and stories on fashionable, 'fast' subjects.

2 Goethe's two novels *Wilhelm Meisters Lehrejahre* and *Wilhelm Meisters Wanderjahre* were published in 1795–6 and 1821 respectively. See note 1 to 1.8. Thomas Carlyle's English translations appeared in 1824 and 1827.

3 See Ralph Waldo Emerson, *English Traits* (1856), chapter 1. Emerson visited Wordsworth at Rydal Mount on 28 August 1833. Henry Crabb Robinson reported that Wordsworth 'always talks ignorantly and there-fore absurdly about G.' *The Correspondence of Henry Crabb Robinson with the Wordsworth Circle (1808–66)*, 2 vols, Oxford, 1927, vol. 1, p. 331.

4 *Sartor Resartus* (1833–4) is a semi-autobiographical work of philosophical fiction by Thomas Carlyle (1795–1881), the English translator of Goethe's *Wilhelm Meister*.

5 Thomas Carlyle, 'Translator's Preface' to his translation of *Meister's Apprenticeship* (1824).

6 Louisa May Alcott (1832–88) was a neighbour and family connection of

the philosopher and poet Ralph Waldo Emerson (1803–82) first at Boston and then at Concord.

7 Thackeray's 'Roundabout Papers' appeared in the *Cornhill Magazine* from January 1860 to February 1863.

8 Matthew Arnold, 'Copyright', *Fortnightly Review* (ns) 27 (March 1880), 319–34.

4

Realism and idealism: the imitation of life

The word 'realism' entered the language in the late 1850s, and from the first it covered a multitude of sins and of virtues. As the French novelist and critic, Champfleury, wittily noted in 1857: 'The word "*realism*" . . . is one of those equivocal terms which lend themselves to all sorts of uses, and can serve at the same time as crowns of laurels or crowns of cabbage-leaves.'[1] The widest sense of the word in English in the period distinguishes the novel of modern life, such as Trollope's *Chronicles of Barsetshire*, Mrs Oliphant's *Chronicles of Carlingford*, Bulwer Lytton's *The Caxtons* and many of Thackeray's novels. In this sense, Dickens is often seen as a 'realist', though many critics discriminate further, and see his sentiment and humour as non-realistic features. This use of 'realism' builds on a well-established set of ideas surrounding the notion of 'truth-to-life' in art, like the test applied to a novel by Margaret Oliphant in 1855, of 'whether it is merely a lying legend of impossible people, or a broad and noble picture of real things and real men'.[2]

A good formulation of this approving sense of 'realism' occurs in 1867 in an article on Trollope – for many the chief practitioner of realistic fiction – in the *Fortnightly Review*, a journal of advanced ideas, co-founded by Trollope and edited by G.H. Lewes:

> realism seems to have reached its limits. Confining himself to actual life in England, and relying implicitly upon his power to inspire interest by the accuracy of his descriptions and the complete verisimilitude of his sketches, Mr. Trollope scorns and rejects all extraneous aid whatever.[3]

A narrower and more technical use of the term refers to fiction written in accordance with certain philosophical standards, most coherently put forward by G.H. Lewes, by which faithful adherence to things, persons and events encountered in the 'real world' ennobles the subject, and the 'real world' of our everyday perceptions and scientific truths is all there is:

The realistic form of art is a legitimate form. When the subject is high, realism is the highest possible form of art; and when the subject is commonplace, realism gives it a warrant. But the only excuse for the artist keeping us amid details of commonplace is, that thereby the commonplace is raised into art; and it can only be so raised by truthful presentation.[4]

Defending realistic art against the charge of 'lack of imagination', Lewes protests that the 'imaginative power' of a work has been 'too frequently estimated according to the extent of a *departure* from ordinary experience in the images selected', pointing out the 'psychological fact that fairies and demons, remote as they are from experience, are not created by a more vigorous effort of imagination than milkmaids and poachers'.[5] These views underlie the passages from Lewes printed as extracts 4.6 and 4.8, and because of the close intellectual relationship between Lewes and George Eliot, they also resemble the views put forward by the narrator of chapter 17 of *Adam Bede* (4.7). The stress on the religious side of human life is more George Eliot's than Lewes's, and Lewes is free of the tone of social condescension which is apparent in the passage from *Adam Bede* – whether George Eliot was conscious of it or not – and which reveals to later readers that it was the educated middle class's version of social reality that was being championed by realistic fiction.

'Realism' is frequently found in opposition to 'idealism', which is the assumption that something lies beyond the world of everyday perceptions and Newtonian, scientific laws, and that this 'something' is grasped by imaginative power, which brings forth ideas clothed in poetic imagery. For the idealist, 'realism' was a term of disparagement, as can be seen in M.E. Braddon's flattery of her mentor, Bulwer Lytton, in March 1866:

The realistic school has been written up so perseveringly of late – always to the disparagement of every thing romantic & imaginative – that I was beginning . . . to bow my head to the idea that the subject of a respectable novel is bound to be all that is trite & commonplace. In you – and Dickens – the art of the novelist has reached its highest perfection – & you alone will I choose for my Gods.[6]

In 2.3 Lytton goes so far as to assert that the fiction of social reform depends upon idealism, since 'low' subjects only achieve a polemical, philanthropic effect when elevated: 'For it is not till Art has told the unthinking that nothing (*rightly treated*) is too low for its breath to vivify, and its wings to raise, that the Herd awaken from their chronic lethargy of contempt, and the Lawgiver is compelled to redress what the Poet has lifted into esteem.' This he says shows the operation of 'the higher and more durable morality which belongs to the Ideal, and instructs us playfully while it interests, in the passions, and through the heart'.

For many, realism was either dull or sordid, and many critics, those of the *Saturday Review* prominent among them, equated realism with lack of imagination and 'mechanical' art. Words like 'photograph', 'kaleidoscope', 'stereotype' and 'Manchester goods' are met with again and again.[7] George Meredith is frequently cited as an example of the 'humourist' whose work rises above mere reality in its pursuit of the 'humours' of mankind:

> There are two classes of novelists . . . and Mr. Meredith is of the *humourist* class, which draws its presentment of mankind in a large degree from its inner consciousness, while the other class paints life phenomenally, as the majority would see it. . . . [H]is characters are more entirely symbols and shadows of his thought than ordinary everyday denizens of the world about him. It would be unfair to try him by the standard relations of novels to life; for, as a humourist, he conceives humourists, and includes them in a world of his own shaping.[8]

Meredith however would have none of this:

> Between realism and idealism there is no natural conflict. This completes that. Realism is the basis of good composition: it implies study, observation, artistic power, and (in those who can do no more) humility. Little writers should be realistic. They would then at least do solid work. They afflict the world because they will attempt that it is given to none but noble workmen to achieve. A great genius must necessarily employ ideal means, for a vast conception cannot be placed bodily before the eye, and remains to be suggested. Idealism is as an atmosphere whose effects of grandeur are wrought out through a series of illusions, that are illusions to the sense within us only when divorced from the groundwork of the real. Need there be exclusion, the one of the other? The artist is incomplete who does this. Men to whom I bow my head (Shakespeare, Goethe; and in their way, Molière, Cervantes) are Realists au fond. But they have the broad arms of Idealism at command. They give us Earth; but it is earth with an atmosphere. One may find as much amusement in a

Kaleidoscope as in a merely idealistic writer: and, just as sound prose is of more worth than pretentious poetry, I hold the man who gives a plain wall of fact higher in esteem than one who is constantly shuffling the clouds and dealing with airy, delicate sentimentalities, headless and tailless imaginings, despising our good, plain strength.

Does not all science (the mammoth balloon, to wit) tell us that when we forsake earth, we reach up to a frosty, inimical Inane? For my part I love and cling to earth, as the one piece of God's handiwork which we possess. I admit that we can refashion; but of earth must be the material.[9]

Departure from 'real life' can be as vigorously attacked as the supposedly slavish imitation of the mundane, as an attack on sentimental writing in the *Saturday Review* in 1860 makes clear:

When Mr. Thackeray sighs over his youth as it seems to slip away from him, when Mr. Dickens drops a tear over a consumptive infant's grave, we sigh with the one and we mourn with the other; for both have a charm with which they fascinate us, and are proficients in the science of softening unwary souls. But we close the book with a feeling that we have been betrayed into a weakness. We blush as we lay it down, for we are conscious that, so far as we have been moved, it has been at the sacrifice of some slight portion of self-respect. When the fit has passed, we take it up again, and wonder at the slightness of the pathos that so stirred us, and, if we are tempted again to succumb, we steel ourselves against the hallucination. . . . when Mr. Dickens is pert, or Mr. Thackeray arch, we think, and think rightly, that we have some cause to be indignant. The great cause why modern humour and modern sentimentalism repel us is, that both are unwarrantably familiar.[10]

The predominant feeling of the age is that the novel 'imitates' life, that a principal test of its success is the criterion of 'truth-to-life', but that unelevated by other considerations, art slides into dulness and is unable to discriminate between good and evil. Consequently formulations of 'truth-to-life' occur which relate 'life' to religious standards, and 'truth-to-life' to a perception of what the critic thinks of as eternal verities:

The object of literature is not the mere delineation of actual men; it is the delineation of men drawn with a full insight into *man*. Wherever individual characters are merely copied without reference to any such vision of man, – wherever, for instance, human evil is pictured without the consciousness that it is also human *degradation*, – wherever meanness is painted without any glimpse of its sadness, – there literature becomes grovelling, decrepit, dead; it chokes and nauseates the mind: it is *human* literature no longer. . . . it is almost inevitable that the habit of taking up all moral and immoral attitudes in turn must dizzy the brain and confound the steadiness of personal convictions, unless there be a real inward hold on that spiritual image, which is the same yesterday, to-day, and for ever. (3.3)

In this passage from 1856, before the word 'realism' entered the critics' vocabulary, the criterion of 'truth-to-life' is united with the highest Victorian moral and religious aspirations. 'Realism', as later construed, has in general a more agnostic tendency.

Notes

1 'Le mot *réalisme* . . . est un de ces termes équivoques qui se prêtent à toutes sortes d'emplois et peuvent servir à la fois de couronne de laurier ou de couronne de choux.' – *Le Réalisme*, 1857. In French, 'cabbage-leaves' are worthless writings.

2 Margaret Oliphant (anon.), 'Modern Novelists – Great and Small', *Blackwood's Edinburgh Magazine* 77 (May 1855), 554–68, p. 554.

3 J. Knight, review of Trollope's *The Claverings*, *Fortnightly Review* (ns) 1 (1 January 1867), 770.

4 G.H. Lewes, 'Causeries', *Fortnightly Review* 4 (15 April 1866), 637.

5 G.H. Lewes, *The Principles of Success in Literature*, Walter Scott Publishing Co Ltd [1898], pp. 58 and 62; reprinted from the *Fortnightly Review* of 1865.

6 Robert L. Wolff, 'Devoted Disciple: The Letters of Mary Elizabeth Braddon to Sir Edward Bulwer-Lytton, 1862–1873', *Harvard Library Bulletin* 12 (1974), 132.

7 See David Skilton, *Anthony Trollope and His Contemporaries*, London, Longman, 1972, pp. 53–5.

8 *The Times* review of *The Ordeal of Richard Feverel*, 14 October 1859, quoted from Maurice Buxton Forman (ed.) *George Meredith: Some Early Appreciations*, 1909, pp. 52 and 53.

9 Letter of 20 September 1864 to the Rev. Augustus Jessopp, *The Letters of George Meredith*, ed W.M. Meredith, 2 vols (1912), vol. 1, pp. 156–7. These remarks arise from a consideration of Meredith's poetic cycle *Modern Love*, but are of more general application.

10 'Sentimental Writing', *Saturday Review* 10 (25 August 1860), 235–6.

4.1 John Forster, unsigned review of Dickens's *Nicholas Nickleby*, *Examiner*, 27 October 1839, 677

John Forster (1812–76), critic, historian and biographer, and now best remembered for his Life of Charles Dickens *(1872–4), was chief literary and dramatic critic of the* Examiner. *He later became its editor. He had met Dickens in 1836, and became the novelist's closest and most enduring friend. His* Life *and* Adventures of Oliver Goldsmith *is the subject of De Quincey's review in extract 1.2. As so much nineteenth-century criticism examines fiction in terms of the 'truth-to-life' of the individual characters, it is refreshing to find Forster – like Bagehot in extract 3.5 – recognising London as an important subject of Dickens's art.*

His style is for the most part admirable. Bating some faults of occasional exaggeration, which we may presently advert to, it is fresh and racy, and has the surpassing charm, of simplicity, earnestness, animal spirits, and good humour. A rare virtue in it is, that it is always, whether grave or gay, thoroughly intelligible, and for the most part thoroughly natural. Its sparkling stream of vivacity or humour glides down by the easiest transition into deeper currents of seriousness and pathos. It is as quick, as warm, as comprehensive, as the sympathies it is taxed to express. We know of none that can paint more powerfully by an apposite epithet, or illustrate more happily by a choice allusion. Whatever Mr. Dickens knows or feels, too, is always at his fingers' ends. There is no beating about the bush for it. It is not carefully deposited, ticketed, labelled, elaborately set apart, to be drawn forth only as formal necessity may suggest, from the various cells of his brain. It is present with him through every passage of his book. It animates old facts with a new life, it breathes into old thoughts a new emotion. Who that has read his description of the various localities of London, as set down in this story of *Nicholas Nickleby*, can ever expect to forget them more? A fresh glow of warmth and light plays over the cheerful and familiar places, a deeper mist of misery and blackness settles on the darker scenes. With him, we pass along misty streets in some cold and foggy morning, while but a few meagre shadows flit to and fro or now and then a heavy outline of coach or cab or cart looms through the dull vapour, yet were it only for the noises he strikes from time to time upon our ears, distantly and indistinctly as though the fog had muffled them, we could not doubt that it was LONDON. We enter with him by night, through long double rows of burning lamps, a noisy, bustling, crowded scene, in which he shows us the rags of the squalid ballad-singer fluttering in the same rich light that shows the goldsmith's glittering treasures, and where one thin sheet of brittle glass is the iron wall by which vast profusions of wealth and food are guarded from starved and pennyless men, and this is the same LONDON as before. At all times, and under every aspect, he gives us to feel and see the great city as it absolutely is. Its interior life is made as familiar to us as its exterior forms. We come to know better the very places we have known best. We observe more smoking and hear more singing in Golden square; the Saracen's Head on Snow hill relaxes into a grim cordiality; the Alphonses of Cadogan place reveal themselves plain Bills to our practised eye;[1] and the sight of even a real butterfly, fluttering among the iron heads of dusty area railings in some retired and noiseless City square, startles us no more.

Note

1 Footmen in fashionable families were frequently given new, more exotic names.

4.2 From the 'Letter of Dedication' to Wilkie Collins's *Basil*, 1852, x–xx

Wilkie Collins (1824-89) became famous as the leading sensation novelist of the period with his Woman in White *(1860), which established a literary fashion. (See extracts 1.6, 5.4 and 5.9.) Many of his works are less well regarded than they were in his own day, but deserve serious attention. He was an intimate friend of Dickens, with whom he collaborated on dramatic ventures, and is also remembered for the complexity of his domestic lives. In the* Longman Companion to Victorian Fiction *John Sutherland aptly describes* Basil *as a 'sexually superheated melodrama'. In this extract Collins defends his choice of a shocking subject with a mundane setting on the grounds of its fidelity to actual experience, and the sort of moral utility which E.S. Dallas mocks in 2.4. His assertion that 'Fancy and Imagination, Grace and Beauty . . . can only grow towards Heaven by taking root in earth' is the sort of image frequently used by writers who wish to collapse what they see as a damaging distinction between realism and idealism.*

I founded the main event out of which this story springs, on a fact in real life which had come within my own knowledge: and in afterwards shaping the course of the narrative thus suggested, guided it as often as I could where I knew by my own experiences, and by the experiences incidentally related to me by others, that it would touch on something real and true, in its progress. My idea was, that the more of the Actual I could garner up as a text to speak from, the more certain I might feel of the genuineness and value of the Ideal which was sure to spring out of it. Fancy and Imagination, Grace and Beauty, all those qualities which are to the work of Art what scent and colour are to the flower, can only grow towards Heaven by taking root in earth. After all, is not the noblest poetry of prose fiction the poetry of every-day truth?

Directing my characters and my story, then, towards the light of Reality wherever I could find it, I have not hesitated to violate some of the conventionalities of sentimental fiction. For instance, the first love-meeting of two of the personages in this book, occurs (where the real love-meeting from which it is drawn, occurred) in the very last place and under the very last circumstances which the artifices of sentimental writing would sanction.[1] Will my lovers excite ridicule instead of interest, because I have truly represented them as seeing each other where hundreds of other lovers have first seen each other, as hundreds of people will readily admit when they read the passage to which I refer? I am sanguine enough to think not.

So again, in certain parts of this book where I have attempted to excite the suspense or pity of the reader, I have admitted as perfectly fit accessories to the scene the most ordinary street-sounds that could be heard, and the most ordinary street-events that could occur, at the time and in the place represented – believing that by adding to truth, they were adding to tragedy – adding by all the force of fair contrast – adding as no artifices of mere writing possibly could add, let them be ever so cunningly introduced, by ever so crafty a hand. . . .

Nobody who admits that the business of fiction is to exhibit human life, can deny that scenes of misery and crime must of necessity, while human nature remains what it is, form part of that exhibition – nobody can assert that such scenes are either useless or immoral in their effect on the reader, when they are turned to a plainly and purely moral purpose. If I am asked why I have written certain scenes in this book, my answer is to be found in the universally-accepted truth which the preceding words express. I have a right to appeal to that truth; for I guided myself by it throughout. In deriving the lesson which the following pages contain, from those examples of error and crime which would most strikingly and naturally teach it, I determined to do justice to the honesty of my object by speaking out. In drawing the two characters, whose actions bring about the darker scenes of my story, I did not forget that it was my duty, while striving to pourtray them naturally, to put them to a good moral use; and at some sacrifice, in certain places, of dramatic effect (though I trust with no sacrifice of truth to Nature), I have shown the conduct of the vile, as always, in a greater or less degree, associated with something that is selfish, contemptible, or cruel in motive. . . .

To those persons who dissent from the broad principles here adverted to; who deny that it is the novelist's vocation to do more than merely amuse them; who shrink from all honest and serious reference, in books, to subjects which they think of in private and talk of in public everywhere; who see covert implications where nothing is implied, and improper allusions where nothing improper is alluded to; whose innocence is in the word, and not in the thought; whose morality stops at the tongue, and never gets on to the heart – to those persons, I should consider it loss of time, and worse, to offer any further explanation of my motives, than the sufficient explanation which I have given already. I do not address myself to them in this book, and shall never think of addressing myself to them in any other.

Note

1   The narrator and Margaret first catch sight of each other in an omnibus.

4.3 George Brimley (anon.), 'Thackeray's *Esmond*', *Spectator* 25 (6 November 1852), 1066–7

George Brimley (1819-57) was a fellow of Thackeray's old college, Trinity, Cambridge, and wrote a good number of excellent articles in the Spectator *and* Fraser's Magazine. *Both through his university background and through* Fraser's, *Brimley was a natural supporter of Thackeray, who considered this review to be the best of the many which greeted* Esmond.[1] *In it Brimley shows a close critical sympathy with Thackeray's irony, which was otherwise very troublesome to his contemporaries, who often found it difficult to reconcile the portrayal of 'low' human traits with acceptable moral standards in the author and his work. All in all Brimley's handling of the relation of the 'real' and the 'ideal' in fiction is particularly sensitive. This extract also alerts us to the importance accorded to historical fiction in the period.*

There is abundance of incident in the book, but not much more plot than in one of Defoe's novels: neither is there, generally speaking, a plot in a man's life, though there may be and often is in sections of it.

Unity is given not by a consecutive and self-developing story, but by the ordinary events of life blended with those peculiar to a stirring time acting on a family group, and bringing out and ripening their qualities; these again controlling the subsequent events, just as happens in life. The book has the great charm of reality. The framework is, as we have said, historical: men with well-known names, political, literary, military, pass and repass; their sayings and doings are interwoven with the sayings and doings of the fictitious characters; and all reads like a genuine memoir of the time. The rock ahead of historical novelists is the danger of reproducing too much of their raw material; making the art visible by which they construct their image of a bygone time; painting its manners and the outside of its life with the sense of contrast with which men of the present naturally view them, or looking at its parties and its politics in the light of modern questions: the rock ahead of Mr. Thackeray, in particular, was the temptation merely to dramatize his lectures:[2] but he has triumphed over these difficulties, and Queen Anne's Colonel writes his life, – and a very interesting life it is, – just as such a Queen Anne's Colonel might be supposed to have written it. We shall give no epitome of the story, because the merit of the book does not lie there, and what story there is readers like to find out for themselves.

Mr. Thackeray's humour does not mainly consist in the creation of oddities of manner, habit, or feeling; but in so representing actual men and women as to excite a sense of incongruity in the reader's mind – a feeling that the follies and vices described are deviations from an ideal of humanity always present to the writer. The real is described vividly, with that perception of individuality which constitutes the artist; but the description implies and suggests a standard higher than itself, not by any direct assertion of such a standard, but by an unmistakeable irony. The moral antithesis of actual and ideal is the root from which springs the peculiar charm of Mr. Thackeray's writings; that mixture of gayety [sic] and seriousness, of sarcasm and tenderness, of enjoyment and cynicism, which reflects so well the contradictory consciousness of man as a being with senses and passions and limited knowledge, yet with a conscience and a reason speaking to him of eternal laws and a moral order of the universe. It is this that makes Mr. Thackeray a profound moralist, just as Hogarth showed his knowledge of perspective by drawing a landscape throughout in violation of its rules.[3] So, in Mr. Thackeray's picture of society as it is, society as it ought to be is implied. He could not have painted Vanity Fair as he has, unless Eden had been shining brightly in his inner eyes. The historian of 'snobs' indicates in every touch his fine sense of a gentleman or a lady. No one could be simply amused with Mr. Thackeray's description or his dialogues. A shame at one's own defects, at the defects of the world in which one was living, was irresistibly aroused along with the reception of the particular portraiture. But while he was dealing with his own age, his keen perceptive faculty prevailed, and the actual predominates in his pictures of modern society. His fine appreciation of high character has hitherto been chiefly shown (though with bright exceptions) by his definition of its contrary. But, getting quite out of the region of his personal experience, he has shown his true nature without this mask of satire and irony. The ideal is no longer implied, but realized, in the two leading characters of *Esmond*. The medal is reversed, and what appeared as scorn of baseness is revealed as love of goodness and nobleness – what appeared as cynicism is presented as a heart-worship of what is pure, affectionate, and unselfish.

Notes

1 G.N. Ray, *Thackeray*, 2 vols, London, Oxford University Press, 1955–8, vol. 2, p. 188.
2 *The English Humorists of the Eighteenth Century*, 1851.
3 The picture in question is William Hogarth's, 'False Perspective', 1753.

4.4 George Brimley (anon.), review of Lytton's *My Novel*, *Spectator* 26 (19 February 1853), 179

For Brimley, see headnote to 4.3, and for Lytton see extracts 1.1, 2.3 and 7.4. My Novel, by Pisistratus Caxton; or Varieties of English Life, to give it its full title, was a comic, four-volume study of provincial life. This review clearly shows an ideological aspect to 'truth-to-life' as a fictional principle, dependent on the myth of an 'organic' society for which convincing presentations of moral, religious, middle-class life would have a particular value. On this basis the supreme novel would seem to display the whole of English life as it is construed by those of Brimley's class and education. To a great extent, as extract 1.8 shows, this desire was to be met by George Eliot's Middlemarch, which continued for many decades to be a favourite with liberal ideologues. In view of the fact that the craving for the Great English Novel was eventually satisfied by a woman novelist, it is ironic that Brimley assumes it will require a 'masculine understanding' to effect it.

A deep and inbred contempt for the middle class would be the only interpretation of a picture of English society which ignored or only sarcastically noticed them, were it not to be explained by a defect in this author's genius and sympathies, alike fatal to him as philosophic politician or as philosophic artist.

And this is, that of the English world, which it is his vocation to paint and to influence, he knows and comprehends and cares for only the lightest froth dancing on the surface. We have seen that in his village he could conceive and describe his characters of squire and parson with their families; below this he could not even go by description, and he fails to exhibit them as actors in the real interests of their lives. It is the same when his scene is transferred to London. Dandies and fine ladies – men and women upon whom life forces no serious duties, and who are not great enough to impose them on themselves – dress, talk, flirt, and intrigue upon his stage. . . . It is needless to add, that of the working lives – and that means the serious portion of the lives – of the merchant, the manufacturer, the lawyer, and other 'working classes,' not the faintest representation is conveyed. . . . He cannot paint the busy classes, even in their pleasure and their family life and their passions – not even those who belong to his 'society' – because the serious occupations and interests of men and women affect their pleasures and their passions; and with these and the characters they form he has no adequate acquaintance and sympathy. So, as we said, he paints the froth of society; and very gay froth it is, and very pretty bubbles he can make of it: but this is not reconciling classes, or giving a philosophic representation in fiction of the great organic being we call the English nation; and so far as *My Novel* pretends to be anything more than a well-wrought story, constructed out of the old Bulwer-Lytton materials, the pretence is fabulous and the performance does not answer to it. We have a novel neither better nor worse than its predecessors; but we have not a great work of art reared on a basis so broad as a general survey of English life in the earlier half of the nineteenth century.

Would such a work of art be possible? A mirror that should show to a nation of workers – to a nation whose family hearth is dear and sacred, to a nation that is earnest, practical, grave and religious – its own life, complex and multitudinous, as it might reflect itself upon the imagination of a great poet, who to masculine understanding trained by observation and study should add the large heart and the clear eye to which nothing human is uninteresting or blank?[1] Homer did something of this sort for the Greece of his day; Dante for the Italy of his; Shakespere for the Europe of his. These men knew not such a word as commonplace or low, except as applied to what is stupid and base. The broad field of human life was to them a field of beauty, richly clothed with food and flowers for the sustenance and nourishment of a vigorous imagination. Art can indeed harmonize classes when the artist is such as these, – when, on the one hand, the dignity and worth of the various callings that minister to the convenience and promote the improvement of a nation, are illustrated by viewing them as harmonious parts of a great whole; and on the other, when the men who pursue these callings are represented with the interesting varieties impressed upon the common humanity by circumstances and education, but still as not having that common humanity obliterated and replaced by some ludicrous or mean features, characteristic, it may be, of their occupation, but not characteristic of men to whom an occupation should be a servant and not a master. Till art deals again as it did in its mighty youth with common life – with that which is the business of a busy struggling world – neither will art regain its strength and renew its youth, nor will common life reappear to us with the freshness and the sacredness which it had to the eye of these who first became self-conscious and burst into song.

Note

1   Compare Terence, 'humani nil a me alienum puto' (Latin): 'I reckon nothing human alien to me'.

4.5 Review of *A Lost Love* by 'Ashford Owen' (pseudonym of Anna C. Ogle), *Saturday Review* 1 (3 November 1855), 17–18

A Lost Love *tells the story of Georgina Sandon who, having broken off an engagement to marry a dull man and promised herself to a man she has always really loved, releases the latter from his engagement to her when she discovers that an earlier love of his, after whom he still hankers, is now a widow. Anna C. Ogle's first novel had a considerable success in literary circles. Walter Bagehot and his wife read it to each other on their honeymoon,*[1] *Browning much admired it, and the* Spectator, *the* Athenaeum *and the* Leader *all devoted serious critical attention to it. This anonymous reviewer in the* Saturday Review *praises Ogle's sad ending, and, like others in his time, considers a tragic story – if true to life – as a sign of the high literary status of a work. Interestingly he goes further and equates tragedy with the actual conditions of 'real life'. He is typical of his class in having had a classical education, which is not only a status marker that gives his fellow university graduates a chance to recognise their shared background in his informed comments on tragedy, but is a rationale for male dominance of critical opinion too, as is seen in a remark later in the article: 'Good writing is, perhaps, more especially difficult to a woman, whose imperfect knowledge of etymology, the ancient languages, and philosophy, may obscure to her the finer sense and exact import of words.' The review is notable too for its attention to point of view, and for its balanced statement on the relation of authorial experience to fiction.*

Most people are glad to be told that another good novel has come into the world. And few are ever sorry to hear in addition that the book is short. We can promise our readers that in the brief volume now before us, entitled *A Lost Love*, they will find a striking and original story, a work of genius and sensibility. The characteristic of the book is, that its scenes are drawn, not from the rose-coloured land of fiction, where all wounds are ultimately healed, and all desires, sooner or later, fulfilled; but from that tragic world in which destiny remains stern to the end, and which is only real life felt more deeply. A story is tragic, as distinguished from being merely painful, in proportion as it conveys a feeling that the sad and afflicting events grow, by a sort of necessity, out of the character and circumstances of the different persons; that no one is entirely and arbitrarily injured, but that there is some justice on both sides; and that even where there is wrong and suffering, it could not have been otherwise. This feeling pervades the present tale, and the writer exhibits throughout a sense of sad irony, dealing truly and powerfully with the mockery of human life, and playing off the contrast between the pettiness of the actual moment and the infinity of our imaginations – between the strength of desire and the impossibility of fulfilment. . . .

[I]t requires no great penetration to see that Ashford Owen is a *nom de guerre*, and that the writer is in reality a woman. All producers of fiction, except perhaps the few great masters of the art, naturally identify themselves with some one of their characters. It is obvious in the book before us, that the character of Georgina is written, so to speak, from the inside. Constance is made vivid and lifelike, and is described, it must be said, with some little spitefulness. James Erskine is a shadowy being, of whom it is impossible to form a very distinct conception – the writer has never analysed him in the way that Georgina and Constance are analysed. He looks, as it were, through a nebulous halo, before the heart and imagination of the author, and while we see that he seemed great and loveable to the women of the tale, we do not know what sort of appearance he would have presented to men like ourselves. These little evidences – but far more the deep sense of reality which attaches to the bitter progress of the story – suggest the inference that the writer is in some sort of way Georgina Sandon, and that a true experience has given the basis on which fancy has built this tale. We say that, in some sort of way, the writer is herself the heroine, but beyond this we cannot go. The most impertinent curiosity cannot penetrate, in cases like these, beyond the general sense of reality. You cannot say of this or that fact that it was literally true. Nothing is more fallacious than the attempt to turn into literal biography the fictions of writers. A great passion does not exactly reproduce itself in a work of art. It gives a stimulus to analogical imagination, it imparts a power of creating analogous situations, and writers feel a secret pleasure in a subtle sense of contrast – in describing what is not real, and yet like the reality – in playing themselves against what is not themselves. An instance of the discrepancy between the authoress and her heroine is afforded by the fact that, while the heroine is represented as unlettered, and of deficient education, and as striving after book-knowledge for James Erskine's sake, the authoress is evidently a person of considerable cultivation; and her acquaintance with foreign literature, and especially with the good sayings of French moralists, is a great source of ornament to her pages. This same fact would lead to the inference that the description of Grainthorpe, the dull home of the heroine, with its cheerless and bookless parlour (in itself an admirable piece of painting), is due, not to reality, but to the analogical imagination.

The one-volume novel has its duties as well as its privileges. While it is allowed to be short, it ought to be very perfect. A single passage of life may suffice to fill it; the story may be simple instead of complex. But, on the other hand, we expect to find in it a well-rounded work of art – by its very form it is calculated to invite criticism. The reader, having eagerly followed to the end the progress of the events and the passion, sits at last with the book in his hand, ready now to turn back, and calmly to review the relation of the parts to the whole. He asks whether there is nothing superfluous or deficient; whether the figures are all definite and well grouped, and their introduction justified by a sort of necessity; whether the story not only excites while it is being read, but afterwards leaves on the mind an impression of beauty, completeness and repose; whether, in short, the book is written for permanence, and for a place in the national literature, or for a one year's notoriety in the circulating libraries. Coming with these high requisitions to Ashford Owen – for to make less than the highest requisitions would be but a poor compliment to a writer who displays so much genius – we cannot pretend to say that she entirely satisfies them.

Note

1   See Mrs Russell Barrington, *Life of Walter Bagehot*, 1914, pp. 263–4.

4.6 G.H. Lewes (anon.), 'Realism in Art: Recent German Fiction', *Westminster Review* 70 (October 1858), 493–6

This part of Lewes's article appears under the running header 'Realism and idealism', which represents one of the earliest uses in English of the word 'realism' as a term of literary criticism. George Henry Lewes (1817–78), was a critic, essayist, novelist and dramatist, and a leading populariser of science and philosophy. He was one of the most important promoters and theorists of literary realism in Britain, and at different times in the 1860s he edited the Cornhill Magazine *and the* Fortnightly Review. *In 1852 he had met the great intellectual Mary Ann Evans, and was instrumental in persuading her to write and publish fiction under the name of 'George Eliot'. As is shown by extract 4.8, he championed Jane Austen's fiction when it was little respected, and his insistence that George Eliot read Austen as well as her beloved Scott is often credited with the increased attention she paid to the nuances of social life in novels such as* Felix Holt, Middlemarch *and* Daniel Deronda. *Lewes and Evans lived together from 1854 to the end of his life.*

. . . [German] libraries swarm with works having but the faintest possible relation to any form of human life, and the strongest infusion of what is considered the 'ideal element.' The hero is never a merchant, a lawyer, an artisan – *Gott bewahre!* [1] He must have a pale face and a thoughtful brow; he must be either a genius or a Herr Baron. The favourite hero is a poet, or an artist, often a young nobleman who has the artistic nature; but always a man of genius; because prose can be found at every street-corner, and art must elevate the public by 'beautifying' life.

This notion of the function of Art is widely spread. It has its advocates in all countries, for it is the natural refuge of incompetence, to which men fly, impelled by the secret sense of their inability to portray Reality so as to make it interesting. A distinction is drawn between Art and Reality, and an antithesis established between Realism and Idealism which would never have gained acceptance had not men in general lost sight of the fact that Art is a Representation of Reality – a Representation which, inasmuch as it is not the thing itself, but only represents it, must necessarily be limited by the nature of its medium; the canvas of the painter, the marble of the sculptor, the chords of the musician, and the language of the writer, each bring with them peculiar laws; but while thus limited, while thus regulated by the necessities imposed on it by each medium of expression, Art always aims at the representation of Reality, *i.e.* of Truth; and no departure from truth is permissible, except such as inevitably lies in the nature of the medium itself. Realism is thus the basis of all Art, and its antithesis is not Idealism, but *Falsism*. When our painters represent peasants with regular features and irreproachable linen; when their milkmaids have the air of Keepsake beauties, whose costume is picturesque, and never old or dirty; when Hodge is made to speak refined sentiments in unexceptionable English, and children utter long speeches of religious and poetic enthusiasm; when the conversation of the parlour and drawing-room is a succession of philosophical remarks, expressed with great clearness and logic, an attempt is made to idealize, but the result is simple falsification and bad art. To misrepresent the forms of ordinary life is no less an offence than to misrepresent the forms of ideal life: a pug-nosed Apollo, or Jupiter in a great-coat, would not be more truly shocking to an artistic mind than are those senseless falsifications of nature into which incompetence is led under the pretence of 'beautifying' nature. Either give us true peasants, or leave them untouched; either paint no drapery at all, or paint it with the utmost fidelity; either keep your people silent, or make them speak the idiom of their class.

Raphael's marvellous picture, the 'Madonna di San Sisto,' presents us with a perfect epitome of illustration. In the figures of the Pope and St. Barbara we have a real man and woman, one of them a portrait, and the other not elevated above sweet womanhood. Below, we have the two exquisite angel children, intensely childlike, yet something *more*, something which renders their wings congruous with our conception of them. In the never-to-be-forgotten divine babe, we have at once the intensest realism of presentation, with the highest idealism of conception: the attitude is at once grand, easy, and natural; the face is that of a child, but the child is divine: in those eyes, and on that brow, there is an indefinable something² which, greater than the expression of the angels' [sic], grander than that of pope or saint, is, to all who see it, a perfect *truth*; we feel that humanity in its highest conceivable form is before us, and that to transcend such a form would be to lose sight of the *human* nature there represented. In the virgin mother, again, we have a real woman, such as the *campagna* of Rome will furnish every day, yet with eyes subdued to a consciousness of her divine mission. Here is a picture which from the first has enchained the hearts of men, which is assuredly in the highest sense real – a real man, a real woman, real angel-children, and a real Divine Child; the last a striking contrast to the ineffectual attempts of other painters to spiritualize and idealize the babe – attempts which represent no babe at all. . . .

We may now come to an understanding on the significance of the phrase Idealism in Art. Suppose two men equally gifted with the perceptive powers and technical skill necessary to the accurate representation of a village group, but the one to be gifted, over and above these qualities, with an emotional sensibility which leads him to sympathize intensely with the emotions playing amid that village group. Both will delight in the forms of external nature, both will lovingly depict the scene and scenery; but the second will not be satisfied therewith: his sympathy will lead him to express something of the emotional life of the group; the mother in his picture will not only hold her child in a graceful attitude, she will look at it with a mother's tenderness; the lovers will be tender; the old people venerable. Without once departing from strict reality, he will have thrown a sentiment into his group which every spectator will recognise as poetry. Is he not more *real* than a Teniers, who, admirable in externals, had little or no sympathy with the internal life, which, however, is as real as the other? But observe, the sentiment must be real, truly expressed as a sentiment, and as the sentiment of the very people represented; the tenderness of *Hodge* must not be that of *Romeo*. . . .

In like manner the novelist . . . expresses his mind in his novels, and according as his emotional sympathy is keen and active, according to his poetic disposition, will the choice and treatment of his subject be poetical: but it must always be real – true. If he select the incidents and characters of ordinary life, he must be rigidly bound down to accuracy in the presentation. He is at liberty to avoid such subjects, if he thinks them prosaic and uninteresting (which will mean that he does not feel their poetry and interest), but having chosen, he is not at liberty to falsify, under pretence of beautifying them; every departure from truth in motive, idiom, or probability, is, to that extent, a defect.

Notes

1 Gott bewahre (German): God preserve!
2 Lewes's footnote: This is only true of the original. No copy or engraving that we have ever seen has even a tolerable accuracy in these finer, subtler beauties.

4.7 George Eliot, 'In which the Story Pauses a Little', *Adam Bede*, first edn, 1859, vol. 1, pp. 259–65

'George Eliot' was the pen-name of Marian Evans (1819–80), who began to publish fiction only after producing a significant number of articles on a variety of serious topics in the Westminster Review, *for which she was for some years Editorial Assistant. Perhaps her greatest contribution to the intellectual life of the age in this earlier stage of her life consisted of two important translations from the German: David Strauss's* Life of Jesus *(1846), which treated Jesus as an historical figure, and Feuerbach's* The Essence of Christianity *(1854), which sought to replace the idea of Christianity as revealed religion with the notion of the human construction of the divine. She also translated Spinoza's* Ethics, *which profoundly influenced her subsequent fiction. It was George Henry Lewes (see 4.6. and 4.8) who persuaded her to enter on her second career as a writer of prose fiction, with* Scenes of Clerical Life *(1858), and his aesthetic and critical ideas were crucially important in her earlier novels.* Adam Bede, *which was published in three volumes in 1859, was her first novel.*

'This Rector of Broxton is little better than a pagan!' I hear one of my lady readers exclaim. 'How much more edifying it would have been if you had made him give Arthur some truly spiritual advice. You might have put into his mouth the most beautiful things – quite as good as reading a sermon.'

Certainly I could, my fair critic, if I were a clever novelist, not obliged to creep servilely after nature and fact, but able to represent things as they never have been and never will be. Then, of course, my characters would be entirely of my own choosing, and I could select the most unexceptionable type of clergyman, and put my own admirable opinions into his mouth on all occasions. But you must have perceived long ago that I have no such lofty vocation, and that I aspire to give no more than a faithful account of men and things as they have mirrored themselves in my mind. The mirror is doubtless defective; the outlines will sometimes be disturbed, the reflection faint or confused; but I feel as much bound to tell you as precisely as I can what that reflection is, as if I were in the witness-box narrating my experience on oath.

Sixty years ago – it is a long time, so no wonder things have changed – all clergymen were not zealous; indeed there is reason to believe that the number of zealous clergymen was small, and it is probable that if one among the small minority had owned the livings of Broxton and Hayslope in the year 1799, you would have liked him no better than you like Mr Irwine. Ten to one, you would have thought him a tasteless, indiscreet, methodistical man. It is so very rarely that facts hit that nice medium required by our own enlightened opinions and refined taste! Perhaps you will say, 'Do improve the facts a little, then; make them more accordant with those correct views which it is our privilege to possess. The world is not just what we like; do touch it up with a tasteful pencil, and make believe it is not quite such a mixed entangled affair. Let all people who hold unexceptionable opinions act unexceptionably. Let your most faulty characters always be on the wrong side, and your virtuous ones on the right. Then we shall see at a glance whom we are to condemn, and whom we are to approve. Then we shall be able to admire, without the slightest disturbance of our prepossessions: we shall hate and despise with that true ruminant relish which belongs to undoubting confidence.'

But, my good friend, what will you do then with your fellow-parishioner who opposes your husband in the vestry? – with your newly-appointed vicar, whose style of preaching you find painfully below that of his regretted predecessor? – with the honest servant who worries your soul with her one failing? – with your neighbour, Mrs Green, who was really kind to you in your last illness, but has said several ill-natured things about you since your convalescence? – nay, with your excellent husband himself, who has other irritating habits besides that of not wiping his shoes? These fellow-mortals, every one, must be accepted as they are: you can neither straighten their noses, nor brighten their wit, nor rectify their dispositions; and it is these people – amongst whom your life is passed – that it is needful you should tolerate, pity, and love: it is these more or less ugly, stupid, inconsistent people, whose movements of goodness you should be able to admire – for whom you should cherish all possible hopes, all possible patience. And I would not, even if I had the choice, be the clever novelist who could create a world so much better than this, in which we get up in the morning to do our daily work, that you would be likely to turn a harder, colder eye on the dusty streets and the common green fields – on the real breathing men and women, who can be chilled by your indifference or injured by your prejudice; who can be cheered and helped onward by your fellow-feeling, your forbearance, your outspoken, brave justice.

So I am content to tell my simple story, without trying to make things seem better than they were; dreading nothing, indeed, but falsity, which, in spite of one's best efforts, there is reason to dread. Falsehood is so easy, truth so difficult. The pencil is conscious of a delightful facility in drawing a griffin – the longer the claws, and the larger the wings, the better; but that marvellous facility which we mistook for genius is apt to forsake us when we want to draw a real unexaggerated lion. Examine your words well, and you will find that even when you have no motive to be false, it is a very hard thing to say the exact truth, even about your own immediate feelings – much harder than to say something fine about them which is *not* the exact truth.

It is for this rare, precious quality of truthfulness that I delight in many Dutch paintings, which lofty-minded people despise. I find a source of delicious sympathy in these faithful pictures of monotonous homely existence, which has been the fate of so many more among my fellow-mortals than a life of pomp or of absolute indigence, of tragic suffering or of world-stirring actions. I turn without shrinking, from cloud-borne angels, from prophets, sibyls, and heroic warriors, to an old woman bending over her flower-pot, or eating her solitary dinner, while the noonday light, softened perhaps by a screen of leaves, falls on her mob-cap, and just touches the rim of her spinning-wheel, and her stone jug, and all those cheap common things which are the precious necessaries of life to her; – or I turn to that village wedding, kept between four brown walls, where an awkward bride-groom opens the dance with a high-shouldered, broad-faced bride, while elderly and middle-aged friends look on, with very irregular noses and lips, and probably with quart-pots in their hands, but with an expression of unmistakable contentment and goodwill. 'Foh!' says my idealistic friend, 'what vulgar details! What good is there in taking all these pains to give an exact likeness of old women and clowns? What a low phase of life! – what clumsy, ugly people!'

But, bless us, things may be lovable that are not altogether handsome, I hope? I am not at all sure that the majority of the human race have not been ugly, and even among those 'lords of their kind,' the British, squat figures, ill-shaped nostrils, and dingy complexions are not startling exceptions. Yet there is a great deal of family love amongst us. I have a friend or two whose class of features is such that the Apollo curl on the summit of their brows would be decidedly trying; yet to my certain knowledge tender hearts have beaten for them, and their miniatures – flattering, but still not lovely – are kissed in secret by motherly lips. I have seen many an excellent matron, who could never in her best days have been handsome, and yet she had a packet of yellow love-letters in a private drawer, and sweet children showered kisses on her sallow cheeks. And I believe there have been plenty of young heroes, of middle stature and feeble beards, who have felt quite sure they could never love anything more insignificant than a Diana, and yet have found themselves in middle life happily settled with a wife who waddles. Yes! thank God; human feeling is like the mighty rivers that bless the earth: it does not wait for beauty – it flows with resistless force and brings beauty with it.

All honour and reverence to the divine beauty of form! Let us cultivate it to the utmost in men, women, and children – in our gardens and in our houses. But let us love that other beauty too, which lies in no secret of proportion, but in the secret of deep human sympathy. Paint us an angel, if you can, with a floating violet robe, and a face paled by the celestial light; paint us yet oftener a Madonna, turning her mild face upward and opening her arms to welcome the divine glory; but do not impose on us any æsthetic rules which shall banish from the region of Art those old women scraping carrots with their work-worn hands, those heavy clowns taking holiday in a dingy pot-house, those rounded backs and stupid weather-beaten faces that have bent over the spade and done the rough work of the world – those homes with their tin pans, their brown pitchers, their rough curs, and their clusters of onions. In this world there are so many of these common, coarse people, who have no picturesque sentimental wretchedness! It is so needful we should remember their existence, else we may happen to leave them quite out of our religion and philosophy, and frame lofty theories which only fit a world of extremes. Therefore let Art always remind us of them; therefore let us always have men ready to give the loving pains of a life to the faithful representing of commonplace things – men who see beauty in these commonplace things, and delight in showing how kindly the light of heaven falls on them. There are few prophets in the world; few sublimely beautiful women; few heroes. I can't afford to give all my love and reverence to such rarities: I want a great deal of those feelings for my everyday fellow-men, especially for the few in the foreground of the great multitude, whose faces I know, whose hands I touch, for whom I have to make way with kindly courtesy. Neither are picturesque lazzaroni or romantic criminals half so frequent as your common labourer, who gets his own bread, and eats it vulgarly but creditably with his own pocket-knife. It is more needful that I should have a fibre of sympathy connecting me with that vulgar citizen who weighs out my sugar in a vilely assorted cravat and waistcoat, than with the handsomest rascal in red scarf and green feathers; – more needful that my heart should swell with loving admiration at some trait of gentle goodness in the faulty people who sit at the same hearth with me, or in the clergyman of my own parish, who is perhaps rather too corpulent, and in other respects is not an Oberlin or a Tillotson,[1] than at the deeds of heroes whom I shall never know except by hearsay, or at the sublimest abstract of all clerical graces that was ever conceived by an able novelist.

Note

1   Johann Friedrich Oberlin, 1740–1826, whose work on the material and moral transformation of some of the poorest parishes in the Vosges in north-eastern France won him a reputation as 'a saint of the protestant church'; John Tillotson (1630–94), Chaplain to Charles II, and later Archbishop of Canterbury, and a noted preacher against Puritanism, Roman Catholicism and atheism.

4.8 George Henry Lewes (anon.), 'The Novels of Jane Austen', *Blackwood's Magazine* 86 (July 1859), 101–7

See the headnote to extract 4.6. For Lewes, Austen exemplifies what can be achieved even in a modest compass by an author cultivating 'the highest department of the novelist's art – namely, the truthful representation of character'. Austen's narrow range of subject, emotion and event, however, prevents him from ranking her with the greatest writers of all: 'There is far greater strain on the intellectual effort to create a Brutus or an Othello, than to create a Vicar of Wakefield or a Squire Western. The higher the aims, the greater is the strain, and the nobler is success.'

If, as probably few will dispute, the art of the novelist be the representation of human life by means of a story; and if the *truest* representation, effected by the *least expenditure* of means, constitutes the highest claim of art, then we say that Miss Austen has carried the art to a point of excellence surpassing that reached by any of her rivals. Observe we say 'the art;' we do not say that she equals many of them in the *interest* excited by the art; that is a separate question. It is probable, nay certain, that the interest excited by the *Antigone* is very inferior to that excited by *Black-eyed Susan*.[1] It is probable that *Uncle Tom* and *Dred* surpassed in interest the *Antiquary* or *Ivanhoe*. It is probable that *Jane Eyre* produced a far greater excitement than the *Vicar of Wakefield*.[2] But the critic justly disregards these fervid elements of immediate success, and fixes his attention mainly on the art which is of eternal substance. Miss Austen has nothing fervid in her works. She is not capable of producing a profound agitation in the mind. In many respects this is a limitation of her powers, a deduction from her claims. But while other writers have had more power over the emotions, more vivid imaginations, deeper sensibilities, deeper insight, and more of what is properly called invention, no novelist has approached her in what we may style the 'economy of art,' by which is meant the easy adaptation of means to ends, with no aid from extraneous or superfluous elements. Indeed, paradoxical as the juxtaposition of the names may perhaps appear to those who have not reflected much on this subject, we venture to say that the only names we can place above Miss Austen, in respect of this economy of art, are Sophocles and Molière (in *Le Misanthrope*). And if any one will examine the terms of the definition, he will perceive that almost all defects in works of art arise from the neglect of this economy. When the *end* is the representation of human nature in its familiar aspects, moving amid every-day scenes, the *means* must likewise be furnished from every-day life: romance and improbabilities must be banished as rigorously as the grotesque exaggeration of peculiar characteristics, or the representation of abstract types. It is easy for the artist to choose a subject from every-day life, but it is *not* easy for him so to represent the characters and their actions that they shall be at once lifelike and interesting; accordingly, whenever ordinary people are introduced, they are either made to speak a language never spoken out of books, and to pursue conduct never observed in life; or else they are intolerably wearisome. . . .

But the real secret of Miss Austen's success lies in her having the exquisite and rare gift of dramatic creation of character. Scott says of her, 'She had a talent for describing the involvements, and feelings, and characters of ordinary life, which is to me the most wonderful I ever met with. The big bow-wow strain I can do myself like any now going; but the exquisite touch, which renders ordinary commonplace things and characters interesting, from the truth of the description and the sentiment, is denied me. What a pity such a gifted creature died so early!'[3] Generously said; but high as the praise is, it is as much below the real excellence of Miss Austen, as the 'big bow-wow strain' is below the incomparable power of the Waverley Novels. Scott felt, but did not define, the excellence of Miss Austen. The very word 'describing' is altogether misplaced and misleading. She seldom describes anything, and is not felicitous when she attempts it. But instead of *description*, the common and easy resource of novelists, she has the rare and difficult art of *dramatic presentation*: instead of telling us what her characters are, and what they feel, she presents the people, and they reveal themselves. In this she has never perhaps been surpassed, not even by Shakespeare himself. If very living beings can be said to have moved across the page of fiction, as they lived, speaking as they spoke, and feeling as they felt, they do so in *Pride and Prejudice*, *Emma*, and *Mansfield Park*. What incomparable noodles she exhibits for our astonishment and laughter! What silly, good-natured women! What softly-selfish men! What lively, amiable, honest men and women, whom one would rejoice to have known! . . .

The absence of breadth, picturesqueness, and passion, will also limit the appreciating audience of Miss Austen to the small circle of cultivated minds; and even these minds are not always capable of greatly relishing her works. We have known very remarkable people who cared little for her pictures of every-day life;[4] and indeed it may be anticipated that those who have little sense of humour, or whose passionate and insurgent activities demand in art a reflection of their own emotions and struggles, will find little pleasure in such homely comedies. Currer Bell may be taken as a type of these. She was utterly without a sense of humour, and was by nature fervid and impetuous. In a letter published in her memoirs she writes, – 'Why do you like Miss Austen so very much? I am puzzled on that point. . . . I had not read *Pride and Prejudice* till I read that sentence of yours, and then I got the book. And what did I find? An accurate daguerreotyped portrait of a commonplace face; a carefully-fenced, highly-cultivated garden, with neat borders and delicate flowers; but no glance of a bright, vivid physiognomy, no open country, no fresh air, no blue hill, no bonny beck. I should hardly like to live with her elegant ladies and gentlemen, in their elegant but confined houses.'[5] The critical reader will not fail to remark the almost contemptuous indifference to the art of truthful portrait-painting which this passage indicates; and he will understand, perhaps, how the writer of such a passage was herself incapable of drawing more than characteristics, even in her most successful efforts. Jane Eyre, Rochester, and Paul Emmanuel, are very vigorous sketches, but the reader observes them from the *outside*, he does not know them. What is said respecting the want of open country, blue hill, and bonny beck, is perfectly true; but the same point has been more felicitously touched by Scott, in his review of *Emma*: 'Upon the whole,' he says, 'the turn of this author's novels bears the same relation to that of the sentimental and romantic cast, that cornfields and cottages and meadows bear to the highly-adorned grounds of a show mansion, or the rugged sublimities of a mountain landscape. It is neither so captivating as the one, nor so grand as the other; but it affords those who frequent it a pleasure nearly allied with the experience of their own social habits.'[6] Scott would also have loudly repudiated the notion of Miss Austen's characters being 'mere daguerreotypes.' Having himself drawn both ideal and real characters, he knew the difficulties of both; and he well says, 'He who paints from *le beau idéal*, if his scenes and sentiments are striking and interesting, is in a great measure exempted from the difficult task of reconciling them with the ordinary probabilities of life; but he who paints a scene of common occurrence, places his composition within that extensive range of criticism which general experience offers to every reader. . . .'

Notes

1 *Black-eyed Susan* (1866) was a burlesque by F.C. Burnand, contributor to and later editor of *Punch*.
2 The distinction Lewes draws between Sophocles and Burnand, and between Harriet Beecher Stowe and Walter Scott remains acceptable, but time has overturned his assumption that *The Vicar of Wakefield* surpasses *Jane Eyre* in 'art'.
3 Quoted from Scott's journal of 14 March 1826, in John Gibson Lockhart, *Life of Scott*, 1838, vol. 8, p. 292.
4 One example in Lewes's mind must have been George Eliot, with whom he was living, and who could not appreciate Austen until he converted her.
5 E.C. Gaskell, *The Life of Charlotte Brontë*, 1857, vol. 2, p. 54. 'Currer Bell' was Brontë's pen-name.
6 This article, which is no longer attributed to Scott, appeared in the *Quarterly Review* in 1815.

4.9 David Masson, *British Novelists and Their Styles: being a critical sketch of the history of British prose fiction*, Cambridge, 1859, pp. 248–51

For David Masson, see headnote to extract 1.4. A consideration of his position in relation to those already seen in this chapter will show the danger of treating mid-Victorian criticism too schematically. Masson's views on Thackeray are interestingly at variance with Brimley's (4.3), while his terms 'Real' and 'Ideal' do not map exactly on to Lewes's 'realism' and 'idealism'.

All [the] differences . . . between Dickens and Thackeray . . . resolve themselves into the one fundamental difference, that they are artists of opposite schools. Thackeray is a novelist of what is called the Real school; Dickens is a novelist of the Ideal or Romantic school. (The terms Real and Ideal have been so run upon of late, that their repetition begins to nauseate; but they must be kept, for all that, till better equivalents are provided.) It is Thackeray's aim to represent life as it is actually and historically – men and women, as they are, in those situations in which they are usually placed, with that mixture of good and evil and of strength and foible which is to be found in their characters, and liable only to those incidents which are of ordinary occurrence. He will have no faultless characters, no demigods – nothing but men and brethren. And from this it results that, when he has conceived a character, he works downwards and inwards in his treatment of it, making it firm and clear at all points in its relations to hard fact, and cutting down, where necessary, to the very foundations. Dickens, on the other hand, with all his keenness of observation, is more light and poetic in his method. Having once caught a hint from actual fact, he generalizes it, runs away with this generalization into a corner, and develops it there into a character to match; which character he then transports, along with others similarly suggested, into a world of semi-fantastic conditions, where the laws need not be those of ordinary probability. He has characters of ideal perfection and beauty, as well as of ideal ugliness and brutality – characters of a human kind verging on the supernatural, as well as characters actually belonging to the supernatural. Even his situations and scenery often lie in a region beyond the margin of everyday life. Now both kinds of art are legitimate; and each writer is to be tried within his own kind by the success he has attained in it. Mr. Thackeray, I believe, is as perfect a master in his kind of art as is to be found in the whole series of British prose writers; a man in whom strength of understanding, acquired knowledge of men, subtlety of perception, deep philosophic humour, and exquisiteness of literary taste, are combined in a degree and after a manner not seen in any known precedent. But the kinds of art are different; and I believe some injustice has been done to Mr. Dickens of late, by forgetting this when comparing him with his rival. It is as if we were to insist that all painters should be of the school of Hogarth. The Ideal or Romantic artist must be true to nature as well as the Real artist, but he may be true in a different fashion. He may take hints from Nature in her extremest moods, and make these hints the germs of creations fitted for a world projected imaginatively beyond the real one, or inserted into the midst of the real one, and yet imaginatively moated round from it. Homer, Shakespeare, and Cervantes, are said to be true to nature; and yet there is not one of their most pronounced characters exactly such as ever was to be found, or ever will be found in nature – not one of them which is not the result of some suggestion snatched from nature, in one or other of her uttermost moments, and then carried away and developed in the void. The question with the Real artist, with respect to what he conceives, is, 'How would this actually be in nature; in what exact setting of surrounding particulars would it appear?' and, with a view to satisfy himself on this question, he dissects, observes, and recollects all that is in historical relation to his conception. The question with the Ideal artist is, 'What can be made out of this; with what human conclusions, ends, and aspirations can it be imaginatively interwoven, so that the whole, though attached to nature by its origin, shall transcend or overlie nature on the side of the possibly existent – the might, could, or should be, or the might, could, or should have been?' All honour to Thackeray and the prose-fiction of social reality; but much honour, too, to Dickens, for maintaining among us, even in the realm of the light and the amusing, some representation in prose of that art of ideal phantasy, the total absence of which in the literature of any age would be a sign nothing short of hideous.

4.10 Richard Holt Hutton (anon.), 'The Genius of Dickens', *Spectator* 43 (18 June 1870), 749–51

This extract from an article summing up Dickens's achievement a few days after his death, is one of the best Victorian attempts to analyse the novelist's humour, and is worthy company for the previous extract (4.9). Hutton is also represented by extracts 3.3 and 6.4.

The great and unfailing wonder is how any novel-writer who gives so absolutely identical a tone to all the characters he conceives, manages to make them so full to overflowing of fresh vitality and infinite humour. No one ever gets tired of Dick Swiveller or Bailey Junior, or Pecksniff, or Mrs. Gamp, or old Mr. Weller, or Fanny Squeers, or Mr. Lillyvick, or Sawyer late Knockemorf, or Barnaby Rudge and his raven, or Simon Tappertit, or even Jenny Wren. And it is marvellous that it should be so, for all these are always precisely consistent with the first glimpse we get of them; and with any genius less rich in variations on the same air than Dickens's we should be sick of them in no time.

But then no writer ever had the power which Dickens had of developing the same fundamental conception in so infinitely humorous a variety of form. Hunt through all Mrs. Gamp's monthly-nurse disquisition, and you will never find there a repetition, – excepting always in those great landmarks of the conception, the vast selfishness and self-admiration, the permanent desire to have the bottle left on 'the chimley piece', for use 'when so dispoged,' and the mutual confidence between her and her mythical friend Mrs. Harris. With these necessary exceptions there is not one single repetition of a speech or a maxim. The central cell, as we may call it, of the character has multiplied itself a thousandfold without a single echo of an old idea. The marvel of Dickens is the exquisite ease, perfect physical consistency, and yet wonderful variety of paths by which he always makes his characters glide back into their leading trait. His greater characters are perfect labyrinths of novel autobiographical experience, all leading back to the same central cell. Mrs. Gamp, for instance, is barely introduced before she introduces also to the reader her great and original contrivance for praising herself and intimating decently to all the world the various stipulations on which alone she agrees to 'sick or monthly,' – that intimate friend whose sayings cannot be verified by direct reference to herself, because she is in reality only the reflex form of No. I, – Mrs. Harris. 'Mrs. Gamp,' says this imaginary lady, as reported by Mrs. Gamp herself, 'if ever there was sober creetur to be got at eighteen-pence a day for working people and three-and-six for gentlefolks – nightwatching,' said Mrs. Gamp, with emphasis, 'being a extra charge, – you are that inwalable person.' 'Mrs. Harris,' I says to her, 'don't name the charge, *for if I could afford to lay all my feller creeturs out for nothink*, I would gladly do it, sech is the love I bears 'em.'[1] But this, we need hardly say, is a great humourist's creation *on a hint* from human life, and not human life itself. . . . The infinite number of avenues by which Mr. Dickens makes Mrs. Gamp, as Hegel would say, *return into herself*,[2] and the absolutely inexhaustible number of physical illustrations all of the monthly-nurse kind by which she effects it, are key-notes to his genius. . . . His power is like that of a moral kaleidoscope, all the various fragments of colour being supplied by actual experience, so that when you turn and turn it and get ever new combinations, you never seem to get away from actual life, but always to be concerned with the most common-place of common-place realities. All the while, however, you are really running the changes on a single conception, but with so vast a power of illustration from the minutest experience, that you are deceived into thinking that you are dealing with a real being. Of course, no man ever really pretended to be so scrupulously candid as Mr. Pecksniff when he complained, 'I have been struck this day with a walking-stick, *which I have every reason to believe* has knobs on it, on that delicate and exquisite portion of the human anatomy, the brain;'[3] nor was there ever any one so persistently desirous of finding disagreeable circumstances under which it would be a credit to be jolly, as Mark Tapley. This is the idealism of the author, idealism only disguised by the infinite resource of common physical detail with which he illustrates it. How little of a realist Dickens actually was in his creations of character, may be seen whenever he attempts to deal with an ordinary man or woman, like Nicholas or Kate Nickleby, or again David Copperfield, who is to us quite as little real as Nicholas Nickleby, even though intended, as has always been said, for the author himself. Mortimer Lightwood and Eugene Wrayburn, in *Our Mutual Friend*, are deplorable failures, and the worthy minor Canon in *The Mystery of Edwin Drood* promised to be so too. The infinite multiplication of detailed illustrations of a single humorous type has always been Mr. Dickens's real secret power. A realist as regards *human* nature, he never was at all.

Notes

1 *Martin Chuzzlewit*, chapter 19.
2 *return into herself*: a reference to the final movement of the Hegelian dialectic, whereby the spirit exists first as undifferentiated universal, then sunders itself into particulars, and then returns by becoming self-conscious (the individual). Thus the 'illustrations of the monthly-nurse kind' constitute the particularisation stage – a self-alienation from which the individual is a profound return.
3 *Martin Chuzzlewit*, chapter 52.

4.11 Anthony Trollope on the language of fiction, *An Autobiography*, written 1875–6, 3 vols, 1883, vol. 2, pp. 59–60

See headnote to extract 2.6. This passage shows how much more accurately the great novelists thought about spoken language than did the critics, who constantly accused writers of bad writing when the speech of their characters failed to obey the 'rules' of grammar and construction learnt at school.

The writer may tell much of his story in conversations, but he may only do so by putting such words into the mouths of his personages as persons so situated would probably use. He is not allowed for the sake of his tale to make his characters give utterance to long speeches, such as are not customarily heard from men and women. The ordinary talk of ordinary people is carried on in short sharp expressive sentences, which very frequently are never completed, – the language of which even among educated people is often incorrect. The novel-writer in constructing his dialogue must so steer between absolute accuracy of language – which would give to his conversation an air of pedantry, and the slovenly inaccuracy of ordinary talkers, which if closely followed would offend by an appearance of grimace – as to produce upon the ear of his readers a sense of reality. If he be quite real he will seem to attempt to be funny. If he be quite correct he will seem to be unreal. And above all, let the speeches be short. No character should utter much above a dozen words at a breath, – unless the writer can justify to himself a longer flood of speech by the speciality of the occasion.

5

Plot and character: realism and sensationalism

'Among English novels of the present day, and among English novelists, a great division is made. There are sensational novels and anti-sensational, sensational novelists and anti-sensational; sensational readers and anti-sensational' (5.8). So wrote Anthony Trollope in 1875–6, commenting on fifteen years which had seen novels – such as his own – based on the ordinary events of everyday, modern life, achieve unprecedented popularity as serials in periodicals like the *Cornhill Magazine*, and had witnessed too a simultaneous explosion of fiction about the sensational aspects of modern life – crime and detection, bigamy, blackmail, drug-addiction and so on. The exploitation of this latter sort of subject-matter was deemed to encourage literary artifice in the contrivance of suspense, surprise and the concealment of information from the reader. Reviewing *Scenes of Clerical Life*, Samuel Lucas describes what later came to be called 'realistic' fiction in the following terms:

> The charm . . . is sustained by an adherence to probability and by the allowance for influences which the incidents alone do not involve, but which we know to make up a large proportion of every man's life. The artificial elements of the story are thus kept within bounds, the tendency to sacrifice to their exigencies is compensated by a reference to the actual results of experience, and a closer resemblance than usual is thus established between the conception of fiction and the realities of the world.[1]

Charles Reade's *White Lies*, on the other hand, Lucas continues,

> resembles closely the plot of a modern French drama in its method and elements. The sacrifice of probabilities to neatness of construction is here pushed to its very furthest limits, so much so that the difference between novels and life which to some extent tells against every work of fiction here widens to a gulf which imagination can barely traverse. It is impossible to

conceive of such things as likely to happen, wherefore, as the purpose of the artist is not to burlesque, his workmanship must be held to be artistically faulty.

The extracts printed here present a variety of views on these fictional trends, and the general opposition between ideas of characterisation and plot-construction. For the mid-Victorian critic, characterisation is usually the basis of convincing imitation of the world, and in 5.1, Hamley castigates Dickens for lack of psychological 'truth-to-life':

> The personages of his stories, having once had particular qualities ascribed to them, are for ever exhibiting these attributes in a way which, were it ever done in real life, would render a knowledge of our species of very easy attainment, since everybody not absolutely idiotic would read everybody else's character . . .

Others, such as an anonymous reviewer of *The Chimes* (2.2) had noticed the possibility that this kind of character might be representative of more than the solitary individual, and be, in fact, 'the type of a class, and the voice and practical exponent of some social error'. More often, successful characterisation is seen in terms of the supposedly immutable facts of 'human nature', and for Bulwer Lytton, the fictional characters deserving the highest praise 'are founded in the preference of generals to particulars; that is, they are enduring types of great subdivisions in the human family, wholly irrespective of mutations in scene and manners'.[2] For Hamley, the development of the characters in the course of a work is the key, and 'in the very highest specimens the principal personages are scarcely fully developed before the end of the book' (5.1). There was a growing recognition – in 1.8 for example – of the 'inner life' of characters as fictional subject-matter, and the mind as the site of fictional action, and George Eliot was readily pressed into service by literary historians of a teleological bent to prepare the way for Henry James. Character, however, remained the fundamental critical term in the period. An author like Meredith, not noted for threatening character by excess of plot, was analysed in terms of a conflict between character and intellectual wit (5.5).

What some of the most perceptive critics did realise was how impossible it was to explain 'truth-to-life' in terms of individual characterisation, and, like Roscoe in 6.1, looked for interpersonal factors too:

> The social human heart, man in relation to his kind – that is his

subject. His actors are distinct and individual, – truthfully, vigorously, felicitously drawn; masterpieces in their way; but the personal character of each is not the supreme object of interest with the author. It is only a contribution to a larger and more abstract subject of contemplation. Man is his study; but man the social animal, man considered with reference to the experiences, the aims, the affections, that find their field in his intercourse with his fellow-men: never man the individual soul.

The presentation of fictional people could be seen as essentially interpersonal. For at least one critic in the *Spectator*, who might have been R.H. Hutton, the social development of a character is carried out through the multiple perspectives of the other characters' consciousnesses, or, in the *Spectator*'s words, 'the construction of the little circumstances, the variations of the angles of the little mental and moral reflectors in which we catch a new glimpse of his characters' nature and essence'. In the case of one character in *Orley Farm* (1861–2), for example, '[t]here is certainly much art in the added vividness which her own sense of guilt takes the moment the pressure of constant concealment is removed, and she sees it reflected back from the minds of friends whom she reveres'. In the realm of social behaviour, the *Spectator* regarded Trollope as a great 'social microscopist' in his 'diagnosis of the true significance of various little *nuances* of social manners, and the influence which he assigns to them in working-out of his story'. 'The whole secret', another review explains,

> seems to be that Mr. Trollope really knows what we may call the *natural history* of every kind of man or woman he seeks to sketch, – by which we mean not so much his or her interior thoughts and feelings, but the outward habits in which these thoughts and feelings are expressed, the local and professional peculiarities of manner and habit in every place and in every trade, nay more, the minutiae of class demeanour, the value that is attached in particular situations to standing up rather than sitting down, to making a statement in one room rather than in another; in short, the characteristic dress in which the small diplomacies of all kinds of social life clothe themselves. . . . Mr. Trollope makes one feel how great a social naturalist he is.

Trollope, concludes the reviewer of *Miss Mackenzie* (1865) in a very suggestive formulation, 'paints those manners best which are almost an artificial language in themselves, which it almost takes an art to interpret'.[3]

Meanwhile plot and the questions of probability and plausibility received equal attention. A general feeling seems to have been that it follows from an elaborate plot that fictional personages will be presented as puppets or victims of events, and hence not be shown making meaningful and 'improving' moral choices. Then again, perhaps the excitement generated by the suspense and surprise of an intricate plot was dangerous in itself – a sort of drug, which the addict perpetually craved in larger and larger doses. The founding father of British empirical psychology, Alexander Bain (5.3), considered the scientific basis of 'the literature of plot-interest', which H.L. Mansel (3.6) attributed to socially and morally low influences. Sensation, it was assumed, involved original plotting, whereas, as Dallas points out:

> The Greek dramatists wrote hundreds of plays, but the tragedians at least had only two stories to work upon. On the tale of Troy and the tale of Thebes they rung innumerable changes, though with all that they had to relate their audiences were perfectly familiar. A modern writer has to provide his readers with much greater novelties. (5.4)

E. Bulwer Lytton proposes that an invented story in non-comic literature is peculiarly the property of the novel.[4] The fact that the Greek tragedians, Shakespeare, Corneille, Racine and Voltaire all used known 'fables' enabled them 'to place the originality there where alone it is essential to the drama – viz., in the analysis of the heart, in the delineation of passion, in the artistic development of the idea and purpose which the drama illustrates through the effects of situation and the poetry of form'. Bulwer Lytton supposes the condition for a novel to be different, for in prose fiction 'an original story is . . . an essential . . . part of artistic invention'. In the 1860s, when this was written, the 'realist' novelists like George Eliot and Trollope were working to combine the 'dramatic' emphasis on 'heart', 'passion', 'idea and purpose' with new stories which would belong specifically to the modern age. In Bulwer Lytton's terms, therefore, 'originality' had to characterise both aspects of this sort of fiction, and invention had a wider field of responsibility indeed.

To the Victorian critic originality might imply a lack of truth to the facts of 'real' life, and so the narrator of Charles Reade's *Autobiography of a Thief* warns the reader not to discount his material as fabrication, and defends (in sensational vein) the 'truth' of sensational subject-matter:

> I feign probabilities; I record improbabilities: the former are conjectures, the latter truths: mixed they make a thing not so true as Gospel nor so false as History: viz., Fiction.
>
> When I startle you most, think twice before you disbelieve me. What able deceiver aims at shocking credulity? Distrust rather my oily probabilities. They should be true too if I could make them; but I can't: they are guesses.[5]

Trollope's plea in 5.8 for 'truth' and 'sensation' to be combined is a rhetorically attractive but intellectually inadequate way out of the problems posed in extracts which make up this chapter.

Notes

1 Samuel Lucas (anon.), review of George Eliot's *Scenes of Clerical Life* and Reade's *White Lies*, *The Times*, 2 January 1858, 9; attribution from *The History of The Times*, 1939, vol. 2, p. 489.
2 E. Bulwer Lytton, 'On Some Authors in whose writings Knowledge of the World is eminently displayed', *Miscellaneous Prose Works*, 3 vols, 1868, vol. 3, p. 453.
3 For these references and a longer account of the *Spectator* on 'social strategy' and the 'language of manners', see David Skilton, *Anthony Trollope and His Contemporaries*, London, Longman, 1972, pp. 114–16.
4 E. Bulwer Lytton, 'On Certain Principles of Art in Works of Imagination', 'Caxtoniana: a Series of Essays on Life, Literature, and Manners. – Part XVI', *Blackwood's Magazine* 93 (May 1863), 554–5, partially reprinted as extract 7.4.
5 Introduction to Charles Reade, *Autobiography of a Thief* (1858).

5.1 Edward Bruce Hamley, 'Remonstrance with Dickens', *Blackwood's Magazine* 81 (April 1857), 495–503

Little Dorrit came out in nineteen monthly parts from December 1855 to June 1857, and in volume form on 30 May 1857. This review was therefore written when only four-fifths of the novel had appeared in serial. The reviewer, E.B. (later Sir Edward) Hamley (1824–93), became a General, a Member of Parliament, and professor of military history at Sandhurst. He was one of a number of notable soldier contributors to Blackwood's Magazine, *and a friend of Thackeray, Lytton and Trollope. He finds* Little Dorrit *distasteful and difficult to deal with, since it is neither a work of humour, nor a novel of character or incident. His reaction to the work illustrates the strength of critical stereotypes in determining critics' responses. Since* Little Dorrit *does not fit into any pre-existing scheme, Hamley views it as a failed mixture of fictional genres. Like most Victorians (including E.S. Dallas and Henry James) he also dismisses fiction which acknowledges an awareness of its own conventions and practices, or allows its technique to be seen rather than seeming to put the reader directly in touch with its 'content'. In an otherwise highly complimentary review of* Our Mutual Friend *in* The Times, *for example, Dallas remarks '[W]hen one thinks more of an artist's manner than of his matter woe to the artist.'[1] Surprisingly, few Victorian critics expressed this worry about Thackeray's fiction. Because* Vanity Fair *was universally regarded as a great work of moral character-study, its self-conscious elements – and in particular the opening and closing passages presenting the novelist as puppeteer – were more easily forgiven. It may also be that Hamley's divergent judgements on Dickens were influenced by his personal allegiance and friendship with Thackeray and other practitioners of a fiction which was socially more prestigious than Dickens's.*

It is because we so cordially recognised, and so keenly enjoyed, his genius in his earlier works, that we now protest against the newer phase he chooses to appear in. Formerly, his impulses came from within. What his unerring eye saw, as it glanced round the world, was represented in a medium of the richest humour. But gradually his old characteristics have slipt from him, supplanted by others totally different in origin and result. All his inspiration now seems to come from without. . . .

[T]his is not a great work of character. Indeed, in the absence of incident, it is difficult to see how character can display itself. Hence arises another prime fault. In a great novel the incidents and characters work together for good, characters producing incident, incident calling forth traits of character, till in the very highest specimens the principal personages are scarcely fully developed before the end of the book. But here a character is minutely described on its first appearance, and henceforward it is a mere repetition, never developing or evolving itself in the least; and whole pages are taken up with the talk about nothing, of people who, if they talked about something, would not be worth listening to. . . . In Dickens's estimation, there is no such thing as insignificance. Throughout the book there is the same tendency apparent to exhaust every part of every subject, whether description, narration, or dialogue, the result being, of course, altogether inadequate to the power exercised, because the material is so worthless. It is like employing some vast machine that is meant for welding iron and cutting steel to macerate old rags.

A novel which, besides being destitute of well-considered plot, is not a novel of incident or character, can scarcely be a great picture of life; indeed, the number of puppets, dummies, and unnatural creations that grimace and jerk their way along the scenes, forbid it to be so considered. 'All the world's a stage,' says Shakespeare, 'and all the men and women merely players.' – 'All the world's a puppet-show,' says Dickens, 'and all the men and women *fantoccini*.[2] See here, ladies and gentlemen, I take this abstract quality, which is one of the characteristics of the present day, and which you will therefore like to see – I select this individual trait from the heap you see lying by me – I add a bit of virtue, because it looks well to detect a soul of goodness in things evil – I dress the combination in these garments, which I got off a man in the street. Observe now, when I pull the strings (and I don't mind letting you see me pulling the strings all through the exhibition – no deception, ladies and gentlemen, none), how natural the action! how effective the character!'

Notes

1   *The Times*, 29 November 1865, 6.
2   *fantoccini* (Italian): stringed puppets. The use of the word connects Dickens's art to popular entertainment – an association quite appropriate in the eyes of many later critics, but perhaps intended by Hamley to reflect badly on Dickens in terms of social status.

5.2 Walter Bagehot, review of *Lost and Won* by Georgiana Marion Craik (Mrs A.W. May), *Saturday Review* 7 (16 April 1859), 474–5

G.M. Craik (1831?–95) specialised in novels presenting the difficulties of love and courtship from the standpoint of a young woman. Critics of the period frequently perceived the narrative devices and techniques novelists were using, but almost always felt obliged to examine them from a moral rather than an aesthetic standpoint. The following example from Bagehot is a case in point. Years later the control of 'point of view' in narrative was to become one of the principal topics in the debate on the art of fiction. In 1859, however, choice of narrative point of view is assumed to have been made for practical and moral reasons, and to have practical and moral consequences, as much as aesthetic ones. Critics in the first half of the twentieth century tended to gloss over the moral, social and political significance of such technical choices, but succeeding generations have once more noticed the implications of technique, this time putting an emphasis on the ideology produced by the text in question. The following discussion on what a young female narrator may decently be allowed to know is worthy of far more extended analysis than would be possible here. Within the confines of this collection it can be usefully compared with the discussions in 7.1 and 7.3 on the subject-matter available to women novelists (and readers), and to the quotation in the introduction to chapter 7 from George Eliot's 'Silly Novels by Lady Novelists'. For Walter Bagehot, see the headnote to 1.3.

[T]here is little in this novel which will require or bear very special criticism. . . . It has, however, one peculiarity, in relation to which it may be instructive to consider it somewhat further. We have said that the narrative professes to have been composed by the quiet heroine, and there are evident advantages which not unfrequently just now induce writers of novels to tell their story from that point of view. It is the greatest of these that the necessary limitations of the life which it is proper to describe in the novel, exactly coincide with the necessary limitations of the knowledge of the person who, on this supposition, professedly writes it. Nothing is, by the received rules, permitted in novels, which does not suit the perusal of young ladies as well as of young gentlemen. Such a writer as Mr. Thackeray is constantly irritated at this restraint. He has evidently to reject illustrations which would be telling, and remarks which would be very appropriate, because they belong to the unladylike and interdicted world. Every man, in proportion to the variety of his acquaintance with life, will feel the same constraint. The obvious remedy is, that the writer should throw himself once for all into the position of a young lady in the story – hear only what she hears, see only what she sees, know only what she knows. His dramatic instincts will then preserve him even from wishing to overstep the prescribed boundary. Whatever he may wish to say himself, he will not wish that a quiet heroine of his delineation should say anything which it would not be quite proper that she should say. If the novel be written, as we know is now not very uncommon, by a young lady, she will find an additional advantage in selecting as the point of delineation the exact point of view with which she is inevitably most familiar, and which is more or less her own. She will be sure of describing only what she can describe, as well as be protected from all risk, if by possibility there should be any, of trespassing on what she ought not to describe.

But there are drawbacks on these advantages. Not only does the extreme limitation of the field of delineation after a time weary all those whose range of knowledge is more varied, but a less evident result follows, of which *Lost and Won* is a striking instance. The narrative becomes very melodramatic. A little reflection will, indeed, enable us to perceive why this must be so. By a melodramatic incident, we mean a startling incident of which no rational or intelligible account is given us. By a melodramatic character, we mean one which has the startling features and exaggerated qualities which tell upon the stage, but of which no real *rationale* is offered. In the case of the event, we have either no idea of its cause, or we perceive that cause to be improbable. In the case of the man, we do not know the inner nature out of which his startling peculiarities arise. These peculiarities are described to us, and we are told that they belong to a certain man, but what that man is we do not know. Some such delineation as this is the inevitable result of that limited knowledge which it is proper to attribute to the favourite narratress of modern fiction – the quiet heroine. A young lady of that kind can only in a modified way understand what passes around her. Not to speak of other limitations, the entire sphere of masculine action is wholly shut out from her perception. Half the incidents in life have their origin in events belonging to the active world, which she has no means of knowing. All around her people move and act from impulses and causes which she only very vaguely, if at all, apprehends, and which never enter her real world of secret thought. In consequence, she acquires a habit of accepting the obvious incidents of life as what they are, without concerning herself with the reasons for them, or much thinking if there are any reasons. As soon as this state of mind is made the point of view from which a narrative is imagined to be told us, we have inevitably one of the principal elements of a melodrama. We have recounted to us events – probably rather striking events, for no one likes telling a story 'about nothing' – of which no rational account is given to us, or, from knowledge appropriate to the imagined narratress, can be given to us. The same result, to an extent even greater, is true of characters. For example, nothing can be more melodramatic than the delineation of Lord Carstairs in *Lost and Won*. He is a very bad but very picturesque young nobleman. He treats Hildred in what may possibly be an attractive sort of way, but it is not a sort of way which enables us to understand his character. He is intended to be a person of much ability, much cultivation, and much daring, but utterly unscrupulous in his relations with women, and much disposed, if they will permit it, to amuse himself at their expense. No one can deny that such a character is possible, or that, in the hands of a master of literary delineation, it might be made a telling subject for the exercise of his art. But it is equally certain that such a character is beyond the mental experience of a common lady. She can have no idea of the early life by which such a man is formed into what he is, or of the more mature life which he leads when he has been so formed. Both conceptions are beyond her sphere. We do not say that a woman of genius may not emancipate herself from these limits; the task is difficult, but we quite believe that it may be possible for an intuitive imagination to divine all that is essential in such a character. But no similar divination must be attributed to an ordinary young heroine. She is not intended to be a woman of genius. Her mind is timid, and its range is narrow. No acquaintance with the real existence of a bad young nobleman can be acquired by such a person except under very peculiar circumstances, or at her own cost. To attribute such knowledge to a gentle young lady who has never had any experience would be monstrous.

5.3 Alexander Bain, from 'Literature of Plot-interest', *The Emotions and the Will*, 1859, pp. 196–7[1]

Alexander Bain (1818–1903) was one of the key figures in the development of British psychology, and is even regarded by some as the founder of the subject in a recognisably modern, empirical form. He found it as a branch of philosophy, and left it with its scope and methodology as a science clearly defined, and its physiological foundations sketched out. He taught grammar, composition, rhetoric, logic and moral philosophy at the university in his native Aberdeen, where he was appointed to the chair of logic in 1860. In 1876 he founded the periodical Mind, *of which he remained the proprietor until 1892. He associated with political radicals, such as J.S. Mill, who approved of Bain's treatment of novel-reading in a review of* The Emotions and the Will.[2] *Bain returns to the subject of fictional plot later in* The Emotions and the Will: *'Among the pleasures incident to Action, we ranked Pursuit and Plot-interest, whose fascination sometimes becomes too great, and requires to be restrained. A certain check must be placed upon the excitement of sport and the engross of story in Youth, as engendering a species of dissipation inconsistent with the sober engagement of life. When allowed to run riot, the interest in mere narrative and plot becomes a source of serious annoyance'* (p. 468).

Before quitting the subject [emotions of action], the Literature of Plot-interest claims some notice. The position of the spectator of moving events is greatly enlarged by language, which can bring before his mind scenes witnessed by other men; and, in so far as he is able to conceive what is thus related, he catches the fire of the actual witness. This is the interest of story, which is such a widely-spread source of excitement. The narrative of a chase, a battle, an adventure, places the hearer under the dominion of the emotion before us. The interesting stake, at first remote and uncertain, but gradually brought nearer as the successive incidents are recounted, keeps up that animated suspense, felt alike by the actor, the looker-on, and the hearer or reader, rendering it difficult for the mind to entertain any new subject till the declaration of the final issue. The recital of what befalls our friends, and the men and societies belonging to our generation, is the commonest and directest mode of stirring up our attention and suspense. We can also be affected by the narratives of past history, some of which are more particularly adapted for this kind of interest. The struggles that have preceded vast changes, contest, revolutions, keep the reader in a state of thrilling expectation; while the inner plots and minor catastrophes serve to discharge at intervals the pent-up currents, and vary the direction of the outlook. Whatever the achievements are that rouse the feelings of a reader – whether wars, conquests, human greatness, or progress and civilization, – the moments, when these were pending in doubtful issue, are to him moments of earnest engrossment.

While the historian is bound by fact and reality, the poet or romancer is able to accommodate his narrative so as to satisfy the exigencies of plot-interest by devices suited thereto. Calculating how much suspense the mind of a reader can easily bear, and how this can be artificially sustained and prolonged; casting about also for the class of events best able to awaken agreeable emotions in a story; the artist in narrative weaves together a tissue of incidents aiming at some one conclusion, which, however, is to be accomplished through many intermediate issues. Epic and dramatic poetry were the first forms of plot fiction; the prose romance or novel is the more modern and perennial variety. Many strings of interest may be touched by a highly-wrought romance, but the dissolution of the plot would destroy what is essential in the structure, and leave the composition lifeless and tedious to the mass of readers.

Notes

1 The second, enlarged edition of *The Emotions and the Will* (1865) is the standard edition to quote in the history of psychology, but the passages used here remain almost unchanged.
2 J.S. Mill, 'Bain's Psychology', *Edinburgh Review* 110 (October 1859), 287–321.

5.4 E.S. Dallas (anon.), review of M.E. Braddon's *Lady Audley's Secret*, *The Times*, 18 November 1862, 8

Lady Audley's Secret was serialised from July 1861 to December 1862 first in Robin Goodfellow *and then in the* Sixpenny Magazine. *It was immensely popular, and ran through no fewer than nine three-volume editions in two months in 1862. The analogy between narrative and the hunt is commonplace, and is also used by the psychologist, Alexander Bain, in extract 5.3. For Dallas see the headnote to 1.6 and for a brief introduction to his aesthetic position see extract 6.5 and its headnote.*

The secret of the imaginary Lady Audley . . . belongs entirely to modern times. It is a good galloping novel, like a good gallop, to be enjoyed rather than criticized. It is full of rapid incident, well put together. When we begin to read we cannot choose but go on; and if, when we come to an end, we observe that we have travelled through well-known country, that the ditches and hedges we have leaped are familiar to us, it is not to be supposed that in passing this criticism we are of necessity depreciating the work of a really clever authoress. The Greek dramatists wrote hundreds of plays, but the tragedians at least had only two stories to work upon. On the tale of Troy and the tale of Thebes they rung innumerable changes, though with all that they had to relate their audiences were perfectly familiar. A modern writer has to provide his readers with much greater novelties; the matter must be fresh and the treatment original; but if it is not entirely so, and if, in spite of that want, the writer succeeds in interesting the public, there is not much room for complaint. In plain English, the present writer has laid her hands upon some well-known materials, but she has turned them to such good account that in the general interest we forget the imperfections of detail, and in the rush of events take little note of what is new or what is hackneyed.

Miss Braddon's story belongs to a class of fiction which Mr. Wilkie Collins has rendered extremely popular, though he can scarcely be said to have invented it. Perhaps Edgar Poe has done more than any other man to show the capacity of exciting the imagination which their species of story affords.[1] There is a secret, generally a crime, to be discovered. There are no apparent means of reaching the discovery. But our modern police regulations have gone far to reduce the detection of crime to a science, and there is nothing which the public are more eager to unravel than such mysteries as every now and then fill the newspapers. Suppose a carpet bag full of mangled remains found on Waterloo-bridge. That secret has never yet been penetrated, but once recognized as a secret, we know how the fascination of crime can be intensified by the fascination of mystery. Every little hint or clue is seized with astonishing avidity; countless suggestions are made and theories are started; millions of readers wait impatiently for more and more news; and the police and the newspaper offices are besieged by correspondents eager to propose new lines of inquiry. The secret which baffles the detectives, it is the province of the novelist to unravel. Whereas the old classical novel always had a villain to make all the mischief and the complications of the plot, and a hero to fight through these complications and to come off victorious by force of bravery or love or some irresistible sentiment; the modern fictions of which we speak delight chiefly in a villain and a villain-finder. The villain is the hero, and the villain-finder is set like a sleuth hound on his path. The fineness of scent which these animals display in fiction is amazing. Where to ordinary perception there is no appearance of anything wrong they detect in a word, in a look, far more than Lord Burleigh ever intended.[2] It is really delightful to see how the evidence accumulates bit by bit, and each bit in its proper place and at the proper time, in the most logical order. The acuteness of the villain-finder is preternatural. He sees a hand you cannot see, he hears a voice you cannot hear. At length, the final link in the chain of evidence is secure. In many cases the hunter has to go across the world for it – to Australia, to America, but he always finds it. The poor hunted beast is driven to bay; the secret is out, and the tale ends. Tell us not that the hunt is an old story, and that one hunt is like another. So it is; but whether over grass or over paper, it comes always new to the keen sportsman, and he who has been at the hunt oftenest enjoys it best. A foxhunter never seems to have enough of it, and a novel-reader will go on reading novels to all eternity, and sometimes even will have several in hand at once – a serial of Mr. Trollope's here, a serial of Mr. Dickens's there, and the last three-volume tale into the bargain.

The most distinguished of the novelists who excite an interest in the analysis of evidence forbade the critics, when his last work appeared, to divulge his secret.[3] To divulge it, however, could have done him no harm, and we do none to Miss Braddon when we say that the secret of Lady Audley is bigamy. We mention it the rather because it is characteristic of the modern novel. That the lady should be the centre of interest, that she should be the sinner of the tale, and that her sin should be a violation of the marriage law are as natural to recent novels as that her guilt should be a secret, and a secret discovered by the most elaborate espionage. This is the age of lady novelists, and lady novelists naturally give the first place to the heroine. But, if the heroines have first place, it will scarcely do to represent them as passive and quite angelic, or insipid – which heroines usually are. They have to be pictured as high-strung women, full of passion, purpose, and movement – and very liable to error. Now, the most interesting side of a woman's character is her relation to the other sex, and the errors of women that are most interesting spring out of this relation. Hence unwonted prominence has of late been given to a theme which novelists used formerly to shrink from; and we are honoured with descriptions of the most hidden feelings of the fair sex which would have made our fathers and grandfathers stare. Truth to tell, however, the novelists have seldom been able to conjoin much analysis of feeling with much analysis of plot. If the novelist gets interested in the analysis of complications and the construction of evidence, he soon finds that he must ignore a good deal of passion, and do continual violence to character. It is needful to keep the two apart, and we generally find female analysis in one class of novels, and the secret police system in another.

Notes

1   Edgar Allan Poe (1809–49) exerted an immense influence over subsequent writers of detective fiction through such tales as 'The Purloined Letter', 'The Mystery of Marie Roget' and 'The Murders in the Rue Morgue'.

2   William Cecil, Baron Burleigh (1520–98) appears as a character in Sheridan's play, *The Critic*, and is seen in Puff's tragedy, a play within a play, in Act III scene i, where he does not speak, but 'comes forward, shakes his head and exit'. Puff explains this as a moment of great subtlety and significance: '[B]y that shake of the head, he gave you to understand that even tho' they had more justice in their cause and wisdom in their

measures – yet, if there was not a greater spirit shown on the part of the people – the country would at last fall a sacrifice to the hostile ambition of the Spanish monarchy.'

3   In the preface to the 1860 edition of *The Woman in White*, Wilkie Collins appealed to critics not 'to let the cat out of the bag', prompting Dallas to reply: 'The cat out of the bag! There are in this novel about a hundred cats contained in a hundred bags, all screaming and mewing to be let out. Every chapter contains a new cat. When we come to the end of it, out goes the animal, and there is a new bag put into our hands which it is the object of the subsequent chapter to open' *(The Times*, 30 October 1860).

5.5 'G' [i.e. Richard Garnett], review of George Meredith's *Emilia in England, Reader* III (no. 69) (23 April 1864), 514–15

Richard Garnett (1835–1906) was a formidable scholar and a librarian who rose to be Keeper of Printed Books at the British Museum (now the British Library). He acutely grasped characteristics of Meredith's work which eluded most of his contemporaries, who did not share his and Garnett's interest in late seventeenth- and early eighteenth-century stage comedy. Because of the signs of this enthusiasm in his fiction, Meredith was unusual in his age in drawing forth discussion of the relation between character on the one hand and intellectual idea and comedy on the other. On its reissue in 1886 Meredith's Emilia in England *was retitled* Sandra Belloni, *the name by which it has continued to be known.*

Mr. Meredith belongs to that select band of humorists who mainly rely for effect upon the pungency and piquancy of their diction, whether uttered in their own character, or placed in the mouths of their *dramatis personae*. Few writers indeed could dispose of resources adequate to so sustained a display of intellectual pyrotechnics as that which has now lasted Mr. Meredith through nine volumes.[1] It is comparatively easy to devise humorous situations; but this is farce. Mr. Meredith's works are the best modern representatives of the genteel comedy of a hundred and fifty years since.[2] Incident and character are not neglected; but both are subordinate to dialogue. The personages have their prototypes in nature, but are still somewhat idealised: they are like and not like people we have seen. They are rather types of character than individuals. Maskwell in Congreve's comedy, for example, is a really scientific combination of the chief traits of a designing villain;[3] but we may perceive at once that these have been ingeniously put together in the study, not copied

131

from the living model. It is a significant circumstance that all Congreve's plays were composed at an age when Mr. Meredith had hardly begun to write. The latter's experience of life is consequently much wider, and there is that in the genius of his time which causes him to be more solicitous about the truth of things. Nevertheless, next to the intellectual brilliancy of his writings, their most salient feature is their artificial aspect. A principle of intelligent selection seems to have presided over their genesis and development. The story is carefully chosen for the sake of some favourite idea snugly bedded in the centre of it – a Psyche-germ, swathed in a rich cocoon of illustration. The personages are all selected with a similar view, and their sayings and doings meted out with the nicest accuracy.

Notes

1 Garnett is presumably counting Meredith's two previous three-volume novels, *The Ordeal of Richard Feverel* (1859) and *Evan Harrington* (1860), and excluding the two earlier pieces of whimsy, *The Shaving of Shagpat* (1855), *Farina* (1857).
2 In 1877 Meredith was to publish an essay on 'The Idea of Comedy', in which, among other things, he sympathetically analysed the comedy of the Restoration and eighteenth century.
3 Maskwell is the chief character in Congreve's play, *The Double-Dealer* (1693).

5.6 Review of Trollope's *The Small House at Allington*, *Spectator*, 9 April 1864, 421–3

The authorship of this review of one of Trollope's best-loved novels is unknown, but in style and method of analysis it bears the imprint – by authorship, rewriting or influence – of the literary editor of the Spectator, *Richard Holt Hutton, whom Trollope called 'of all the critics of my work . . . the most observant, and generally the most eulogistic'.[1] In this extract the reviewer goes beyond the commonplace analysis of fiction in terms of individual characters, to a consideration of the rules by which social behaviour can be analysed. This method of reading recognises manners, social conventions and gestures as constituting signifying systems by which, whether they are aware of it or not, people communicate, and it strikingly anticipates semiological approaches of the following century. The critic is not developing this insight unaided, but is responding to an analysis Trollope makes of such phenomena when he is guiding us as to how to 'read' his social world.*

Mr. Trollope has written nothing more true or entertaining than this admirable representation of our modern social world, with its special temptations, special vices, and special kinds of retribution. It is not so much a story, though it has a certain current of story quite sufficient to lead the reader on, as a fragment of complicated social strategy that he describes in these pages, – and describes with a delicacy of observation and a moral thoughtfulness which matters apparently so trifling probably never before received. The utter defeat of a man of the world in virtue of his too great worldliness, or rather in consequence of a dash of better and purer tastes being mixed up with that utter worldliness of purpose, the faint degree in which motives higher than merely worldly motives affect the feelings and estimates of worldly men, the stronger degree in which worldly thoughts and motives affect the feelings and estimates of unworldly men, the shades of advantage given by purely accidental circumstances and associations to either combatant in a conflict for social ascendancy, the extent to which a defeated man may, if he has courage, even though he may not deserve it, save himself from utter ruin, and retire, not indeed with the honours of war, but without all the disgrace of defeat that retributive appetite might demand for him, and with a prospect of partially retrieving his heavy losses in future, – these are the themes which Mr. Trollope embodies for us in pictures of wonderful skill, fidelity, and humour. There is scarcely a chapter in the book which does not in some way illustrate the laws of success and failure in what we may call social tactics, – from the great advantage given by perfect frigidity and utter heartlessness to the splendid strategy of Lady Dumbello, to the slight advantage gained by Lily in her little contest with Hopkins, the gardener, through the device of luring him out of the garden and the immediate vicinity of his plants into the overawing neighbourhood of chairs and tables. 'I always like,' says Lily, 'to get him into the house, because he feels himself a little abashed by the chairs and tables; or perhaps it is the carpet that is too much for him. Out on the gravel walks he is such a terrible tyrant, and in the greenhouse he almost tramples on one.' And this subtle estimate of the strategical worth of a 'situation,' whether it be merely in trivial circumstances like this, – or one which depends on the moral claims which trouble and grief confer, such as the same young lady uses so playfully and yet tyrannically over her mother and sister, – or one which springs from superior courage, such as Eames gained over Cradell, – or one which arises from homage conceded to mere position and rank, such as the Countess de Courcy wields over poor Crosbie during the preparations for his wedding, where 'she throws her head a little back' as she accosts him, and he instantly perceives that he is 'enveloped in the fumes of an affectionate but somewhat contemptuous patronage,' – or one of a purely moral kind, such as Lady Julia de Guest gains over Crosbie for a moment at Courcy Castle, until his superior address and presence of mind redress the balance of advantage, – this subtle estimate of the value of the less obvious elements in the strategy of social life is, after all, what gives the chief humour as well as charm to this amusing book.

Mr. Trollope's intellectual grasp of his characters, so far as he goes (which is only now and then much below the surface), is nearly perfect; but then he chooses to display that grasp almost exclusively in the hold they get or fail to get over other characters, and in the hold they yield to other characters over them. It is in his command of what we may call the moral 'hooks and eyes' of life that Mr. Trollope's greatest power lies. And his characters are more or less interesting almost exactly in proportion to the degree in which their mode of influencing or failing to influence other people is unique and characteristic. For example, perhaps the most skilful chapters in this book are those which give an account of Mr. Plantagenet Palliser's faint attentions to Lady Dumbello, and of the Duke of Omnium's efforts to deter his nephew from advances in that quarter. And the reason is, that in Lady Dumbello's marble frigidity of nature and the Duke of Omnium's magnificent way of managing a menace through the hints of his man of business, Mr. Trollope has found almost a new medium for expressing the influence wielded by character over character, and one so exceedingly slight and indirect that no novelist but himself would have thought of availing himself of it at all. Indeed, Mr. Trollope's greatest power is, in this respect, in unison with the greatest power of cultivated modern society, namely, to make a great use of little means in expressing his meaning, – nay, to make more use, if one may so speak, of unused social weapons by faintly indicating their far-off existence than of those which are actually brought into play. There is nothing which Mr. Trollope draws with greater humour than the difference between the strategic value of a vague unexpended resource, and of the same resource if actually put into requisition. There is nothing which he loves better to paint than the wise self-restraint and reticence of true men or women of the world, in doling out gradually their doses of worldly motive to those whom they wish to influence, and their great caution and almost dread of expending that motive power. He evidently knows that the power of motives, like the power of money, is greatest in prospect, and even in his own art he always *hoards*, like the world, his rewards and penalties with the greatest care, adding to the sense of his power by the self-restraint with which he deals out his poetical justice. In this respect Mr. Trollope is like the Duke of Omnium himself; – he hints to his characters that if they do certain things there may be 'some change in the arrangements;' he uses that menace, however, most charily, reluctant to exhaust its power; and if at length he is compelled to make that 'change in the arrangements' he does so with studious moderation, relaxing his heaviest punishments almost immediately, and always reminding us of the great difference between the sharp moral retribution of fancy and the diluted moral sentences, modified by a hundred different counteracting circumstances, of actual life.

Note

1   *An Autobiography*, 1883, vol. 2, p. 12.

5.7 E.S. Dallas, *The Gay Science*, 2 vols, London, 1866, vol. 2, pp. 292–9

For Dallas and The Gay Science *see headnotes to 1.6 and 2.4, and for a brief introduction to his aesthetic position see extract 6.5 and its headnote. The witty tone in which he writes should not distract from the importance of what he is saying. In particular he points out that a connection is made between the 'realistic' novel of character and human potential to master circumstances. This connection forms part of many later attempts to distinguish between realism and naturalism, and may also be the ancestor of the assumption (still frequently voiced) that it is a characteristic of realism that it makes the alarming flux of human experience understandable. He is also sensitive to the difficulties involved in presenting active women characters who are not to fall foul of Victorian moral conventions. It is worth observing that Edith Simcox (1.8) attaches great importance to George Eliot's development of the 'inner life' in* Middlemarch.

Not only does Thackeray . . . insist upon a theory of character which implies in the sense of the poet the withering of the individual;[1] we see precisely the same tendency in the school of fiction, which is the right opposite of his – what is called the sensation school. In that school the first consideration is given to the plot; and the characters must succumb to the exigencies of the plot. This is so clearly necessary that at length it has become a matter of course to find in a sensation novel a fine display of idiocy. There is always, in a sensation novel, one, or it may be two, half-witted creatures. The utility of these crazy beings is beyond belief. The things they see which nobody thought they would see, and remember which nobody thought that they would remember, are even more remarkable than the things which, do what their friends will, they cannot be made to comprehend, and cannot be counted upon to repeat. Now, this species of novel is very much sneered at by persons of supposed enlightenment, and certainly it is more satisfactory to the pride of human nature to write and to read a novel of character. But I am not sure that, viewed in the abstract, such a work is either more true or more philosophical than the species of fiction in which the plot is of most importance. Suppose we attempt to state in abstract terms the difference between the two kinds of fiction.

Both profess to give us pictures of life, and both have to do with certain characters going through certain actions. The difference between the two lies solely in the relation of the characters portrayed to the actions described. In the novel of character man appears moulding circumstances to his will, directing the action for himself, supreme over incident and plot. In the opposite class of novel man is represented as made and ruled by circumstance; he is the victim of change and the puppet of intrigue. Is either of these views wholly true or wholly false? We may like the one better than the other. We may like to see men generally represented as possessed of decided character, masters of their destiny, and superior to circumstance; but is this view of life a whit more true than that which pictures the mass of men as endowed with faint characters, and as tossed hither and thither by the accidents of life, which we sometimes call fate and sometimes fortune? The art of fiction, which makes character succumb to the exigencies of plot, is just as defensible as that which breaks down incident before the weight of character. In point of fact, however, most novelists attempt to mix up the two extreme views of life, though they cannot help leaning to the one side or to the other; and the chief weakness of the plotting novels, as they are now written, is, that while they represent circumstances and incidents as all-important, and characters amid the current of events as corks upon the waves, they generally introduce one character, who, in violent contrast to all the others, is superior to the plot, plans the events, guides the storm, and holds the winds in the hollow of his hand. It is quite wonderful to see what one picked character can do in these stories in comparison with the others, who can do nothing. He predominates over the plot, and the plot predominates over all else. The violence of this contrast is an artistic error; but the views themselves which are thus contrasted are not necessarily false. To show man as the sport of circumstance may be a depressing view of human nature; but it is not fair to regard it as immoral nor to denounce it as utterly untrue. And whether it be true or false, still, as a popular view of life, it is one of the facts which we have to regard, when we consider either the Laureate's view, that the individual withers, or Archdeacon Hare's view, that this is an age of superficial character.[2] . . .

There was a time when the chief characters in fiction were men, and when to find a female portrait well drawn, especially if she was intended to rank as a heroine, was a rare exception. How colourless, for example, are most of Sir Walter Scott's heroines, when compared with the men in whom he delights. Now all the more important characters seem to be women. Our novelists have suddenly discovered that feminine character is an unworked mine of wealth, and they give us jewels of women in many a casket. This is all the more natural, seeing that most of our novelists just now seem to belong to the fair sex. But their masculine rivals follow in the same track. . . .

It must be allowed that this feminine tendency in our literature is not all for good. But the evil which belongs to it is not what one would expect. Woman embodies our highest ideas of purity and refinement. . . . And now, when the influence of women is being poured into our literature, we expect to feel within it an evident access of refinement. We find the very opposite. The first object of the novelist is to get personages in whom we can be interested; the next is to put them in action. But when women are the chief characters, how are you to set them in motion? The life of women cannot well be described as a life of action. When women are thus put forward to lead the action of a plot, they must be urged into a false position. To get vigorous action they are described as rushing into crime, and doing masculine deeds. Thus they come forward in the worst light, and the novelist finds that to make an effect he has to give up his heroine to bigamy, to murder, to child-bearing by stealth in the Tyrol, and to all sorts of adventures which can only signify her fall. The very prominence of the position which women occupy in recent fiction leads by a natural process to their appearing in a light which is not good. This is what is called sensation. It is not wrong to make a sensation; but if the novelist depends for his sensation upon the action of a woman, the chances are that he will attain his end by unnatural means.

Notes

1 Tennyson, 'Locksley Hall' (1842): 'And the individual withers and the world is all in all' (l.144).
2 Julius Charles Hare (1795–1855), archdeacon of Lewes, author of two very popular series of essays, *Guesses at Truth* (1827 and 1848), the earlier of which he wrote with his brother Augustus William (1792–1834).

5.8 Anthony Trollope, *An Autobiography*, written 1875–6, 3 vols, 1883, vol. 2, pp. 41–4

For Anthony Trollope, see the headnote to extract 2.6.

Among English novels of the present day, and among English novelists, a great division is made. There are sensational novels and anti-sensational, sensational novelists and anti-sensational; sensational readers and anti-sensational. The novelists who are considered to be anti-sensational are generally called realistic. I am realistic. My friend Wilkie Collins is generally supposed to be sensational. The readers who prefer the one are supposed to take delight in the elucidation of character. They who hold by the other are charmed by the construction and gradual development of a plot. All this is, I think, a mistake, – which mistake arises from the inability of the imperfect artist to be at the same time realistic and sensational. A good novel should be both, and both in the highest degree. If a novel fail in either, there is a failure in art. Let those readers who believe that they do not like sensational scenes in novels think of some of those passages from our great novelists which have charmed them most: – of Rebecca in the castle with Ivanhoe; of Burley in the cave with Morton; of the mad lady tearing the veil of the expectant bride, in *Jane Eyre*; of Lady Castlewood as, in her indignation, she explains to the Duke of Hamilton Henry Esmond's right to be present at the marriage of his Grace with Beatrix; – may I add, of Lady Mason, as she makes her confession at the feet of Sir Peregrine Orme? Will any one say that the authors of these passages have sinned in being over-sensational? No doubt, a string of horrible incidents, bound together without truth in detail, and told as affecting personages without character, – wooden blocks, who cannot make themselves known to the reader as men and women, – does not instruct or amuse, or even fill the mind with awe. Horrors heaped upon horrors, and which are horrors only in themselves, and not as touching any recognized and known person, are not tragic, and soon cease even to horrify. . . . No novel is anything, for purposes either of comedy or tragedy, unless the reader can sympathise with the characters whose names he finds upon the pages. Let an author so tell his tale as to touch his reader's heart and draw his tears, and he has, so far, done his work well. Truth let there be, – truth of description, truth of character, human truth as to men and women. If there be such truth, I do not know that a novel can be too sensational.

5.9 John Ruskin, from 'Fiction, Fair and Foul', parts 1 and 5, *Nineteenth Century* 7 (June 1880), 944–6 and 10 (October 1881), 520–1

The passages printed here find the great fine-art critic and radical social prophet, John Ruskin (1819-1900), objecting in the strongest terms to the ugliness of the subject-matter of most modern fiction, and hence both to sensationalism and to realism's willingness to deal with 'low' subjects. In this he is following a line of attack laid down years before by critics of quite different political, social and religious persuasions. We learn from such examples not to classify Victorian reactions to complex cultural phenomena on a simplistic scale of 'left to right'. Ruskin's particular variant on this widespread critical position naturally grows out of his general concern with the moral and cultural degradation of the age, particularly as exemplified in and brought about by mechanisation and urbanisation. The resemblance of Ruskin's position to High Church Tory lines of thought, may be an example of 'convergent evolution' – a process whereby the response of different species to similar environments produces apparently similar characteristics, even if these species are not closely related. (The numbering of the paragraphs is Ruskin's.)

7.(III.) The monotony of life in the central streets of any great modern city, but especially in those of London, where every emotion intended to be derived by men from the sight of nature, or the sense of art, is forbidden for ever, leaves the craving of the heart for a sincere, yet changeful, interest, to be fed from one source only. Under natural conditions the degree of mental excitement necessary to bodily health is provided by the course of the seasons, and the various skill and fortune of agriculture. In the country every morning of the year brings with it a new aspect of springing or fading nature; a new duty to be fulfilled upon earth, and a new promise or warning in heaven. No day is without its innocent hope, its special prudence, its kindly gift, and its sublime danger; and in every process of wise husbandry, and every effort of contending or remedial courage, the wholesome passions, pride, and bodily power of the labourer are excited and exerted in happiest unison. The companionship of domestic, the care of serviceable, animals, soften and enlarge his life with lowly charities, and discipline him in familiar wisdoms and unboastful fortitudes; while the divine laws of seed-time which cannot be recalled, harvest which cannot be hastened, and winter in which no man can work, compel the impatiences and coveting of his heart into labour too submissive to be anxious, and rest too sweet to be wanton. What thought can enough comprehend the contrast between such life, and that in streets where summer and winter are only alternations of heat and cold; where snow never fell white, not sunshine clear; where the ground is only a pavement, and the sky no more than the glass roof of an arcade; where the utmost power of a storm is to choke the gutters, and the finest magic of spring, to change mud into dust: where – chief and most fatal difference in state – there is no interest of occupation for any of the inhabitants but the routine of counter or desk within doors, and the effort to pass each other without collision outside; so that from morning to evening the only possible variation of the monotony of the hours, and lightening of the penalty of existence, must be some kind of mischief, limited, unless by more than ordinary godsend of fatality, to the fall of a horse, or the slitting of a pocket?

8. I said that under these laws of inanition, the craving of the human heart for some kind of excitement could by supplied from *one* source only. It might have been thought by any other than a sternly tentative philosopher, that the denial of their natural food to human feelings would have provoked a reactionary desire for it; and that the dreariness of the street would have been gilded by dreams of pastoral felicity. Experience has shown the fact to be otherwise; the thoroughly trained Londoner can enjoy no other excitement than that to which he has been accustomed, but asks for *that* in continually more ardent or more virulent concentration; and the ultimate power of fiction to entertain him is by varying to his fancy the modes, and defining for his dulness the horrors, of Death. In the single novel of *Bleak House* there are nine deaths (or left for deaths, in the drop scene) carefully wrought out or led up to, either by way

of pleasing surprise, as the baby's at the brickmaker's,[1] or finished in their threatenings and sufferings, with as much enjoyment as can be contrived in the anticipation, and as much pathology as can be concentrated in the description. Under the following varieties of method:–

One by assassination .... Mr. Tulkinghorn.
One by starvation, with phthisis .... Joe.
One by chagrin .... Richard.
One by spontaneous combustion .... Mr. Krook.
One by sorrow .... Lady Dedlock's lover.
One by remorse .... Lady Dedlock.
One by insanity .... Miss Flite.
One by paralysis..................................... Sir Leicester.

Besides the baby, by fever, and a lively Frenchwoman left to be hanged.[2]

And all this, observe, not in a tragic, adventurous, or military story, but merely as the further enlivenment of a narrative intended to be amusing; and as a properly representative average of the statistics of civilian mortality in the centre of London.

9. Observe further, and chiefly. It is not the mere number of deaths (which, if we count the odd troopers in the last scene, is exceeded in *Old Mortality*, and reached, within one or two, both in *Waverley* and *Guy Mannering*)[3] that marks the peculiar tone of the modern novel. It is the fact that all these deaths, but one, are of inoffensive, or at least in the world's estimate, respectable persons; and that they are all grotesquely either violent or miserable, purporting thus to illustrate the modern theology that the appointed destiny of a large average of our population is to die like rats in a drain, either by trap or poison. Not, indeed, that a lawyer in full practice can be usually supposed as faultless in the eye of Heaven as a dove or a woodcock; but it is not, in former divinities, though the will of Providence that he should be dropped by a shot from a client behind his fire-screen, and retrieved in the morning by his housemaid under the chandelier. Neither is Lady Dedlock less reprehensible in her conduct than many women of fashion have been and will be: but it would not therefore have been thought poetically just, in old-fashioned morality, that she should be found by her daughter lying dead, with her face in the mud of a St. Giles's churchyard.

* * *

108. All healthy and helpful literature sets simple bars between right and wrong; assumes the possibility, in men and women, of having healthy minds in healthy bodies, and loses no time in the diagnosis of fever or dyspepsia in either; least of all in the particular kind of fever which signifies the ungoverned excess of any appetite or passion. The 'dulness' which many modern readers inevitably feel, and some modern blockheads think it creditable to allege, in Scott, consists not a little in his absolute purity from every loathsome element or excitement of the lower passions; so that people who live habitually in Satyric or hircine[4] conditions of thought find him as insipid as they would a picture of Angelico's.[5] The accurate and trenchant separation between him and the common railroad-station novelist is that, in his total method of conception, only lofty character is worth describing at all; and it becomes interesting, not by its faults, but by the difficulties and accidents of the fortune through which it passes, while, in the railway novel, interest is obtained with the vulgar reader for the vilest character, because the author describes carefully to his recognition the blotches, burrs and pimples in which the paltry nature resembles his own. *The Mill on the Floss* is perhaps the most striking instance extant of this study of cutaneous disease. There is not a single person in the book of the smallest importance to anybody in the world but themselves, or whose qualities deserved so much as a line of printer's type in their description. There is no girl alive, fairly clever, half educated, and unluckily related, whose life has not at least as much in it as Maggie's, to be described and to be pitied. Tom is a clumsy and cruel lout, with the making of better things in him (and the same may be said of nearly every Englishman at present smoking and elbowing his way through the ugly world his blunders have contributed to the making of); while the rest of the characters are simply the sweepings out of a Pentonville omnibus.

109. And it is very necessary that we should distinguish this essentially Cockney literature, – developed only in the London suburbs, and feeding the demands of the rows of similar brick houses, which branch in devouring cancer round every manufacturing town, – from the really romantic literature of France. Georges [sic] Sand is often immoral; but she is always beautiful, and in the characteristic novel ... *Le Péché de Mons. Antoine*, the five principal characters, the old Cavalier Marquis, – the Carpenter, – M. de Chateaubrun, – Gilberte, – and the really passionate and generous lover, are all as heroic and radiantly ideal as Scott's Colonel Mannering, Catherine Seyton, and Roland Graeme;[6] while the landscape is rich and true with

the emotion of years of life passed in glens of Norman granite and beside bays of Italian sea. But in the English Cockney school, which consummates itself in George Eliot, the personages are picked up from behind the counter and out of the gutter; and the landscape, by excursion train to Gravesend, with return ticket for City-road.

Notes

1 *Bleak House*, chapter 8.
2 Hortense, arrested for the murder of Mr Tulkinghorn.
3 Ruskin holds up Scott's novels as in general a healthy contrast to most later fiction.
4 Satyric or hircine: pertaining to a satyr or to a goat.
5 Fra Angelico, Dominican friar and didactic painter, active 1428–55.
6 Characters in *Guy Mannering* and *The Abbot*.

6

The imagination and the creative process

All the concerns of the foregoing chapters come together in a consideration of the literary imagination and the creative process. If this truly was the age of the novel, it was a matter of grave concern to estimate the worth of prose fiction as a genre by all possible criteria, including the amount of creative energy writers displayed. Few commentators agreed with G.H. Lewes's complaint that the 'imaginative power' of a work had traditionally been 'too frequently estimated according to the extent of a *departure* from ordinary experience in the images selected', in defiance of the 'psychological fact that fairies and demons, remote as they are from experience, are not created by a more vigorous effort of imagination than milkmaids and poachers'.[1] 'Realism', Lewes argued, was *per se* no less 'imaginative' than other forms of literature. Not bothering to rebut this claim, critics continued to assume that realism involved 'copying' from 'reality', and that this was a mechanical or reproductive rather than an aesthetic process. The broad distinction in images of creativity which M.H. Abrams notes between the mid-eighteenth century and the Romantic period, from the mirror to the flame or the fountain or some other natural process,[2] is paralleled here, with the Romantic values intact. Poetry, the Ideal, characterisation which 'penetrates to the soul', fiction which treats of Eternity – these are 'imaginative', and attract images of creativity or depth. 'Truth-to-life' and 'society fiction' on the other hand, are damned with images of superficiality and mechanical processes: steam-manufacture or printing, stereotyping, photography, *bas-relief*, the kaleidoscope, and, of course, the looking-glass. By and large Emily Brontë, though 'revolting', is imaginative (6.2), and Thackeray is superficial (6.1), while Trollope – by virtue of his very success in presenting a recognisable world – is the exemplum of all that is mechanical, as 6.6 makes clear. The knowledge required to be a social novelist sounds less than grand, as Masson concludes when he proposes that 'prose-fiction of social reality' depends upon 'acquired knowledge of men' (4.9).

144

R.H. Hutton debates the issue of depth and superficiality at length in the article from which 6.4 is derived. In various remarks too dispersed to be represented here, he also puts forward the view that men can be presented by 'superficial' means because they have full social existences, but that women require more 'poetic' characterisation, since he presumes them to have no intellectual 'position' *vis-à-vis* the world by which they can be recognised.[3] Women writers, of course, are hampered – or aided – by a narrowness of experience which may keep them pure, while limiting the 'truth' of their 'pictures' (5.2). For G.H. Lewes, Gaskell approaches the subject of the 'fallen woman' in *Ruth* 'like a woman, and a truly delicate-minded woman',[4] while for Dallas, as I point out in the introduction to chapter 7, women's fiction has a natural tendency to concern 'pap & primers'. As one woman novelist put it:

> This, which is the age of so many things – of enlightenment, of science, of progress – is quite as distinctly the age of female novelists; and women, who rarely or never find their way to the loftiest class, have a natural right and claim to rank foremost in the second. The vexed questions of social morality, the grand problems of human experience, are seldom so summarily discussed and settled as in the novels of this day which are written by women; and, though we have little reason to complain of the first group of experienced novelists who lead our lists, we tremble to encounter the sweeping theories of the very strange world revealed to us in the books of many of the younger sisterhood.[5]

A far more interesting model of the creative process than that assumed by the majority of Victorian critics is that developed by E.S. Dallas in his *Gay Science* of 1866, and which is supplied in skeletal form as extract 6.5. He was alone among his British contemporaries to recognise the rôle of the subconscious in artistic process, and has remained under-appreciated to this day, as a kind of Victorian intellectual misfit.

Notes

1 G.H. Lewes, *The Principles of Success in Literature*; see introduction to chapter 4.
2 M.H. Abrams, *The Mirror and the Lamp*, New York, Oxford University Press, 1953.
3 See David Skilton, *Anthony Trollope and His Contemporaries*, London, Longman, 1972, pp. 118–22.

4   G.H. Lewes (anon.), '*Ruth* and *Villette*', *Westminster Review* (ns) 3 (April 1853), 476.
5   Margaret Oliphant (anon.), 'Modern Novelists – Great and Small', *Blackwood's Edinburgh Magazine* 77 (May 1855), 555.

6.1 William Caldwell Roscoe (anon.), 'W.M. Thackeray, Artist and Moralist', review of *The Newcomes* and *Miscellanies, Prose and Verse*, *National Review* 2 (January 1856), 177–213, pp. 179–80

This and the succeeding extract are by the poet and essayist William Caldwell Roscoe (1823–59), who was brother-in-law to R.H. Hutton. (See headnotes to 3.3, 5.6 and 6.4.) His description of Thackeray's powers was either highly influential or typical of the age, since not only the general form of his argument but some of the very phrasing of this article is met with time and again over the next twenty years, particularly in accounts of Thackeray and Trollope. Roscoe judges Thackeray to be observant but not imaginatively penetrating, and holds that he deals with social phenomena rather than individual character, and hence with worldly matters rather than the 'higher' subject of human relations with God. Imaginative power was clearly a matter of importance in the period, partly because it was used as one of the measures of the cultural status of the age. As is usual at the time, the analysis of literature centres on the discussion of characterisation, and this and other factors in the novel are attributed directly to personal qualities of the novelist. By this standard, Thackeray (and, later, Trollope) are defective in imagination but supremely strong in 'truth-to-life', while the Brontës are strong in imagination, but lack the skill of checking their production against the observable facts of 'real' life.

The social human heart, man in relation to his kind – that is his subject. His actors are distinct and individual, – truthfully, vigorously, felicitously drawn; masterpieces in their way; but the personal character of each is not the supreme object of interest with the author. It is only a contribution to a larger and more abstract subject of contemplation. Man is his study; but man the social animal, man considered with reference to the experiences, the aims, the affections, that find their field in his intercourse with his fellow-men: never man the individual soul. He never penetrates into the interior, secret, *real* life that every man leads in isolation from his fellows, that chamber of being open only upwards to heaven and downwards to hell. He is wise to abstain; he does well to hold the ground where his pre-eminence is unapproached, – to be true to his own genius. But this genius is of a lower order than the other. The faculty that deals with and represents the individual soul in its complete relations is higher than that which we have ascribed to Mr. Thackeray. There is a common confusion on this subject. We hear it advanced on the one side, that to penetrate to the hidden centre of character, and draw from thence, – which of course can only be done by imagination, – is higher than to work from the external details which can be gathered by experience and observation; and on the other hand, that it is much easier to have recourse to the imagination than to accumulate stores from a knowledge of actual life, – to draw on the fancy than to reproduce the living scene around us. The answer is not difficult. It is easier, no doubt, to produce faint vague images of character from the imagination than to sketch from the real external manifestations of life before our eyes; and easier to make such shadows pass current, just because they are shadows, and have not, like the others, the realities ready to confront them. But take a higher degree of power, and the scale turns. It is easier to be Ben Jonson, or even Goethe, than Shakespeare. In general we may say, that the less elementary the materials of his art-structure, the less imagination does the artist require, and of the less creative kind; – the architect less than the sculptor, the historian less than the poet, the novelist less than the dramatist. Reproducers of social life have generally rather a marshalling than a creative power. And in the plot and conduct of his story Mr. Thackeray does not exhibit more than a very high power of grouping his figures and arranging his incidents; but his best characters are certainly creations, living breathing beings, characteristic not only by certain traits, but by that atmosphere of individuality which only genius can impart. Their distinctive feature and their defect, as we have before stated, is this, that not one of them is complete; each is only so much of an individual as is embraced in a certain abstract whole. We never know any one of them completely, in the way we know ourselves, in the way we imagine others. We know just so much of them as we can gather by an intercourse in society. Mr. Thackeray does not penetrate further; he does not profess to show more. He says openly this is all he knows of them. He relates their behaviour, displays as much of the feelings and character as the outward demeanour, the actions, the voice, can bear witness to, and no more. It is exactly as if you had met the people in actual life, mixed constantly with them, known them as we know our most intimate friends. Of course this is all we can *know* of a man; but not all we can imagine, not all the artist can, if he chooses, convey to us. We don't know our nearest friends; we are always dependent on our imagination. From the imperfect materials that observation and sympathy can furnish we construct a whole of our own, more or less conformable to the reality according to our opportunities of knowledge, and with more or less completeness and distinctness according to our imaginative faculty; and every man, of course, is something really different from that which every man around him conceives him to be. But without this imaginative conception we should not know one another at all, we should only have disconnected hints of contemporary existence.

It is perhaps the highest distinguishing prerogative of poetry or fiction, or whatever we choose as the most comprehensive name for that art which has language for its medium, that it gives the artist the power of delineating the actual interior life and individual character of a living soul. It is the only art that does so. The dramatist and the novelist have the power of imagining a complete character, and of presenting before you their conception of it; and the more complete this is, and the more unmistakably they can impress you with the idea of it in its fullness and in its most secret depths, the nearer they attain to the perfection of their art. Thackeray leaves the reader to his own imagination. He gives no clues to his characters, as such; he is not leading to an image of his own. He probably has a very distinct, but no complete conception of them himself; he knows no more of them than he tells us. He is interested more in the external exhibitions of character and the feelings than in character itself; his aim is not to reproduce any single nature, but the image that the whole phenomenon of social life has left impressed on his mind. . . .

If the power of producing the impression of reality were the test of the highest creative power, Thackeray would perhaps rank higher than any one who has ever lived.

6.2 William Caldwell Roscoe, 'The Miss Brontës', review of Gaskell's *Life of Charlotte Brontë* and Charlotte Brontë's collected novels, *National Review* 5 (July 1857), 127–64, pp. 134–6

See headnote to extract 6.1. Roscoe starts this extract by discussing Wuthering Heights.

It is idle to deny that the book is revolting. That a wickedness, whose only claim to attention is its intensity, that the most frightful excesses of degrading vices, snarling hyopocrisy, an almost idiotic imbecility of mind and body, combined with a cruel and utterly selfish nature, – that these things should not excite abhorrence is impossible; and they occupy so large a space in the book, they seem displayed so much for their own sake, that it is impossible the whole work should not obtain a share of the sentiment. We may admire, but not without horror, the stern, unflinching hand with which the author drives her keen plough through the worst recesses of the human heart, nothing surprised at what she finds there, nothing concerned at what she uproots; accepting every thing as the simple bent of nature, referring to no higher standard, and letting no sign escape her either of approval or condemnation. Unsparing vindictiveness and savage brutality are depicted in all their native deformity. Art throws aside her prerogative to dwell on beautiful and hint at hideous things, and lays bare to day the base actualities of coarse natures and degraded lives. The way in which the imagination of the author is imbued with the fierce uncontrolled tone of the work is shown remarkably in its overriding essential probabilities, as for instance, in the way in which Isabella Linton's and the younger Catherine's temper and character become so immediately assimilated in coarseness and malice to those of Heathcliff's household. We dare not question Charlotte Brontë's judgement, when she says of her sisters that they were 'genuinely good and truly great.' How the will and the life may have moulded the character, we are not competent to discern; and therefore we do not say that in the character, but that in the original temperament of Emily, there must have been some strange sympathy with the fierce natures she revels in delineating. We cannot help shrinking from a mind which could conceive and describe, even as occurring in a dream, the rubbing backwards and forwards of a child's hand along the jagged glass in a broken window-pane till the blood flowed down upon the bed. 'Having formed these beings,' says Charlotte, 'she did not know what she had done. If the auditor of her work, when read in the manuscript, shuddered under the grinding influence of natures so relentless and implacable, of spirits so lost and fallen; if it was complained that the mere hearing of certain vivid and fearful scenes banished sleep by night, and disturbed mental peace by day, – Ellis Bell would wonder what was meant, and suspect the complainant of affectation.'[1]

Her sister goes on to prophesy that the matured fruits of her mind would have thrown into the shade this early and immature production. But we doubt it. We doubt, at least, whether she could ever have taken any very high place in dramatic literature. In *Wuthering Heights* there is an unmistakable tendency to subordinate differences of character to vividness of narration. Rather, we should say, it shows the absence of any power of intuitive insight into characters widely differing from one another and from the author. All the characters described in the book are within a very narrow range, and have a tendency to run into one another. Yet the whole story embodies a wonderful effort of imagination. It is not painted in detail from observation or reflection, but caught up, as it were, into the highest heaven of imagination, and flung out from thence into the world, with scornful indifference to the restrictions of Art and the judgement of men. All is fused together as by fire; and the reader has neither power not inclination to weigh probabilities or discuss defects. He shudders as he reads, and feels as one may imagine a modern Englishman would feel in gazing at the gladiatorial shows of ancient Rome; but the laceration of his feelings deadens him to the bearings of details.

Note

1 In using her sister's pen-name, Ellis Bell, Charlotte Brontë may be drawing a distinction (uncommon at the time) between the novelist as creative artist and as social and family being.

6.3 Elizabeth Gaskell, *Life of Charlotte Brontë*, second edn, 1857, vol. 2, pp. 114–15

Elizabeth Gaskell's Life of Charlotte Brontë, *which has been referred to in several of the previous extracts and headnotes, was, alongside* Lockhart's Life of Scott *(1838) and Forster's biography of Dickens (1872-4), one of the most important extended works on a nineteenth-century novelist. Gaskell (1810-65) was herself one of the great novelists of the age, who by this date had published the larger part of her fiction. In this extract she is discussing Brontë's* Shirley *(1849).*

She was anxious to write of things she had known and seen; and among the number was the West Yorkshire character, for which any tale laid among the Luddites would afford full scope. In 'Shirley' she took the idea of most of her characters from life, although the incidents and situations were, of course, fictitious. She thought that if these last were purely imaginary, she might draw from the real without detection, but in this she was mistaken; her studies were too closely accurate. This occasionally led her into difficulties. People recognised themselves, or were recognised by others, in her graphic descriptions of their personal appearance, and modes of actions and turns of thought; though they were placed in new positions, and figured away in scenes far different to those in which their actual life had been passed. Miss Brontë was struck by the force or peculiarity of the character of some one whom she knew; she studied it, and analysed it with subtle power; and having traced it to its germ, she took that germ as the nucleus of an imaginary character, and worked outwards; – thus reversing the process of analysation, and unconsciously reproducing the same external development. The 'three curates' were real living men, haunting Haworth and the neighbouring district; and so obtuse in perception that, after the first burst of anger at having their ways and habits chronicled was over, they rather enjoyed the joke of calling each other by the name she had given them. 'Mrs. Pryor' was well known to many who loved the original dearly. The whole family of the Yorkes were, I have been assured, almost daguerreotypes.

6.4 R.H. Hutton, 'The Novels of George Eliot', *National Review* 11 (July 1860), 191–219

Richard Holt Hutton devoted a great deal of effort to examining varieties of characterisation in literature, and – perhaps following W.C. Roscoe – generally drew a distinction between the full rendering of the social aspects of personality of many characters on the one hand and 'depth of portraiture' of individuals on the other. The latter pictures emotional and religious life more fully, and in his view is particularly necessary in presenting women characters, since, he claims, women are not necessarily 'in position' as regards the world.[1] The undoubted value he perceived in the works of Austen, Gaskell, Trollope and Thackeray made him consider alternatives to the imitation of character as a model of fiction, and under Trollope's influence in particular he later speculated brilliantly on the possibility that novels might imitate aspects of society by the fictional presentation of the verbal and behavioural codes and conventions of interpersonal interaction – a sort of fictional social anthropology. (See 5.6.) The extract printed below from his long article on George Eliot in the National Review *contrasts the 'imaginative' intensity of Charlotte Brontë with the 'superficiality' of the treatment of manners by the 'society-novelists'.*

The essay from which an extract is printed here, was collected in Hutton's Essays Theological and Literary *(2 vols, 1871), but because it predates* Middlemarch, *and was based only on George Eliot's early fiction, Hutton did not include it in the later single-volume edition of his* Literary Essays. *One example of a judgement which he later modified was that George Eliot had 'little . . . capacity for catching the under-tones and allusive complexity' of polite society – a remark which must have seemed quite inappropriate after the publication of* Middlemarch *and* Daniel Deronda. *It is interesting to read an example of a critic trying to establish the terms to use in dealing with someone he recognises as a major writer, when with the hindsight of posterity we know that she is yet to produce her greatest works. On George Eliot's death Hutton declared, 'I should rank George Eliot second only in her own proper field . . . to Sir Walter Scott, and second to him only because her imagination, though it penetrates far deeper, had neither the same splendid vigour of movement, nor the same bright serenity of tone.'* [2]

What is remarkable in George Eliot is the striking combination in her of very deep speculative power with a very great and realistic imagination. It is rare to find an intellect so skilled in the analysis of the deepest psychological problems, so completely at home in the conception and delineation of real characters. . . . It is, indeed, a great help towards understanding her true genius to compare George Eliot with the school of society-novelists of whom I have spoken [Austen, Gaskell, Trollope and Thackeray]. What one remarks about the works of those who have studied any particular society as a whole far more deeply than they have studied the individual characters in it, is that their creations all stand on one level, are delineated, with great accuracy, down to the same not very considerable depth, and no further; that all, in short, are bas-reliefs cut out on the same surface. The novelists of this school are perfectly inexhaustible in resource on the special social ground they choose, and quite incapable of varying it. And all of them disappoint us in not giving more insight into those deeper roots of character which lie beneath the social surface. Probably the mobile sympathies which are so essential to artists of this class, and the faculty of readily realising, and of being easily satisfied with realising, the workings of other minds, are to some extent inconsistent with that imaginative intensity and tenacity which is needful for the deeper insight into human character. Certainly the accomplished artists I have named carve out their marvellously life-like groups in a very shallow though sufficiently plastic material. How perfect and how infinitely various are the images left on the mind by the characters in Miss Austen's novels! . . . but it is equally remarkable that all of them are drawn just to the same depth, all delineated out of the same social elements.[3] None of their minds are exhibited in any direct contact with the ultimate realities of life; none of them are seen grasping at the truth by which they seek to live, struggling with a single deadly temptation, – or, in short, with any of the deeper elements of human life. The same may almost be said of Thackeray's, Mr. Trollope's, and Mrs. Gaskell's sketches. These authors, indeed, sometimes probe the motives of their leading characters, but they generally report that at a very small depth below the surface the analysis fails to detect any certain result. The whole graphic effect of their art is produced with scarcely any disturbance of the smooth surface of social usage. The artist's graver just scratches off the wax in a few given directions till the personal bias of taste and bearing is sufficiently revealed, while the pervading principle of the society in which the artist lives is strictly preserved.

It was very different with Miss Brontë. Her imagination was not, and under the circumstances of her life could not have been, at home with the light play of social influences. There is even an abruptness of outline, a total want of social cohesion among her characters. They are sternly drawn, with much strong shading, and kept in isolated spheres. They break, or rather burst, in upon each other, when they exert mutual influences at all, with a rude effort, that is significant enough of the shyness of a solitary creative imagination. Still, for this very reason, what characters Miss Brontë does conceive truly, she reveals much more deeply than the society-novelists of whom I have been speaking. She has no familiarity with the delicate touches and shades by which they succeed in conveying a distinct impression without laying bare the deeper secrets of character. She has not, like them, any power of giving in her delineations *traces* of thought and feeling which lie beyond her actual grasp. She has a full and conscious hold of all the moods she paints; and though her paintings are in nine cases out of ten far less lifelike, yet *when* lifelike they are far more profoundly imagined than those of Mr. Trollope, Miss Austen, Mrs. Gaskell or even Thackeray himself. There is as little common life, diffused atmosphere of thought, and there are as few connecting social ideas, amongst the various figures in Miss Brontë's tales as is possible to conceive among fellow-men and fellow-countrymen. But what personal life there is, is of the deepest sort, though it is apt to be too exceptional and individual, and too little composed out of elements of universal experience.

The novelists of the society-school, who delineate not so much individual figures as a complete phase of society, have what one may call a *medium* ready to their hand in which to trace the characteristic features of the natures they delineate. They have a familiar world of manners to paint, in which a modulation, an omission, or an emphasis here and there, are quite sufficient to mark a character, or indicate a latent emotion. Not so an author who, like Miss Brontë, endeavoured to fit all her characters with a new and appropriate outward manner of their own as distinct and special as the inward nature it expressed. With her there was necessarily a *directness* of delineation, a strong downrightness in the drawing which is in very marked contrast with the method that charms us so much in the pictures of Miss Austen and her modern successors. Much of the art of the drawing-room novelists consists in the indirectness, the allusiveness, the educated reticence of the artists. They portray a society; they *indicate* an individuality. They delight in fine strokes; they will give a long conversation which scarcely advances the narrative at all, for the sake of a few delicate touches of shade or colour on an individual character. In the power to paint this play of common social life, in which there are comparatively but few key-notes of distinct personality, the charm of this school of art consists; while Miss Brontë's lay in the Rembrandt-like distinctness with which all that the mind conceived was brought into the full blaze of light, and the direct vigour with which all the prominent features were marked out. . . .

George Eliot's genius is exceedingly different. Her genial, broad delineations of human life have . . . more perhaps of the breadth of Fielding than of any of the manners-painters of the present day. For these imagine life only as it appears in a certain dress and sphere, which are a kind of artificial medium for their art, – life as affected by drawing-rooms. George Eliot has little, if any, of their capacity for catching the under-tones and allusive complexity of this sort of society. She has, however, observed the phases of a more natural and straightforward class of life, and she draws her external world as much as possible from observation . . . instead of *imagining* it, like Miss Brontë, out of the heart of the characters she wishes to paint. The English mannners she delights in are chiefly of the simplest and most homely kind, – of the rural farmers and labourers, – of the half-educated portion of the country middle-class, who have learnt no educated reticence, – and of the resident country gentry and clergy in their relations with these rough-mannered neighbours. This is a world in which she could not but learn a direct style of treatment. . . .

George Eliot's pictures are not only directer and simpler than those of the drawing-room novelists, but her deeper and frequently poetic imagination discriminates finely betwixt the various degrees of depth which she gives to her characters, and throws more of universality and breadth into them. The manners of 'good society' are a kind of social costume or disguise, which is, in fact, much more effective in concealing how much of depth ordinary characters have, and in restraining the expression of universal human instincts and feelings, than in hiding the individualities, the distinguishing inclinations, talents, bias, and tastes of those who assume them. The slight restraints which are imposed by society upon the expression of individual bias are, in fact, only a new excitement to its more subtle and various, though less straightforward, development. Instead of speaking itself simply out, it gleams out in a hundred ways by the side-paths of a more elaborate medium. To avail yourself skilfully of all the opportunities which these social manners admit of *being yourself*, adds a fresh, though very egotistic, interest to life, and gives much of the zest to the sort of study in which Thackeray and Mr. Trollope are the acknowledged masters. But this applies only to the lighter and more superficial part of human personality. Those stronger passions and emotions in which all men share more or less deeply; which are in the strictest sense personal, and yet in the strictest sense universal; which are private, because either the objects or the occasions which excite them more deeply are different for every different person, and universal, because towards some objects, or on some occasions, they are felt alike by all; – these most personal and most widely diffused of all the elements of human nature are sedulously suppressed in cultivated society; and even the most skilful of the drawing-room novelists find little room for delineating the comparative depth of their roots in different minds.[4]

And yet these deepest portions of human character, which the simpler and less educated grades of society, in their comparative indifference to the sympathy they receive, do not care to hide, and which educated society half suppresses, or expresses only by received formulas quite without personal significance, are far truer measures of force and mass in human character than any other elements. They are, in fact, the only *common* measures which are applicable to all in nearly equal degree. After all, what we care chiefly to know of men and women, is not so much their special tastes, bias, gifts, humours, or even the exact proportions in which these characteristics are combined, – as the general depth and mass of human nature that is in them, – the breadth and the power of their life, – its comprehensiveness of grasp, its tenacity of instinct, its capacity for love, its need of trust. A thousand skilful outlines of character based on mere individualities of taste and talent and temper, are not near as moving to us as one vivid picture of a massive nature stirred to the very depths of its commonplace instinct and commonplace faith.

Notes

1 R.H. Hutton, *Essays Theological and Literary*, 2 vols, 1871, vol. 2, pp. 205–6. See David Skilton, *Anthony Trollope and His Contemporaries*, London, Longman, 1972, pp. 100–25.
2 *Brief Literary Criticisms Selected from the Spectator* (1906), pp. 181–2.
3 These remarks refer specifically to Austen's young clerical characters, but are also given general application.
4 In an essay on Wordsworth, Hutton summarises an idea from Book 13d *The Prelude* (1805–6) in another formulation of this point: 'There are two selfs [sic] in every man – the private and the universal; – the source of personal crochets, and our humanity that is our bond with our fellow-men . . .' – *Essays Theological and Literary*, 1871, vol. 2, p. 135.

6.5 E.S. Dallas, *The Gay Science*, 2 vols, London, 1866, vol. 1, pp. 207–8, 315–16 and 331–2

For Dallas, see headnote to 1.6. The present selection consists of three brief extracts which will serve to introduce Dallas's brilliantly original work on the unconscious in art. Although 'unconscious cerebration' was a phenomenon fairly often discussed from 1853 onwards,[1] Dallas was the only critic in English to make unconscious activity central to an account of artistic creativity (or 'imagination') and, to a lesser extent, of the reception of works of art. The first extract below gives the barest bones of Dallas's general psychological hypothesis, while the second shows how he applies it in his aesthetic theory. The final extract shows what happens when he relates his notion of the unconscious to prose fiction, and uses it to reformulate a standard nineteenth-century distinction between works of 'imagination' (expressive works) and works 'imitating' the world (mimetic works). Defoe is the standard example for any Victorian critic of a writer supposedly lacking imagination and using purely reproductive or 'photographic' procedures. Dallas himself disapproves of the prominence given to imitation in most aesthetic theory since Aristotle, and the aim of The Gay Science *is to base an aesthetic on the principle of pleasure, to which he finds the unconscious immediately relevant. His philosophical position (and perhaps his Scottish education too) lead him to value the mysterious and the 'weird' as the most 'poetic' qualities in literature. Consequently the application of a theory of the unconscious to*

English prose fiction, with its strong inclination to realism, had to wait some time, but no account of 'creativity' or 'imagination' in the period is complete without a glance at Dallas's position.

I hope to avoid the nonsense and the jargon of those who have discoursed most on the sphere of the transcendental – that is, the sphere of our mental existence which transcends or spreads beyond our consciousness; but that consciousness is not our entire world, that the mind stretches in full play far beyond the bourne of consciousness, there will be little difficulty in proving. Outside consciousness there rolls a vast tide of life, which is, perhaps, even more important to us than the little isle of our thoughts which lies within our ken. Comparisons, however, between the two are vain, because each is necessary to the other. The thing to be firmly seized is, that we live in two concentric worlds of thought, – an inner ring, of which we are conscious, and which may be described as illuminated; an outer one, of which we are unconscious, and which may be described as in the dark. Between the outer and the inner ring, between our unconscious and our conscious existence, there is a free and a constant but unobserved traffic for ever carried on. Trains of thought are continually passing to and fro, from the light into the dark, and back from the dark into the light. When the current of thought flows from within our ken to beyond our ken, it is gone, we forget it, we know not what has become of it. After a time it comes back to us changed and grown, as if it were a new thought, and we know not whence it comes. So the fish, that leaves our rivers a smolt, goes forth into the sea to recruit its energy, and in due season returns a salmon, so unlike its former self that anglers and naturalists long refused to believe in its identity. What passes in the outside world of thought, without will and for the most part beyond ken, is just that which we commonly understand as the inscrutable work of imagination; is just that which we should understand as the action of the hidden soul.

* * *

If the object of art were to make known and to explain its ideas, it would no longer be art, but science. Its object is very different. The true artist recognises, however dimly, the existence within us of a double world of thought, and his object is, by subtle forms, tones, words, allusions, associations, to establish a connection with the unconscious hemisphere of the mind, and to make us feel a mysterious energy there in the hidden soul. For this purpose he doubtless makes

157

use of the known. He paints what we have seen, he describes what we have heard; but his use of knowledge is ever to suggest something beyond knowledge. If he be merely dealing with the known and making it better known, then it becomes necessary to ask wherein does his work differ from science? Through knowledge, through consciousness, the artist appeals to the unconscious part of us. The poet's words, the artist's touches, are electric; and we feel those words, and the shock of those touches, going through us in a way we cannot define, but always giving us a thrill of pleasure, awakening distant associations, and filling us with the sense of a mental possession beyond that of which we are daily and hourly conscious. Art is poetical in proportion as it has this power of appealing to what I may call the absent mind, as distinct from the present mind, on which falls the great glare of consciousness, and to which alone science appeals.

* * *

If there be artists who content themselves with adhesion to bare fact, who are never able to transcend fact and to move the imagination, then we must think of them as of Defoe. We take an interest in what Defoe tells us, but it is not the interest excited by art. He sees things clearly and describes them sharply; but the complaint against him is that he has no imagination – that he never touches the hidden sense, which we have been trying to analyze. And as a man may tell a story well (it is done every day in the newspapers), and yet his clear story-telling is not poetry; so a man may paint a picture well, and yet his picture for all the clearness and fulness of knowledge it exhibits may not be art, because it wants that something which a great artist once described by snapping his fingers. 'It wants,['] said Sir Joshua Reynolds, 'it wants *that*.'

Note

1 The phrase 'unconscious cerebration' was coined in 1853 by William B. Carpenter (1813–85), and had entered common usage by 1870. It is one of the principle subjects of Carpenter's *Principles of Mental Physiology* (1874). One of the works which indirectly exerted a large influence on the development of European ideas was Eduard von Hartmann's *Philosophy of the Unconscious* – a survey of the unconscious in Western, and particularly German, thought – which was published in the same year as Dallas's *Gay Science*, but was not available in English translation until 1884.

6.6 Review of Trollope's *An Eye For An Eye*, *Saturday Review* 47 (29 March 1879), 410–11

The Saturday Review *ran regular attacks on Trollope, amounting almost to a campaign, accusing him of 'mechanical' work, starting in 1860 with a generalised assault on serial fiction, and on Thackeray, Trollope and the* Cornhill Magazine *in particular. Then, when Trollope published* The Belton Estate *in the* Fortnightly Review *in 1865–6 to exemplify the 'realistic' fiction which he and the* Fortnightly's *editor, G.H. Lewes, were advocating, the* Saturday *took the opportunity of linking 'realism' to the concept of 'mechanical' art: '[I]f Mr. Trollope only looks upon his art as a manufacture, there can be no reason why he should not take as just a pride in turning so many novels out of his brain in the twelvemonth as a machine-maker takes in turning so many locomotives or looms out of his shed.'* [1] *During the 1860s and 1870s certain images recur when critics contrast what they regard as the product of true imagination with the lower function of reproductive, or repetitive art, all of them denying human creativity: 'stereotype', 'photograph', 'kaleidoscope' and 'Manchester goods'.* [2] *The following passage is taken from a review of one of Trollope's novels with an Irish setting, and it is possible that this also alienates the English reviewer from the characters. For this critic successful literature allows the reader to reach through the work to the personality of the author, in accordance with Tristram Shandy's image of a novel as a form of 'conversation'.* [3] *Also lying behind this passage is the Horatian maxim from* The Art of Poetry *that a writer who wishes to make the reader weep must first feel grief himself.* [4]

The literary invention which has established a regular manufactory of its wares and devised an easy method of producing fiction congenial to the popular taste – fiction neatly turned, signalized by marks of the original achievement which got the author his name and fame, bearing the impress of a master's hand, and thus winning a certain amount of success – yet fails uniformly in one point, and for the obvious reason that the interest and feeling of the artificer is less apparent in machine-made work than in the model which it imitates. The work has been carried through without that intimate partnership between heart and soul and hand, which is apparent in the past efforts of genius, whether the thing be handicraft or headwork. Habit makes the brain even more obedient than before to the calls made upon it, and facility comes with practice; but enthusiasm fails. The emotions of the author are less equal than before to the demands upon them; they take matters easily, and will not wait upon invention with a zealous interest; and because the sympathy of the writer with his creations flags, the heart of the reader takes their trials and sorrows in quite a different spirit from that which first brought him into relation with their author. This is one supreme advantage which early efforts have over the later productions of a prolific fancy. The tiro is absorbed in the creatures of his fancy; their adventures, their griefs, are his own; he is full of them; and the reader, while believing himself to sympathize with ideal personages, is really sympathizing with the imagination that invents them. We do not suppose it possible to be keenly interested in any story which has not awakened an intensity of feeling in its narrator. Such intensity is certainly wanting in the tragical story before us; and therefore the reader takes the calamities of its leading characters not only dry-eyed, but with an easy composure.

Notes

1 *Saturday Review* 21 (3 February 1866), 140–2.
2 See David Skilton, *Anthony Trollope and His Contemporaries*, London, Longman, 1972, pp. 142–3.
3 'Writing, when properly managed, (as you may be sure I think mine is) is but a different name for conversation' – Laurence Sterne, *Tristram Shandy* (1759–67), II.xi.
4 Horace, *Ars Poetica*, 102: 'si vis me flere, dolendum est/primum ipsi tibi' (Latin): 'if you wish me to weep it is first necessary to feel grief yourself'.

7

The office of novelist

'Now, the fault I find chiefly with novelists is their own contempt for their craft', wrote Bulwer Lytton in 1863 (7.4), and it used once to be generally held that early and mid-Victorian novelists paid little attention to what they were doing. The acknowledged 'greats' among them were then supposed to be entirely instinctive, and to operate like Shakespeare in Milton's description of him, warbling 'his native wood-notes wild'.[1] Serious consideration of the art of the novel, in this account, only appeared with Henry James, who brought a French concentration to bear on the subject, and with it a plausible claim for intellectual respect for the novelist. George Eliot, who as usual had been exempted from the general low esteem accorded her fellows, was thought to be unusual in referring to 'the sacredness of the writer's art' as early as 1856. (See 7.7.) A closer examination of the works of Dickens, Gaskell and Trollope, to name but three, shows a very considerable attention to structure, point-of-view and reader relations, amounting to unending experimentation, which belies the strictures of early commentators. It is however true that there was neither the forum nor the well-developed vocabulary for a complete public discussion of these things, and, as has been pointed out throughout, the present volume is in part an effort to assemble some of the best attempts to overcome these disabilities.

George Eliot was clear on the position:

> Every art which has its absolute technique is, to a certain extent, guarded from the intrusions of mere left-handed imbecility. But in novel-writing there are no barriers for incapacity to stumble against, no external criteria to prevent a writer from mistaking foolish facility for mastery.[2]

The 'dignity' of a profession correlates strongly with the difficulty of entry to it, whether by virtue of the cost of entry, the social status demanded, or the level of training and education required. George

Eliot's blunt assessment of the qualifications of second-rate novelists partly explains why the public did not in general regard novel-writing as socially on a par with the learned professions. As the general introduction to this volume indicates, the writers of fiction themselves tended to concentrate their attention on commonsensical advice to those embarking on their career, in apparent recognition of the fact that entry to the calling was unrestricted by ability and experience. Novel-writing was clearly regarded by public and practitioners alike as not having reached the dignity of a full 'profession'. For this reason 7.2 is an extract from a book by H. Byerley Thomson giving advice to middle-class young men and their parents about the most momentous decision of their lives, the 'choice of a profession'. Literature is there assessed as a calling in strongly utilitarian terms:

> Book-writing has never been looked upon by the public as a profitable calling, and with great justice. Yet there is no reason that it should not be so to a man of sufficient talent. Recent examples have occurred of the possibility of making a large income, or even a fortune, in the persons of Scott, Byron, Macaulay, Dickens, Thackeray.

For the calling to be an honest one, of course, material gain had to take second place to moral purpose and integrity, as the *Economist* recognised in 1845, during the worst decade of the century for human suffering:

> If at the moment when the heart of England is filled to overflowing with intense woe, in spite of 'facts and figures' announcing a flourishing revenue, proving that the interest of men in office is terribly at variance with the interest of the industrious people, Dickens could have touched the national misery and its sources with no other object than to tickle his readers into a forgetfulness of their duty, and to put a few pieces of paltry coin into his own pocket, as has been more unworthily and ignorantly imputed to him – he would have been in our estimation one of the meanest spirits, and one of the most degraded writers, of the day. But he aspires to be a social reformer, to make each year happier than the last, by making all classes better. (2.2)

The combination of money and morality almost constitutes a definition of Victorian respectability.

What is less obvious in the discussion is a sense of high aesthetic purpose. As the *Saturday Review* remarked in 1866, 'novel-writing has not yet been recognised in its true position, as one of the loftiest and most capacious of all the arts'.[3] Indeed, in their efforts to have novel-writing recognised as demanding application, experience and expertise, novelists sometimes gave the impression that it might not be an art at all, but a trade like shoe-making or calico weaving. (See Lytton, Trollope and George Eliot in 7.4, 7.5 and 7.6.) In fact the discussion of the office and status of the novelist had two strands: socio-economic status and aesthetic integrity. Both are involved in something as apparently simple as Trollope's use of his shoe-maker image to make mock of the pseudo-romantic view that good writing was produced by 'inspiration' (7.5).

Later writers would claim a high intellectual and aesthetic status for themselves and their work, but would recognise that this could only be granted by an élite. Early and mid-Victorian novelists, on the other hand, were not only popular with the educated middle class, but proud to be so. The commonplace assumption that there existed a close social identity between readers, authors and their subject-matter was most prevalent in the 1860s, and it was an important factor in the popularity of Thackeray and Trollope, for example, that they projected the image of middle-class gentlemen addressing their equals. Meredith, in contrast, was not accepted with the same easy familiarity. As George Gissing remarked in 1885:

> It is amazing that such a man is so neglected. For the last thirty years he has been producing work unspeakably above the best of any living writer and yet no one reads him outside a small circle of highly cultivated people. Perhaps that is better than being popular, a hateful word.[4]

Popularity with the well-to-do was certainly not 'hateful' to most novelists before 1880, and it is interesting to contrast their attitude with that of Robert Louis Stevenson, in an essay composed in 1887–8 and published posthumously under the title which nearly echoes H. Byerley Thomson's (7.2): 'On the Choice of a Profession'. Stevenson is clear not only that a parent would resist a son's desire to become a creative artist (this would have been true in the 1860s), but that to become an artist provided an attractive answer to the terrible alternative of being asked to become successfully middle-class. 'You are now come to that time of life,' writes Stevenson's typical father to his son, 'and have reason within yourself to consider the absolute necessity of making provision for the time when it will be asked, Who is this man? Is he doing any good in the world? Has he the means of being "One of us?" ' The pose adopted by Stevenson and many of his contemporaries was that nothing worse could be contemplated than this 'being "One of us" '; but for many earlier writers one of the obvious motives in writing fiction was to make money and achieve a secure social status – that is to be considered 'One of us' by the respectable bourgeoisie.[5] The creation of specialist readerships for fiction later in the century, and the loss of the concept of the 'general reader', were vitally important in the formation of the twentieth-century novel.

So much for social standing. Aesthetic integrity was held to involve equal proportions of hard work, humanity and sound morality:

> [W]e will call that book good whose author is competent and conscientious. A writer who has heart and brain will produce a good book if he put the best powers of his heart and brain into his work. But if his aim is nothing more than to turn out so many sheets of 'copy' with the least labour to himself, then, depend upon it, whatever be his talents and his reputation, the product will be bad. That is what we find so much of in the present-day – careless and worthless work; and only once and again a conscientious, true BOOK. . . . For the rest, we may trust the young people that their morals – when they have any – will not be corrupted by the reading of any books whose authors in the writing of them have been *honest*. (3.8)

A further quality much prized in male novelists was 'knowledge of the world'. Trollope, said the *Spectator* admiringly when reviewing *Sir Harry Hotspur of Humblethwaite*, 'is, before all things, a man of the world, and as a man of the world he understands to the core every passion involved' in his principal male character.[6] Such dangerous knowledge was conventionally prohibited to women, since, as E.S. Dallas remarked (5.7), 'Woman embodies our highest ideas of purity and refinement.' Women novelists were at a serious disadvantage in being deemed either lacking in refinement or ignorant of their subject-matter. Dallas was scornful of the fictional possibilities of the subjects which were unequivocally permissible: 'From all that babble about the nursery, & all the weary detail of pap & primers – Good Lord deliver us' (headnote to 7.1).

In this period the potential for a worthwhile literature especially belonging to women was discussed in advanced circles. In an attack on 'Silly Novels by Lady Novelists', George Eliot pointed out the greatness of much fiction by women, and proposed that there did indeed exist subjects and approaches specific to women:

Happily, we are not dependent on argument to prove that Fiction is a department of literature in which women can, after their kind, fully equal men. A cluster of great names, both living and dead, rush to our memories in evidence that women can produce novels not only fine, but among the very finest; – novels, too, that have a precious speciality, lying quite apart from masculine aptitudes and experience. No educational restrictions can shut women out from the materials of fiction, and there is no species of art which is so free from rigid requirements.[7]

John Stuart Mill took up the subject in his influential book, *The Subjection Of Women*:

[T]here is a very obvious reason why women's literature is, in its general conception and in its main features, an imitation of men's. . . . If women lived in a different country from men, and had never read any of their writings, they would have had a literature of their own. As it is, they have not created one, because they found a highly advanced literature already created. . . . If a women's literature is destined to have a different collective character from that of men, depending on any differ-ence of natural tendencies, much longer time is necessary than has yet elapsed, before it can emancipate itself from the influence of accepted models, and guide itself by its own impulses. But if, as I believe, there will not prove to be any natural tendencies common to women, and distinguishing their genius from that of men, yet every individual writer among them has her individual tendencies, which at present are still subdued by the influence of precedent and example: and it will require generations more, before their individuality is sufficiently developed to make head against that influence.[8]

It is characteristic of the period that we should find a recognisably modern debate taking place alongside the expression of old and powerful prejudices.

Notes

1   Milton, 'L'Allegro', l.133.
2   George Eliot (anon.), 'Silly Novels by Lady Novelists', *Westminster Review* 66 (October 1856), 461.
3   *Saturday Review* notice of Trollope's *The Belton Estate*, 21 (3 March 1866), 140–2.
4   *Letters of George Gissing to Members of His Family*, 1927, pp. 171–2.

5 R.L. Stevenson, 'On the Choice of a Profession', *Essays Literary and Critical (Tusitala Edition*, 1923), p. 17.
6 *Spectator* 43 (26 November 1870), 1415.
7 Eliot, 'Silly Novels by Lady Novelists', 461. See also 7.7 below.
8 J.S. Mill, *The Subjection Of Women*, 2nd edn, 1869, pp. 132–3.

7.1 E.S. Dallas (anon.), 'Currer Bell', *Blackwood's Magazine* 82 (July 1857), 78–80

This is an extract from another review of Gaskell's biography of Charlotte Brontë. In a letter to John Blackwood, the reviewer says that he has attacked Gaskell 'in the interest' of Charlotte Brontë, 'whom she has miserably betrayed for the gratification of her own vanities. . . . the dead Charlotte Brontes are sacrificed to the living E.C. Gaskells'.[1] He explains his objections in another passage of the review:

> Mrs Gaskell is, indeed, lavish of her sympathy; but it is of the patronising apologetic kind, feeling for rather than with the sufferer; crushing her with condescension, overpowering her with affection, and rejoicing itself with a copious discharge of those cheap protestations which Sairey Gamp, over her brown teapot, might offer to Betsy Prig.[2]

She writes, Dallas complains, too much of ' "myself," "my husband," "our little girls," "an aunt of mine," "a visit I paid," "a letter I received," "what I partly knew," and "what my feelings were" ' (p. 78). Attitudes to the visibility of the biographer over the ages would make a fascinating study. It appears that this review was originally even more negative, and that Dallas toned it down at the behest of the editor and proprietor, John Blackwood:

> I hope that I have attended to all your suggestions as you wish, not excepting your remark as to female novelists. I was thinking chiefly of M[rs] Gore, Miss Muloch & all the rubbish that Smith, Elder & Co delight to publish chiefly from the hands of women. From all that babble about the nursery, & all the weary detail of pap & primers – Good Lord deliver us.[3]

For E.S. Dallas, see the headnotes of 1.6 and 2.4, and for a brief introduction to his aesthetic position see extract 6.5 and its headnote.

The Life of Charlotte Bronte is full of interest, as that of an intellectual woman combating with adverse fortune, and determined to win her way in the world. Although her success was extraordinary, her struggles were by no means peculiar; and in the simple facts of her life we have touching evidence of what hundreds of young women have to undergo, who have no proper outlet for their mental activities. If the employments to which women in this country can turn their hands are few enough, how very few are the occupations for educated women! What private professions can they adopt, putting public ones out of the question? They can become either governesses or authoresses. But every one does not succeed as a governess. Like poor Charlotte Bronte, who tried scheme after scheme, some may have a positive inaptitude for dealing with children. What then? Like the three sisters, Currer, Ellis, and Acton Bell, they, in a great number of cases, take to writing novels. Interesting as this fact is with regard to the occupations of women who, by necessity of education demand, whether they have families or not to look after, some higher gymnastic than the knitting of stockings, and the invention of puddings, it is not less so as involving the most singular literary phenomenon of the day – the feminine aspect of our fictitious literature. To this exceedingly voluminous literature, the quantity contributed by women is enormous; and where they are not the writers, they in most instances prescribe the tone of sentiment, which is Pindaric[4] and superhuman, as well as the character of the incidents, which are domestic and infantine. That women can succeed greatly in fiction, he who is in the slightest degree acquainted with the publications of only the last ten years would be a bold man to deny, not to speak of such classical authors as Miss Austen, Miss Edgeworth, and Miss Ferrier, whose works will be read, and deserve to be read, as long as those of any brother novelist. Still it must be evident that, from that inexperience of life which no amount of imagination, no force of sympathy, can ever compensate, women labour under serious disadvantages in attempting the novel. Everybody knows that men almost always fail in drawing the character of ideal women; the thing has scarcely ever been done. Shakespeare well-nigh stands alone as a faithful delineator of the sex; and yet even he sometimes places his heroines in the most dubious positions – in which we see, not so much the lady as the boy actress of the period affecting the lady, while all the paint on his face cannot conceal the incipient beard. And just as men fail in describing women, they in turn fail in describing men. It is their weakness; it is a weakness which must always prevent them from attaining the very highest success as writers of that class of fiction to which the modern novel belongs. What success they do attain – and it is of no mean order – is principally from the development of female character. No doubt there are instances in which, as in the Rochester and Paul Emanuel of Currer Bell,[5] the masculine character is treated with considerable power and truth; but these are exceptions to the rule; and it must be confessed that the great majority of novels from the hands of women are by no means satisfactory. It could scarcely be otherwise in the circumstances under which they are written. How many women are there who pursue this style of writing from a decided inclination for it? Yet surely, if there is one department of literature more than another which ought not to be followed without a sense of enjoyment on the part of the writer, it is that which includes the highest exercise of the imagination. Charlotte Bronte succeeded, because, as we shall presently see, she was born a novelist. As soon as she could write, she began to write tales. But after reading these volumes, and seeing how desperately the poor Brontes clutched at one scheme after another in order to make a little money, it is difficult not to believe that an immense number of the novels with which the press now groans are not thrown down before the public as vainglorious challenges for fame, but are wrung from the sickness of woman's heart amid the weariness and discomforts of poverty, the cares and griefs of nursing, in order to win daily bread, or to purchase a few luxuries for those who are dearer than life. God knows what these poor women have to undergo who have been placed by education on a level with the best of us, and who are placed by adverse circumstances in a position which very often is not half so good as that of a cook or a housemaid; and in estimating the effects of their influence upon the literature of the time, if sometimes, as critics, we are disposed to call for bell, book, and candle, and solemnly to excommunicate the offenders, let us also, as men, remember the trials which many of them have to undergo, and the desperation which drives some into slavery of the pen, as others still more unfortunate, are driven into slavery of the needle.

Notes

1   National Library of Scotland MS 4123, f105, E.S. Dallas to John Blackwood, 7 July [1857].
2   Sairey Gamp, the greedy, drunken and dishonest nurse in Dickens's *Martin Chuzzlewit*, who maintains a pretence of respectability, is discussed in 4.10.
3   National Library of Scotland MS 4123, f103, E.S. Dallas to John Blackwood, no date [1857].
4   Pindaric: imitative of the Greek poet Pindar (4th century BC), and characterised by elevated language, brilliant metaphor and

expressive periphrasis. Matthew Arnold called 'pindarism' an 'intoxication of style'.

5   The chief male characters in Charlotte Brontë's *Jane Eyre* (1847) and *Villette* (1852) respectively.

7.2 H. Byerley Thomson, *The Choice of a Profession. A Concise Account and Comparative Review of the English Professions*, 1857, pp. 336–8

Henry Byerley Thomson (1822–67) was a barrister who became a colonial judge. His Choice of a Profession *consists of advice to parents who wish to place their sons in one of the professions, and contains information on the cost of gaining the necessary qualifications and on the income to be expected. Thomson's contention that good writers never need be financially hard up at the time is plausible in view of the enormous expansion of periodical publications. It is not, however, the case that writers could necessarily then, any more than at any other period, earn a living by cultivating their chosen field of literature. A case in point is the poet James Thomson ('B.V.') (1834–82) who at this stage was a teacher in the army education service, and later supported himself by writing articles for the house magazine of a Liverpool tobacco importer.*

The 'profession of literature' is a term that has been applied of late years to the large body of authors, journalists, compilers, and translators, who live by the pen. But this important occupation does, in fact, contain none of the elements of a regular profession. It has no form, no combination, no special education, and no linking society, with the exception of a charitable institution, termed the 'Literary Fund.' It is an occupation that is entered upon by chance rather than by design. A subject for illustration occurs to an educated and intelligent man, and the result is an article or a book, for which he has more or less difficulty in obtaining a publisher. If he succeeds, the incipient writer often then, and then for the first time, thinks of becoming an author by profession. Some, indeed, but not many, feel a natural wish to a literary career from their earliest years, and then embrace it with enthusiasm and success. These few are the only persons who may be said to follow literature as a profession in its higher walks. The chance author has generally some other calling, or even a private competence of his own, and leaves his path of letters readily on the first temptation to do so. Book-writing has never been looked upon by the public as a profitable calling, and with great justice. Yet there is no reason that it should not be so to a man of sufficient talent. Recent examples have occurred of the possibility of making a large income, or even a fortune, in the persons of Scott, Byron, Macaulay, Dickens, Thackeray, &c., in England; Dumas, Huc,[1] and others in France; and Longfellow and Prescott[2] in America. These gentlemen have succeeded in realising the profits of a profession, because they have pursued literature in somewhat of that form. Men of equal, or not inferior talent, have in their own days starved upon the products of their genius, greatly because they have not followed the same prudent course.

Whatever may be the amount of personal talent, success in a calling requires a long apprenticeship, and practice, and experience, as well as knowledge and ability. Every man who, therefore, when he discovers in himself a talent for writing, rushes at once into print, cannot expect to produce anything except that which is ephemeral and only of partial interest, and therefore of no great value either in fame, or pecuniary reward to himself.

But if, on the other hand, the aspiring author unhastily and carefully prepares himself for his literary labour, in the same manner as he would consider himself bound to prepare himself for following the law, or practising medicine, he can promise himself some measure of success and reward. Even if he has the misfortune to be a dull writer, he may bring forth a work of great value in other respects, that will find favour with some classes of readers.

The large class of mediocre writers, – hasty intruders on the sacred soil of learning, – finding their frail labours unappreciated, are but too apt to exclaim that literature is not encouraged in their country. As well might the three thousand briefless barristers say that the law is not encouraged. Good literature is not only encouraged, but highly prized and amply rewarded; and, strange to say, indifferent literature receives no small amount of encouragement also. If it were otherwise, would there be such a continuous stream of trashy novels, travels over well-known lands, and shallow memoirs. It is impossible to show a single example in the present day of a distinguished writer neglected in the way suggested. The enormous increase of readers, and the avidity of whole classes that of late years joined the reading community, has put a stop to any chance of the kind. Valuable literature will always receive a valuable reward.

Notes

1 Évariste Régis Huc (1813–60), prolific travel writer, most famous for his accounts of Central Asia and Tibet.
2 William Hickling Prescott (1796–1859), historian, best known for his *History of the Conquest of Mexico* (1843) and *The Conquest of Peru* (1847).

7.3 W.R. Greg (anon.), 'False Morality of Lady Novelists', *National Review* 1 (1859), 147–9

This article, which is a review of Gaskell's Ruth, *and four other novels, is by William Rathbone Greg (1809–81), an essayist on social and political questions, for eighteen years a millowner, and at different times a Commissioner of Customs and Comptroller of the Stationery Office. He approaches the subject of this extract – the prevalence of women novelists – from a sociological point of view, coloured by dominant Victorian assumptions about the experience possible or proper to women of a certain class and age, and about their supposed propensity to high-flown sentiment in youth. The form of his argument is familiar to those who study the mechanisms of patriarchy: an observable effect (that there are many weak novels written by women) is attributed to 'natural' deficiencies in women, and not to social convention and ideology. Moreover, the ostensible reason for paying attention to a subject which might otherwise be deemed to be beneath the notice of Greg's educated male readers is that women require protection from bad influences, since, as he explains*

> *novels constitute a principal part of the reading of women, who are always impressionable, in whom at all times the emotional element is more awake and more powerful than the critical, whose feelings are more easily aroused and whose estimates are more easily influenced than ours, while at the same time the correctness of their feelings and the justice of their estimates are matters of the more special and preeminent concern. (pp. 145–6)*

There are vast numbers of lady novelists, for much the same reason that there are vast numbers of sempstresses. Thousands of women have nothing to do, and yet are under the necessity of doing something. Every woman can handle a needle *tant bien que mal*:[1] every unemployed woman, therefore, takes to sewing. Hundreds of educated ladies have nothing to do, and yet are tormented with a most natural desire, nay are often under a positive obligation, to do something. Every educated lady can handle a pen *tant bien que mal*: all such, therefore, take to writing – and to novel-writing, both as the kind which requires the least special qualifications and the least severe study, and also as the only kind which will sell. The number of youthful novelists, and of young lady novelists, extant at this moment passes calculation, and was unparalleled at any former epoch.[2] Indeed the supply of the fiction market has mainly fallen into their hands; and it speaks well for the general taste and cultivation of the age, that, under such circumstances, so many of the new novels that pour forth weekly from the press should be really interesting and clever, and that so few should be utterly poor or bad. But it is in the nature of things impossible that productions of such a character, from such a source, however able or however captivating, should not be radically and inherently defective. The plot may be exciting, the style may be flowing, the sentiments may be pleasing and even stirring, and the characters may be natural, interesting, and well sustained; but the views of life and the judgements of conduct must be imperfect and superficial, and will often be thoroughly unsound. These things cannot be surely deduced, as is too often fancied, from certain fixed rules and principles which may be learned *a priori*; they depend in a great measure on observation and experience, on knowledge of the world and of the characters that move and act there, and on the ascertained consequences of actions and influences of qualities. Now here the young are necessarily wanting. If the writer be a young man, his experience of life must be brief, imperfect, and inadequate. If the writer be a young lady, her experience must be not only all this, but must be partial in addition. Whole spheres of observation, whole branches of character and conduct, are almost inevitably closed to her. Nay, even with respect to the one topic which forms the staple of most novels, and a main ingredient in all, viz., love, and its various phases, varieties, and developments, – her means of judgement and of delineating must be always scanty and generally superficial. She may have felt the passion, it is true; but she will have felt it only in one form, – the form congenial to her own nature; – she will be able, therefore, in all likelihood, to depict it only under one aspect, and will estimate its character and consequences from a personal point of view. She may possibly have enjoyed (or suffered) opportunities of observing the workings of the sentiment in some one of her friends; but its wilder issues and its fiercer crises are necessarily and righteously hidden from her sight. She may, by dint of that marvellous faculty of sympathy and intuition which is given to those who have felt profoundly and suffered long, be able to divine much which she cannot discover, and to conceive much which she has never seen or heard; and the pure and God-given instincts which some women possess in so rare a measure may enable her to distinguish between the genuine and the false, the noble and the low; – but many of the saddest and deepest truths in the strange science of sexual affection are to her mysteriously and mercifully veiled; and the knowledge of them can only be purchased at such a fearful cost, that we cannot wish it otherwise. The inevitable consequence, however, is, that in treating of that science she labours under all the disadvantages of partial study and superficial insight. She is describing a country of which she knows only the more frequented and the safer roads, with a few of the sweet scenes and the prettier by-paths and more picturesque *détours* which lie not far from the broad and beaten thoroughfares; while the rockier and loftier mountains, the more rugged tracks, the more sombre valleys, and the darker and more dangerous chasms, are never trodden by her feet and scarcely even dreamed of by her fancy.

In youth, moreover, and in the youth of women more especially, there is a degree of exaltation of mind and temper which – beautiful as it is, and deeply as we should grieve over its absence – partakes of, or at least has a strong tendency to degenerate into, the morbid and unsound. It may add to the interest of a tale, but it renders it unfaithful as a picture of life, unsafe as a guide to the judgement, and often noxious in its influence on the feelings. In short – and to sum up in a single sentence the gist of all that we have said – that branch of the literature of our day which exercises the widest and most penetrating influence on the age, – from which the young and impressionable (nearly all of us, in short, at one period or other) chiefly draw their notions of life, their canons of judgement, their habitual sentiments and feelings (so far as these are drawn from literature at all), and their impressions as to what is admirable and right and what is detestable and wrong, – is in the hands of writers whose experience of life is seldom wide and never deep, whose sympathies have not yet been chastened or corrected, whose philosophy is inevitably superficial, whose judgement cannot possibly be matured, and is not very likely to be sound. The result is, that we are constantly gazing on inaccurate pictures, constantly sympathising with artificial or reprehensible emotions, constantly admiring culpable conduct, constantly imbibing false morality.

Notes

1   *tant bien que mal* (French): so-so; more or less adequately.

2   Using census returns, H.B. Thomson (see 7.2) gives the number of
persons claiming to be solely dependent on their pens: 'The authors,
writers, and literary men, number 2866, of whom 436 are authors, 1302
editors, or writers.' He does not comment on the number of *women*
professional writers, as he does on the importance of 'the fair sex' in
education. Presumably few of those of whom Greg is writing were
returned as bread-winners, however essential their literary earnings may
have been to their households.

7.4 Edward Bulwer Lytton, 'On Certain Principles of Art in Works of Imagination', 'Caxtoniana: a Series of Essays on Life, Literature, and Manners. – Part XVI', *Blackwood's Magazine*, 93 (May 1863), 554–5

*For the author, see the headnote to 1.1. The idea of devotion to the art
of fiction was not unusual at this time, and George Eliot among others
was clear on 'the sacredness of the writer's art' (see 7.7). Later
generations however tended to believe that it was their own discovery.
The difference is that in the late nineteenth and early twentieth
centuries this devotion was expressed in terms of the cultivation of
certain features then held dear, especially the invisibility of the
novelist in the novel, an appearance of 'structure' in the work of art,
and a style which clearly distinguished prose fiction from everyday
transactional uses of the English language.*

Now, the fault I find chiefly with novelists is their own contempt for
their craft. A clever and scholarlike man enters into it with a dignified
contempt. 'I am not going to write,' he says, 'a mere novel.' What,
then, is he going to write? What fish's tail will he add to the horse's
head? A tragic poet might as well say, 'I am not going to write a mere
tragedy.' The first essential to success in the art you practise is respect
for the art itself. Who could ever become a good shoemaker if he did
not have a profound respect for the art of making shoes? There is an
ideal even in the humblest mechanical craft. A shoemaker destined to
excel his rivals will always have before his eye the vision of a perfect
shoe, which he is always striving to realise, and never can.[1] It was well
said by Mr. Hazlitt, 'That the city prentice who did not think the Lord
Mayor in his gilded coach was the greatest of human beings would
come to be hanged.'[2] Whatever our calling be, we can never rise in it
unless we exalt, even to an exaggerated dignity, the elevation of the
calling itself. We are noble peasants or noble kings just in proportion

as we form a lofty estimate of the nobility that belongs to peasants or the nobility that belongs to kings.

We may despair of the novelist who does not look upon a novel as a consummate work of art – who does not apply to it, as Fielding theoretically, as Scott practically, did, the rules which belong to the highest order of imagination. Of course he may fail of his standard, but he will fail less in proportion as the height of his standard elevates his eye and nerves his sinews.

The first object of a novelist is to interest his reader; the next object is the quality of the interest. Interest in his story is essential, or he will not be read; but if the quality of the interest be not high, he will not be read a second time. And if he be not read a second time by his own contemporaries, the chance is that he will not be read once by posterity. The degree of interest is for the many – the quality of interest is for the few. But the many are proverbially fickle, the few are constant. Steadfast minorities secure, at last, the fame of great writings.

Notes

1 The comparison between the devotion necessary to novel-writing and to shoe-making was one of Anthony Trollope's favourite points throughout the 1860s, and it reappears in *Autobiography*, 1883. See 7.5.
2 This remark by the critic and essayist William Hazlitt (1778–1830) has not been identified.

7.5 Anthony Trollope, *An Autobiography*, written 1875–6, 3 vols, 1883, vol. 1, pp. 162–3

Trollope's comparison of the craft of writing a novel with the making of shoes is famous, and may originally have been a response to an attack from the Saturday Review *in 1860:*

> *Mr. Trollope has reached the stage in which he may justly claim the character of an excellent literary workman (though the style of his workmanship is certainly open to some criticism) but that he has also arrived at the point when he makes a novel just as he might make a pair of shoes, with a certain workmanlike satisfaction in turning out a good article, but with little of the freshness and zest which marked his earlier productions.[1]*

See 7.4 for Lytton's slightly different use of the comparison of the novelist and the shoemaker. For Trollope's Autobiography *see 2.6.*

The humour in the following passage has often been missed by later, censorious critics.

There are those who would be ashamed to subject themselves to such a taskmaster [as a writing schedule], and who think that the man who works with his imagination should allow himself to wait till – inspiration moves him. When I have heard such doctrine preached, I have hardly been able to repress my scorn. To me it would not be more absurd if the shoemaker were to wait for inspiration, or the tallow-chandler for the divine moment of melting. If the man whose business it is to write has eaten too many good things, or has drunk too much, or smoked too many cigars, – as men who write sometimes will do, – then his condition may be unfavourable for work; but so will be the condition of a shoemaker who has been similarly imprudent. I have sometimes thought that the inspiration wanted has been the remedy which time will give to the evil results of such imprudence. – *Mens sana in corpore sano!*[2] The author wants that as does every other workman, – that and a habit of industry. I was once told that the surest aid to the writing of a book was a piece of cobbler's wax on my chair. I certainly believe in the cobbler's wax much more than the inspiration.

Notes

1 Review of *Castle Richmond, Saturday Review* 9 (19 May 1860), 643–4.
2 *Mens sana in corpore sano* (Latin): 'A healthy mind in a healthy body'.

7.6 George Eliot, 'Authorship', from 'Leaves from a Notebook', written 1872–8, *Essays*, 'Standard Edition' of *The Works of George Eliot*, 1888, pp. 288–92

According to Charles Lee Lewis, George Eliot's editor in 1888, the notes comprising 'Leaves from a note-book' were written 'some time between the appearance of "Middlemarch" and that of "Theophrastus Such" ' – i.e. during the years 1872–8. They were published in 1888. In the extract printed below George Eliot looks briefly at the moral position of the writer in a capitalist system, to see whether the operation of the market can exercise sufficient regulation over authorship. It provides a socio-economic gloss on the discussion of the office and responsibility of the novelist.

Among those callings which have not yet acquired anything near a full-grown conscience in the public mind is Authorship. Yet the changes brought about by the spread of instruction and the consequent struggles of an uneasy ambition, are, or at least might well be, forcing on many minds the need of some regulating principle with regard to the publication of intellectual products, which would override the rule of the market: a principle, that is, which should be derived from a fixing of the author's vocation according to those characteristics in which it differs from the other bread-winning professions. Let this be done, if possible, without any cant, which would carry the subject into Utopia away from existing needs. The guidance wanted is a clear notion of what should justify men and women in assuming public authorship, and of the way in which they should be determined by what is usually called success. But the forms of authorship must be distinguished; journalism, for example, carrying a necessity for that continuous production which in other kinds of writing is precisely the evil to be fought against, and judicious careful compilation, which is a great public service, holding in its modest diligence a guarantee against those deductions of vanity and idleness which draw many a young gentleman into reviewing, instead of the sorting and copying which his small talents could not rise to with any vigour and completeness.

A manufacturer goes on producing calicoes as long and as fast as he can find a market for them; and in obeying this indication of demand he gives his factory its utmost usefulness to the world in general and to himself in particular. Another manufacturer buys a new invention of some light kind likely to attract the public fancy, is successful in finding a multitude who will give their testers for the transiently desirable commodity, and before the fashion is out, pockets a considerable sum: the commodity was coloured with a green which had arsenic in it that damaged the factory workers and the purchasers. What then? These, he contends (or does not know or care to contend), are superficial effects, which it is folly to dwell upon while we have epidemic diseases and bad government.

The first manufacturer we will suppose blameless. Is an author simply on a par with him, as to the rules of production?

The author's capital is his brain-power – power of invention, power of writing. The manufacturer's capital, in fortunate cases, is being continually produced and increased. Here is the first grand difference between the capital which is turned into calico and the brain capital which is turned into literature. The calico scarcely varies in appropriateness of quality, no consumer is in danger of getting too much of it, and neglecting his boots, hats, and flannel-shirts in consequence. That there should be large quantities of the same sort in the calico manufacture is an advantage: the sameness is desirable, and nobody is likely to roll his person in so many folds of calico as to become a mere bale of cotton goods, and nullify his senses of hearing and touch, while his morbid passion for Manchester shirtings makes him still cry 'More!' The wise manufacturer gets richer and richer, and the consumers he supplies have their real wants satisfied and no more. . . .To write prose or verse as a private exercise and satisfaction is not social activity; nobody is culpable for this any more than for learning other people's verse by heart if he does not neglect his proper business in consequence. . . . But a man or woman who publishes writings inevitably assumes the office of teacher or influencer of the public mind. Let him protest as he will that he only seeks to amuse, and has no pretension to do more than wile away an hour of leisure or weariness – 'the idle singer of an empty day'[1] – he can no more escape influencing the moral taste, and with the action of the intelligence, than a setter of fashions in furniture and dress can fill the shops with his designs and leave the garniture of persons and houses unaffected by his industry.

For a man who has a certain gift of writing to say, 'I will make the most of it while the public likes my wares – as long as the market is open and I am able to supply it at a money profit – such profit being the sign of liking' – he should have a belief that his wares have nothing akin to the arsenic green in them, and also that his continuous supply is secure from a degradation in quality which the habit of consumption encouraged in the buyers may hinder them from marking their sense of by rejection; so that they complain, but pay, and read while they complain. Unless he has that belief, he is on a level with the manufacturer who gets rich by fancy-wares coloured with arsenic green. He really cares for nothing but his income. He carries on authorship on the principle of the gin-palace.

And bad literature of the sort called amusing is spiritual gin.

A writer capable of being popular can only escape this social culpability by first of all getting a profound sense that literature is good-for-nothing, if it is not admirably good: he must detest bad literature too heartily to be indifferent about producing it if only other people don't detest it. And if he has this sign of the divine afflatus[2] within him, he must make up his mind that he must not pursue authorship as a vocation with a trading determination to get rich by it. It is in the highest sense lawful for him to get as good a price as he honourably can for the best work he is capable of; but not for him to force or hurry his production, or even do over again what has already been done, either by himself or others, so as to render his work of no real contribution, for the sake of bringing his income to the fancy pitch. An author who would keep a pure and noble conscience, and with that a developing instead of degenerating intellect and taste, must cast out of his aims the aim to be rich. And therefore he must keep his expenditure low – he must make for himself no dire necessity to earn sums in order to pay bills.

Notes

1   William Morris, *The Earthly Paradise* (1868–70), 'An Apology'.
2   'divine afflatus': inspiration by supernatural power (e.g. the muses).

7.7 Edith Simcox (signed), 'George Eliot', *Nineteenth Century* 9 (May 1881), 782 and 797–8

For Edith Simcox, see headnote to extract 1.8.

It is of course interesting to possess George Eliot's opinions as to other women novelists, written before she was silenced by her own greater fame. As an artist, she wrote in 1852, Miss Austen surpasses all the male novelists that ever lived, and for eloquence and depth of feeling no man approaches George Sand. But in general the literature of women 'may be compared to that of Rome – a literature of imitation;' and she insists both in this article and in one on a kindred subject, some years later, on the importance rather of recognising and using to vary and extend the range of literature, whatever specific differences there might be in the perceptions and intuitions of men and women. . . .

   She gave unqualified and unhesitating assent to what might be called the most 'advanced' opinions on this subject [i.e. the whole subject of the rights and position of women]; only the opinions had to be advocated in practice with large tolerance and disinterestedness, and she wished to be assured that nothing of what is valuable in the social order of the past should be sacrificed in the quest of even certain future good. In matters intellectual she had, what is perhaps equally rare in men and women, the same standard for both sexes. In an article in which we trace her hand on 'Silly Novels by Lady Novelists' (*West. Rev.* October 1856) we read: 'It must be plain to every one who looks impartially and extensively into feminine literature, that its greatest deficiencies are due hardly more to the want of intellectual power than to the want of those moral qualities that contribute to literary excellence, patient diligence, a sense of the responsibility involved in publication, and an appreciation of the sacredness of the writer's art.' Upon the two latter points she felt with peculiar strength, though reluctant, as herself a successful writer, to express all she thought. No amount of demand for the 'trash that smothers excellence' seemed to her a justification for the manufacture of slipshod compilation or trivial torrents of small talk in print. As a step towards the recognition of a higher standard, at least by women, she naturally looked towards an improved education, and it will be remembered that among the first gifts towards the foundation of the college which is now Girton was 100*l.* from 'the author of *Adam Bede*,' with whom at that date such sums were not superfluously plentiful. With her delight in the mere acquisition of knowledge of all kinds for its own sake, there was necessarily something almost comic in questions as to the capacity of feminine brains; but it must be admitted that she is the first woman who has carried so complete a panoply of learning without being oppressed, not to say smothered, under its weight.

Further reading

It is not possible to give a list of suggested further reading to cover what has happened in criticism of early and mid-Victorian fiction since the 1880s. Further guidance on criticism of these novels by their contemporaries, and information on economic and social aspects of the literary system can be gained from the following:

Robin Gilmore, *The Novel in the Victorian Age: A Modern Introduction*, London: Edward Arnold, 1986

Kenneth Graham, *English Criticism of the Novel 1856–1900*, London: Oxford University Press, 1965

Guinevere Griest, *Mudie's Circulating Library and the Victorian Novel*, Newton Abbot: David & Charles, 1970

David Skilton, *Anthony Trollope and His Contemporaries: a Study in the Theory and Conventions of Mid-Victorian Fiction*, Harlow: Longman; New York: St Martin's, 1972

Richard Stang, *The Theory of the Novel in England 1850–1870*, London: Routledge & Kegan Paul, 1959

John Sutherland, *Victorian Novelists and Publishers*, London: Athlone Press, 1976

John Sutherland (ed.) *The Longman Companion to Victorian Fiction*, London: Longman, 1988

Routledge's Critical Heritage Series reprints large amounts of original criticism, with useful introductions and commentaries. Relevant authors who are covered in the series include:

The Brontës, ed Miriam Allott
Wilkie Collins, ed Norman Page
Dickens, ed Philip Collins
George Eliot, ed David Carroll
Elizabeth Gaskell, ed Angus Easson

Thomas Hardy, ed R.G. Cox
Meredith, ed Ioan Williams
Thackeray, ed Geoffrey Tillotson and Donald Hawes
Anthony Trollope, ed Donald Smalley